Adva...

The Lo...

MW01132096

Candidates for public office, *and* the voters who elect them, should be required to read John Michael Greer's accurate diagnosis of the terminal illness our fossil-energy subsidized industrial civilization has too long denied. He shows how stubborn belief in perpetual progress blinded us to the abyss toward which we were speeding and thus impeded wise preparation for our unavoidable descent into a deindustrial age. We must hope that the array of mitigating tools he prescribes may yet render that descent down the back side of Hubbert's peak less devastating than it will be if we insistently claim a right to be prodigal in using this finite Earth.

— William R. Catton, Jr.
author of *Overshoot: The Ecological
Basis of Revolutionary Change*

This is a very wise and timely message for a nation facing enormous practical challenges. Greer's generosity of spirit and essential kindness are habits of mind and heart very much worth emulating.

— James Howard Kunstler
author of *World Made by Hand*
and *The Long Emergency*

When we find ourselves falling off the lofty peak of infinite progress, our civilization's mythology predisposes our imaginations to bypass reality altogether, and to roll straight for the equally profound abyss of the Apocalypse. Greer breaks this spell, and instead offers us a view on our deindustrial future that is both carefully reasoned and grounded in spirituality.

— Dmitry Orlov
author of *Reinventing Collapse:
The Soviet Experience and American Prospects*

If, as Greer suggests, our "prolonged brush with ecological reality" is not a slide or a free-fall, but a stair-step, then we have time to see this book made required reading in every U.S. high school. This is both a past and future history book, written from a perspective that is rare now, but will soon be widely shared.

— Albert Bates,
author of *The Post-Petroleum
Survival Guide and Cookbook*

"Sweeping historical vision" is not generally a term applied to books about peak oil, which tend to imagine the coming crisis in terms as a culmination and a single event. John Michael Greer offers a useful corrective to this narrow vision in a book that is both pragmatic and visionary. In this deeply engaging book, Greer places us not at the end of our historical narrative, but at the beginning of a sometimes harrowing, but potentially fascinating transition.

— Sharon Astyk
author of *Depletion & Abundance: Life on the New Home Front* and blogger, SharonAstyk.com

At once erudite and entertaining, Greer's exploration of the dynamics of societal collapse couldn't be more timely. Resource depletion and climate change guarantee that industrial societies will contract in the decades ahead. Do we face a universally destructive calamity, or a long transition to a sustainable future? That's one of the most important questions facing us, and this book is one of the very few to address it on the basis of clear reasoning and historical precedents.

— Richard Heinberg
Senior Fellow, Post Carbon Institute,
and author of *The Party's Over* and *Peak Everything*

The fall of civilization, according to Greer, does not look like falling off a cliff but rather "a slide down statistical curves that will ease modern industrial civilization into history's dumpster." Presenting the concept of "catabolic collapse", Greer brilliantly assists the reader in deciphering an illusory intellectual polarity consisting on one side of the infinite progress of civilization and on the other, apocalypse. Not unlike the journey through the mythical Scylla and Charybdis, Greer appropriately names this odyssey the Long Descent, and for it, he offers us not only an excellent read, but tangible tools for navigating the transition.

— Carolyn Baker
author of *Speaking Truth to Power*
www.carolynbaker.net

THE LONG DESCENT

THE LONG DESCENT

John Michael Greer

A User's Guide to
the End of the
Industrial
Age

NEW SOCIETY PUBLISHERS

Cataloging in Publication Data:
A catalog record for this publication is available from
the National Library of Canada.

Copyright © 2008 by John Michael Greer.
All rights reserved.

Cover design by Diane McIntosh.
Images: iStock/Dan Tero

Printed in Canada.
First printing July 2008.

Paperback isbn: 978-0-86571-609-4

Inquiries regarding requests to reprint all or part of *The Long Descent*
should be addressed to New Society Publishers at the address below.

To order directly from the publishers, please call toll-free (North America)
1-800-567-6772, or order online at www.newsociety.com

Any other inquiries can be directed by mail to:

New Society Publishers
P.O. Box 189, Gabriola Island, BC V0R 1X0, Canada
(250) 247-9737

New Society Publishers' mission is to publish books that contribute in
fundamental ways to building an ecologically sustainable and just society, and
to do so with the least possible impact on the environment, in a manner that
models this vision. We are committed to doing this not just through education,
but through action. This book is one step toward ending global deforestation
and climate change. It is printed on Forest Stewardship Council-certified
acid-free paper that is **100% post-consumer recycled** (100% old growth
forest-free), processed chlorine free, and printed with vegetable-based, low-
VOC inks, with covers produced using FSC-certified stock. Additionally,
New Society purchases carbon offsets based on an annual audit, operating
with a carbon-neutral footprint. For further information, or to browse our full
list of books and purchase securely, visit our website at: www.newsociety.com

NEW SOCIETY PUBLISHERS
www.newsociety.com

Contents

Preface

The difference between Europeans and Americans, some wag has suggested, is that Europeans think a hundred miles is a long distance, and Americans think a hundred years is a long time. I had a cogent reminder of that witticism in the summer of 2003 when my wife and I climbed a rocky hill in the Welsh town of Caernarfon. Spread out below us in an unexpected glory of sunlight was the whole recorded history of that little corner of the world.

The ground beneath us still rippled with earthworks from the Celtic hill fort that guarded the Menai Strait more than two and a half millennia ago. The Roman fort that replaced it was now the dim brown mark of an old archeological site on low hills off to the left. Edward I's great gray castle rose up in the middle foreground, and the high contrails of RAF jets on a training exercise out over the Irish Sea showed that the town's current overlords still maintained the old watch. Houses and shops from more than half a dozen centuries spread eastward as they rose through the waters of time, from the cramped medieval buildings of the old castle town straight ahead to the gaudy sign and sprawling parking lot of the supermarket back behind us.

It's been popular in recent centuries to take such sights as snapshots of some panorama of human progress, but as Caernarfon unfolded its past to me that afternoon, the view I saw was a different one. The green traces of the hill fort showed the highwater mark of a wave of Celtic expansion that flooded most of Europe in its day. The Roman fort marked the crest of another wave whose long ebbing — we call it the Dark Ages today — still offers up a potent reminder that history doesn't always lead to better things. The castle rose as medieval England's Plantagenet empire neared its own peak, only to break on the battlefields of Scotland and France and fall back into the long ordeal of the Wars of the Roses. The comfortable brick houses of the Victorian era marked the zenith of another vanished empire, and it didn't take too much effort just then to see, in the brash American architecture of the supermarket, the imprint of a fifth empire headed for the same fate as the others.

Views like this are hard to find in North America. The suburban houses and schools where I spent my childhood were all built after the Second World War, on land that had been unbroken old growth forest three quarters of a century before that. In that setting, it was easy to believe the narrative of linear progress served up by the schools, the media, and the popular culture of the time. Even in the handful of Atlantic coast cities old enough to have a history worth mentioning in Old World terms, the marks of the past are buried deep enough beneath the detritus of the present that the same narrative seems to make sense. The energy crises of the 1970s shook this easy faith in progress, but the following decade saw that moment of uncertainty dismissed as an aberration, or rather a nightmare of sorts from which we had all thankfully awakened.

Readers who hope to see those same reassuring sentiments repeated here will be disappointed. The energy crises of the 1970s, as this book will show, were anything but an aberration. Rather, they marked industrial civilization's first brush with an unwelcome reality that will dominate the decades and centuries ahead of us. We have lived so long in a dream of perpetual economic and technological expansion that most people nowadays take progress for granted as the inevitable shape of the future. Our collective awakening from that fantasy may prove bitter — after sweet dreams, the cold light of morning is rarely a welcome sight — but at this turn of history's wheel, few things are more necessary.

No heresy raises hackles in the contemporary world quite so effectively as the suggestion that the soaring towers and equally lofty pretensions of the industrial world could become the crumbling ruins and dim memories of some future age. At the core of the modern world's identity is the conviction that our civilization is exempt from the slow trajectories of rise and fall that defined all of human history before the industrial revolution. It's an article of contemporary faith, as deeply and sincerely held as any religious creed, that we have been singled out for some larger destiny — perhaps a science fiction future among the stars, perhaps a grand catastrophe bigger and brighter than any other civilization has managed for itself, but certainly not the slow ebb of a tide of expansion that has been flowing since our ancestors figured out how to tap into the Earth's reserves of fossil fuels. This conviction colors nearly all modern attempts to make sense of the future.

The word "decline" has been absent from our historical sense for so long that most people nowadays find the possibility of economic, cultural, and technological decline impossible to grasp. Still, that unacknowledged possibility defines the most probable future for the modern industrial world. We have to face the fact that our civilization may not be exempt from the common fate, and could very well follow the great civilizations of the past down the long slope into history's dumpster.

In the view from that Caernarfon hilltop, the similarities that united the empires of past and present stood out clearly enough to bring that awareness within reach. In the pages that follow, I hope to provide a similar view from a more abstract height. The topography in question was originally surveyed by an American petroleum geologist in the middle years of the 20th century. Its name is Hubbert's peak, and the road that leads down from it traces out the most likely future we face today — a future I've named the Long Descent.

Making sense of that future will require a reassessment of many aspects of the recent past and careful attention to the cultural narratives we use to impose structure on the inkblot patterns of human history. Those tasks will be taken up in the first two chapters of this book, "The End of the Industrial Age" and "The Stories We Tell Ourselves." The chapter that follows, "Briefing for the Descent," outlines the likely shape of our approaching decline into a deindustrial future. The next two chapters, "Facing the Deindustrial Age" and "Tools for the Transition," map out the strategies and technologies that will be needed in an age of decline.

A final chapter, "The Spiritual Dimension," is an attempt to make sense of the Long Descent in the context of that realm of ultimate meanings we awkwardly call "spiritual" or, perhaps, "religious." An appendix, more technical in nature, outlines the theory of societal collapse that underlies the argument of this book.

No book is the product of a single mind, and this one in particular has benefited from the help I have received from many other people. Dr. Richard Duncan and the members of the Third Place Society introduced me to the world of peak oil and encouraged the first rough outlines of the ideas presented here. Richard Heinberg offered valuable feedback at several stages of the process; he and Wijnandt de Vries also arranged for online publication of my initial essay "How Societies Fall: A Theory of Catabolic Collapse" when other options fell through. Many people provided valuable feedback on that essay and on subsequent posts on my blog, "The Archdruid Report," where many of the ideas discussed in this book were first aired. All the staff of New Society Publishers, especially publisher Chris Plant and editor Linda Glass, were unfailingly enthusiastic and helpful.

Another series of intellectual debts begins with Corby Ingold, who introduced me to the modern Druid tradition. Philip Carr-Gomm, Chosen Chief of the Order of Bards Ovates and Druids (OBOD), helped me make sense of Druidry and posed cogent questions about the interface between Druid spirituality and the fate of the industrial world. The visit to Caernarfon described at the beginning of this introduction was made possible by OBOD's Mount Haemus award for Druid scholarship, for which I also must thank the Order's Patroness Dwina Murphy-Gibb. Dr. John Gilbert welcomed me into the Ancient Order of Druids in America (AODA), the Druid order I now head. He and many other members of AODA have played crucial roles in shaping my ideas on this and many other subjects. My wife Sara, finally, has had a central part in helping to shape this book, and in the rest of my life. My thanks go to all.

The End
of the
Industrial Age

F **or those of us** who grew up during the energy crises of the 1970s, recent headlines have taken on an eerie degree of familiarity. Now as then, soaring energy costs make the news almost daily, part of a wider economic shift that's sending the prices of many raw materials through the roof. The countries that export the oil we in North America waste so casually (OPEC then; Iran, Venezuela, and Russia now) are showing an uncomfortable eagerness to cash in their economic chips for the headier coin of international power. Meanwhile the US balance of trade sinks further into a sea of red ink as imported consumer goods from our largest Asian trading partner (Japan then, China now) overwhelm what's left of American exports, sending the dollar skidding against most foreign currencies. In Yogi Berra's famous words, it's déjà vu all over again.

Then as now, too, the rising cost of oil isn't simply the result of market vagaries or the wickedness of oil companies. It comes out of a disastrous mismatch between our economic system and the hard facts of petroleum geology. In 1970, petroleum production in the

I

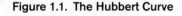

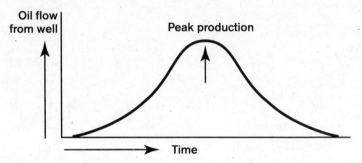

One of the basic tools of petroleum geology, the Hubbert curve predicts the total production of petroleum from an oil well. Peak production comes when about half of total production has already taken place.

United States reached its all-time peak and began the steady decline that continues to this day. This decline forced American society, raised on fantasies of endless supplies of cheap home-grown energy, to retool its foreign policy, its economy, and its culture to deal with the unwelcome new reality of dependence on overseas reserves. Much of the economic and cultural turmoil of the decade after 1970 came out of the wrenching changes demanded by that new reality.

The peak of US oil production came as a surprise only to those who weren't paying attention. Decades before, a petroleum geologist named M. King Hubbert worked out equations that predict in advance how much oil you can get from a well.[1] Oil is viscous stuff, and it takes time to move through pores and crevices in the rock that contains it. When an oil well pierces the rock and starts drawing out oil, the flow starts off slowly, gradually rises to peak production, and dwindles away just as gradually to nothing. Normally this works out to a bell-shaped curve, the Hubbert curve, that ranks today as one of the basic tools of petroleum geology.

Hubbert's discovery, however, had wider implications. The same curve, he found, was just as effective a way of tracking production from oil fields, oil provinces (regions with similar geological features), and the oil reserves of entire nations. It's worth taking the time to understand how this works, because both the crisis of the 1970s and the larger crisis taking shape around us today both unfold from it. Production from a field, an oil province, or a country starts off slowly, just as with an oil well, because it takes time and investment to find the right places to drill. As the first few wells start producing, more wells are drilled, and total production rises. Eventually, though, the rising curve of production runs into the awkward fact that any given field, oil province, or country only contains so much oil.

This impacts production in two ways. First, as the number of wells rises, it gets harder to find more places where oil can be drilled. Second, old wells start to run dry as each one follows its own Hubbert curve, and so rising production from new wells starts to be offset by dwindling production from older ones. Sooner or later, these two factors overtake the rate of new oil production, and the field, province, or nation tips into decline. On average, this happens when about half the recoverable oil has been pumped out. There's still plenty of oil in the ground when this happens, and much of it may not even be discovered by then, but each new well drilled after the peak simply helps take up some of the slack from older wells that are running dry.

All through the early 1950s, Hubbert tried out his curve on oil field data from around the world and refined his equations. In 1956 he took the next step by predicting publicly that oil production in the United States would peak about 1970, and then enter a permanent decline. Almost everyone in the oil industry dismissed his claim as nonsense. The conventional wisdom insisted that better technology and increased investment would keep US domestic oil production rising into the far future.

As the numbers came in during the early 1970s, though, it became clear that Hubbert was right. Despite immense investment, dramatic new technological advances, and federal tax policies that amounted to a trillion-dollar giveaway to the American oil industry, production peaked and then began to shrink right on schedule. That peak and decline gave the newly founded Organization of Petroleum Exporting Countries (OPEC) the leverage they needed to force the price of oil upward. Then, when the United States sided with Israel in the 1973 Yom Kippur War, OPEC was able to impose an oil embargo that came close to bringing the US economy to its knees.

Hubbert was not finished, though. In 1970, armed with the best current estimates of world oil reserves, he took his curve one step further and applied it to the entire world. His calculations predicted that oil production for the entire planet would crest around 2000, and decline thereafter. This was bad news for a global economy that depended on oil for close to half its energy and nearly all its transportation. How bad the news might be, though, did not become clear until a few years later, when a study sponsored by the Club of Rome put the concepts of limits to growth on the Western world's cognitive map.

The Limits To Growth

The Club of Rome was founded in 1968 by Aurelio Peccei, a former CEO of Italian auto manufacturer Fiat. Its mission was to find constructive responses to what Peccei called "the global problematique" — the spiral of converging crises that he, along with many leading figures in economic and scientific fields, saw closing in on industrial society in the second half of the 20th century. Shortly after its founding, the Club hired a team of MIT scientists and computer engineers for a daring project — an attempt to predict the future course of industrial society. The results of the project saw print in 1972 as the controversial bestseller *The Limits to Growth*, one of the defining books of the decade and the storm center of bitter debates that continue to this day.

What the *Limits to Growth* team found was that, in simplest terms, unlimited growth on a finite planet is a recipe for disaster. As population increases and economic growth unfolds, the world has to provide ever greater supplies of food, water, energy, and raw materials for industry. The Earth, though, only has so much oil, so much coal, so much topsoil, and so on through the sprawling list of resources used by industrial society, and it can only absorb so much pollution before the natural systems that support the global economy begin to break down. Since these systems include the weather patterns, water and nutrient cycles, and ecological interactions that produce food for people to eat, wood and other raw materials for them to use, and even the oxygen they breathe, this is not a small matter.

None of this is a problem as long as a society stays within what ecologists call the *carrying capacity* of its environment (the level of resource use and pollution the environment can support indefinitely). Once growth outstrips carrying capacity, though, resources become scarcer while demand rises, and so the costs of supplying the economy with what it needs climb steadily. Meanwhile, rising population and economic growth churn out ever greater amounts of pollution and put increasing strains on economically important natural systems. As these natural systems begin coming apart, the global economy either has to pay to do things nature once did for free or it has to fund pollution control measures to keep natural systems operating. Either way, costs go up.

The *Limits to Growth* team found that the twin economic burdens of resource depletion and pollution turn a growth-oriented economy into its own nemesis. The MIT team's computer models showed that once an economy overshoots the carrying capacity of its environment, the costs of resource depletion and pollution rise faster than the rate of economic growth. In the end the economic burden of dealing with the consequences of growth overwhelms growth itself and brings the global economy to its knees.

All this posed a stark contradiction to one of the most widely held beliefs in modern economics — the conviction that economic growth is the answer to all the problems of human society. The *Limits to Growth* demonstrated that you can't grow your way out of a crisis if growth is what's causing the crisis in the first place. The study concluded with the sobering assessment that unless something changed drastically, the limits to economic growth would arrive sometime in the first half of the 21st century and push industrial society over the edge into a long period of catastrophic decline.

From the day of its publication, *The Limits to Growth* became the focus of a firestorm of criticism, much of it politically motivated and not all of it fair or well informed. Economists dismissed it out of hand; conservative politicians denounced it as something close to a Communist plot; and plenty of people from all walks of life found its conclusions impossible to accept. Still, it found receptive audiences all over the world. While the use of sophisticated computer models was new, the risks charted by the MIT team were simply a restatement of problems already discussed in educated circles in Europe and America for most of a century before *Limits to Growth* was published.

By the late 19th century, in fact, perceptive people in Europe and America were already comparing the modern West to ancient Rome and other vanished civilizations and suggesting that industrial civilization was already on the downslope of its history.[2] The crises of the 1970s brought these uncomfortable possibilities to center stage. The industrial world found itself confronted with a succession of economic crises — soaring energy costs driven by depletion at home and the rising power of OPEC overseas, and the American military failure in Vietnam. These troubles drove many people to take a hard second look at their assumptions about the future, kickstarting a flurry of projects aimed at retooling industrial society so that it could survive in an age of resource depletion and ecological limits.

Some of those projects were follies from the start, and others that could have succeeded foundered on the inevitable problems facing any innovative venture. Fingerpointing and scapegoat hunting played as large a part in the collective dialogue then as it does today, but despite all that, a remarkable amount of effort went into constructive responses to the crisis. The 1970s were a boomtime for the now-forgotten "appropriate technology movement," which developed an impressive toolkit of methods for conserving energy and raw materials. Two other movements — organic agriculture and recycling — moved off the drawing boards and became profitable industries during that decade.

Conservation and energy efficiency in general had a pervasive presence on the cultural radar screens of the time. Most Americans in those years knew about insulation and weatherstripping and at least glanced at the miles-per-gallon numbers when shopping for a car. The result was an unprecedented decline in energy use — for example, petroleum consumption worldwide went down some 15% in the decade after 1973.[3] For a brief moment in the late 1970s, it seemed possible that the industrial world might move forward to a future of sustainable prosperity.

The successes of 1970s conservation, however, represented only the first baby steps toward that goal. By the end of the 1970s most serious students of energy policy saw only two realistic options for going further. The first would have thrown the full weight of government policy and funding into a transition toward a "conserver society," in which stability rather than growth would be the watchword. The second would have launched a transition to nuclear power, gambling the future of the industrial world on the success and safety of untried breeder reactor and fusion technologies. Both options were major challenges with huge financial and political price tags.[4]

The Reagan/Thatcher era saw politicians across the industrial world choose a third option, breathtaking in its simplicity — or rather, in its simple-mindedness. Where the conserver society and the nuclear options accepted severe short-term costs to ensure the long-term survival of industrial society, 1980s political leaders across the industrial world pursued short-term strategies that forced energy prices down in order to keep the electorate and business interests happy; the politicians simply hoped that things would somehow work out in the long term.

The conservation successes of the 1970s helped make this decline in energy costs possible by bringing down the demand for oil. The reckless overproduction of newly discovered oil fields in the North Sea and Alaska's North Slope finished the process by allowing American and British governments to turn the oil spigot all the way on, sending the price of oil crashing to levels that were (in constant dollars or pounds) lower than ever before. As a short-term strategy, it proved overwhelmingly successful: energy prices plummeted; economies shook themselves out of the "stagflation" of the 1970s; and the Soviet Union lurched into bankruptcy and political collapse as oil — its one reliable source of hard currency — no longer propped up the inefficiencies of the Communist system.

The blowback from these successes, though, is only just coming due today. As energy prices plunged, efforts to find a replacement for fossil fuels withered on the vine. Alternative energy companies went bankrupt by the score as the market for their products evaporated. The nuclear industry took just as severe a hit; only massive government subsidies kept nuclear plants functioning as the price of electricity dropped below the cost of producing it by splitting atoms. The 1982 bankruptcy of the Washington Public Power Supply System, a grandiose, and wildly overpriced nuclear power project, convinced investors around the world that the nuclear industry was a sucker's bet.

Some of those who pushed the short-term economic fixes of the 1980s likely did so out of sheer political opportunism — it's almost always a good election strategy to tell voters what they want to hear. Still, it's only fair to say that some of those who supported the energy policies of Reagan, Thatcher, and their equivalents in other industrial nations had more respectable reasons for doing so. Faith in the free market's ability to solve all problems was at an all-time high. Influential conservative intellectuals of the period such as Julian Simon and Herman Kahn argued that the exhaustion of petroleum reserves was a nonproblem. Once government regulations got out of the way (the claim went) entrepreneurs would come up with abundant new energy sources and all would be well.

Those of us who were around in the 1980s may still remember the Laffer Curve, the theory floated by Reagan's economic officials that tax revenues could actually be increased by cutting taxes. The theory was that excessive taxes stifled business activity and lower rates would spur so much economic expansion that they would actually bring in more revenue. Although it looked plausible at the time, it didn't work. Instead, the Reagan tax cuts landed the United States in a cycle of reckless deficit spending that continues today. The energy policy embraced by industrial nations in the 1980s followed a similar logic. It looked just as plausible to many people at the time, and it turned out to be just as misguided in the long run.

For most of the 1980s and 1990s, though, it looked to many as though both the energy shortages and the visions of sustainability seen in the 1970s were an aberration best forgotten. That was where matters stood in the late 1990s, when Hubbert's nearly forgotten 1970 prediction suddenly took on a great deal of new urgency and a new phrase — "peak oil" — started moving in whispers through the intellectual back alleys of the industrial world.

The Coming of Peak Oil

At the time, nothing seemed sillier than concern about the future of the world's energy supply. Oil prices were at historic lows, bumping along just above the $10 a barrel level. Gasoline was so cheap that huge, gas-guzzling SUVs had become America's latest automotive obsession, and they were starting to find a market overseas. Energy had cost so little for so long that most of the conservation programs put in place during the 1970s had long since been scrapped. Hubbert's curve, while it remained a standard tool among working petroleum geologists, had dropped so far out of public awareness that even the best discussions of energy in the 1990s routinely missed the fact that oil production would peak

and decline a long time before the last of the world's oil was extracted from the ground.[5]

The only thing wrong with the comfortable picture of abundant oil was the troubling numbers coming from the oil industry. Despite huge investments in exploration and discovery, it was
becoming harder and harder to find new oil fields, while existing
oil fields all over the world moved closer to their Hubbert peaks
and the world's thirst for oil kept climbing. Those who took the
time to put the numbers together discovered that the volume of
oil pumped out of the ground overshot the volume of new oil discovered in every year since 1964, and the gap was growing — by
2000, for example, new discoveries only equaled a quarter of the
oil drawn from existing wells that year. Since oil has to be found
before it can be pumped, and it can only be pumped out of the
ground once, a slump in the rate of oil field discovery is the prover-
bial canary in the mine shaft of the petroleum economy.

These unwelcome figures brought belated attention to
Hubbert's 1970 prediction of a 2000 peak. During the late 1990s,
several teams of independent researchers set out to update
Hubbert's figures. This was a challenging task, not least because
oil in the ground is an asset that affects stock prices and the value
of national currencies. Oil companies and oil-exporting nations
alike have strong incentives to inflate their reserves and no reason
at all to reveal details that might puncture the bubble of apparent prosperity. As a result, many oil-producing nations keep the
size of their oil reserves secret, and the estimates published by various government and industry sources are unreliable, at best. Still,
as the teams crunched numbers and found ways to estimate figures they could not locate, it became clear that unless the world
had much more oil than the evidence showed, the world's Hubbert
peak was much closer than anyone had guessed.

The imminence of the peak was bad news because the entire
modern way of life runs on oil. Industrial civilization demands
fantastic inputs of energy. Oil, more than anything else, keeps it

running. Oil is nearly the perfect energy source: there was originally a huge amount of it, it contains a huge amount of energy per
unit of volume, it can be extracted from the ground very cheaply,
it's just as easy to transport and store, it's even easier to use, and
it's *fungible* — that is, it can be easily put to work in many different
ways; you can burn it to produce heat, power motors, fuel cars or
planes, generate electricity, or anything else you want. Oil provides
40% of all energy used by human beings on Earth, and it powers
nearly all transportation in the industrial world. It's also the most
important raw material for plastics, agricultural and industrial
chemicals, lubricants, and asphalt roads.

As the first peak oil researchers and activists began work, two
objectives took center stage in their work: figuring out when the
worldwide peak of petroleum production would arrive, and com-
municating the unwelcome news to the rest of the world. The first
of these tasks proved to be the easiest. A loose network of retired
petroleum geologists and engineers — Colin Campbell, Kenneth
Deffeyes, Richard Duncan, Walter Youngquist, and others — took
the lead in sorting through the data on oil reserves. Taking advantage of the great strides made in computer technology in the 1990s,
they developed analytical models as accurate as the ones used by
the major oil companies. As the end of the decade closed in, the results of these new models converged, placing peak between 2005
and 2010. As the imminence of the peak became clearer, the focus
shifted steadily toward the second objective — getting the word
out to governments and the public that a new round of energy crises might soon be in the offing.

At first, these warnings fell on deaf ears. The same business
and government interests that had been fighting tooth and nail
against the recognition of global warming quickly turned on peak
oil as well. In the resulting debate, official figures on oil reserves
too often reflected political expediency rather than accurate science. Thus the Energy Information Agency (EIA), a branch of the
US Department of Energy, has long been one of the major sources

used by debunkers of the peak oil theory. Its own documents, however, show that the figures it offers for future oil production are generated by estimating future demand for oil and then assuming that the supply will be there when it's needed.[6] To say that this begs the question is to understate matters considerably.

One of the many ironies of these debates is that while the EIA and other government agencies massaged the data, the peak oil message had already found an audience in the highest levels of the American political system. One of the experts who began speaking out about peak oil in the late 1990s was Matthew Simmons, a banker to the energy industry who served as energy advisor to Vice President Cheney in the months immediately before and after the 2000 election. Many astute observers of the American political scene have argued that peak oil has been the hidden subtext behind much of American foreign policy since that time.[7] This would certainly go far to explain the Bush administration's obsession with launching an invasion of Iraq, a country that probably has more untapped oil reserves than any other nation in the world.

If access to oil supplies was the point of America's recent Middle East entanglements, the results have not been worth the cost in money, lives, and international prestige. The Afghanistan and Iraq invasions put American troops in control of the world's last remaining major undeveloped oil fields. In both cases, however, American military power drove a hostile government from power but proved unable to make peace in their absence, much less secure access to oil reserves. Moreover, these military adventures have pushed America into exactly the sort of imperial overstretch that Paul Kennedy warned about in his widely respected book *The Rise and Fall of the Great Powers*.

Meanwhile, the energy, materials, and time expended on these ventures were desperately needed to help make the transition to a post-peak economy. One of the central themes of *The Limits to Growth* was precisely that modern civilization cannot turn on a dime. Changing from one energy resource to another isn't simply a matter of pouring something different into our gas tanks, because much of today's energy infrastructure is fuel-specific — that is, you can't burn coal in a nuclear reactor or dispense hydrogen through a gasoline pump. It took 150 years and some of the biggest investments in history to build the industrial, economic, and human infrastructure that turns petroleum from black goo in the ground to the key power source of modern society. To replace all that infrastructure with a new system designed to run on some other form of energy would take roughly the same level of investment, as well as a great deal of time.

In a widely cited 2005 study, a team of researchers headed by Robert Hirsch determined that even given the full resources of the US government, a program to head off the worst consequences of peak oil would have to be launched fully twenty years before peak to keep the inevitable production declines from having severe impacts on economy and society.[8] The problem here is that we don't have twenty years. We probably don't have ten. We may not have five. As I write these words, world petroleum production appears to have peaked in late 2005 and declined since then, despite sky-high prices that make even the most marginal oil wells paying propositions. Several more years will need to pass before it's clear whether those declines are a temporary fluke or the beginning of the end of the Petroleum Age, but it's possible that peak oil has already arrived.

Replacing Petroleum?

The obvious solution to the peak oil problem is to find something to replace oil, and this became a third major topic for discussions within the peak oil community as soon as the scale of the problem became clear. The problem peak oil researchers found, as their equivalents in the 1970s discovered before them, is that replacing oil with anything else is much more difficult than it looks. Sheer volume poses the first of many difficulties. The world burns

84 million barrels of petroleum — more than three and a half billion gallons — every single day, with about a quarter of that going to the United States. Replacing even a small fraction of that vast flood of energy and material from any other source poses staggering challenges.

To start with, the three other fuels that, together with oil, provide most of the world's energy — coal, natural gas, and uranium — are already being exploited at a breakneck pace. Official statements about reserves of these resources suffer from the same distortions as oil, for similar reasons, and statements that there will be plenty of these fuels for many years to come need to be assessed with this in mind. These sanguine estimates also fail to take into account what would happen if production has to be increased in order to make up for dwindling supplies of oil.

As things stand today, uranium reserves are severely depleted worldwide (roughly half of the reactor fuel used today comes from dismantled Russian warheads, not from mines) and prices have soared accordingly in recent years.[9] Unless huge new reserves turn up unexpectedly, the supply of reactor fuel will start to fall short of demand sometime before 2010 — in other words, around the same time oil does. Natural gas is expected to hit its worldwide Hubbert peak around ten years after oil, and North American natural gas production will most likely begin dropping before that. Furthermore, a growing fraction of Canadian gas now gets burned to power the plants that extract oil from Alberta's tar sands, which decreases the amount of gas available for other uses and accelerates the depletion rate.

The one fossil fuel we can expect to have left in large quantities after oil peaks is coal, the most abundant of all the fossil fuels — and also the dirtiest. For many years, claims that the world had virtually endless supplies of coal have been part of conventional wisdom, but recent studies have cast serious doubts on that comforting faith; the National Academy of Sciences, for example, has issued a report warning that current estimates of the amount of coal left in the United States are wildly inflated.[10] Furthermore, unlike oil or natural gas, coal's energy content varies dramatically from one variety to another. Anthracite, the most energy-rich grade of coal, contains about half the energy as the same weight of petroleum, while lignite, the lowest grade, contains as little as a sixth.[11] Sensibly enough, mining firms have concentrated on extracting the best grades of coal first, and so most of what's left is low-grade "brown coal" full of sulfur and other impurities. In recent years the ratio between the amount of energy provided by coal and the amount of energy needed to mine it has been dropping rapidly — so rapidly, according to some studies, that by 2040 coal will take about twice as much energy to mine as it produces when burned.

The problems with coal are a good example of the crucial problem of *net energy*, the least discussed and most challenging part of the energy equation. To get energy out of any resource, you have to put energy in. To access the energy in oil, for example, you have to invest the energy needed to drill and maintain an oil well. The energy you get out minus the energy you put in equals the net energy of the resource. Net energy varies from one fuel to another, and it also varies from one source to another — oil from a newly drilled well producing light sweet crude under natural pressure can have a net energy of 200 or more (that is, burning the oil yields 200 or more times as much energy as it takes to drill and maintain the well). On the other hand, oil from an old well that has to be pumped out of the ground often has net energy down in single digits.

A net energy of 1 is the breakeven point — the resource yields exactly as much energy as went into extracting it — and many of the proposed "solutions" to the energy crisis have lower net energy than that. This makes them energy sinks, not energy sources. Hydrogen, the "wonder fuel" ballyhooed by so many pundits in recent years, could be the poster child for this particular problem because there are no reserves of hydrogen gas lying around waiting

for us to tap into them — not this side of the planet Jupiter, anyway. Pure hydrogen must be manufactured from water or natural gas, and you have to put slightly more energy into extracting it
from these sources than you will get back from burning it; the result is negative net energy. Trying to run an economy on energy
sources with negative net energy is like trying to support yourself
by buying $1 bills for $2 each. No matter how you calculate it, it's a
losing proposition.

More insidious is the fact that all other fuels and energy resources receive a hidden "energy subsidy" from oil. For example, coal is excavated and transported by machinery powered by
petroleum-derived diesel fuel, not by coal. Coal contains much less
energy than oil does. As mentioned earlier, it takes about twice as
much coal as oil to do the same amount of work, even with anthracite, and if you're burning brown coal it takes much more. If coal
has to be mined, processed, and shipped using machinery powered by coal or a coal-derived diesel substitute, costs soar and ef-
ficiencies slump by at least a factor of two. Of course, if you have
to turn the coal into a liquid fuel, or build new mining machinery to run on coal, the energy needed for either process also has to
be factored into the equation. If oil prices itself out of the market,
in other words, coal reserves have to be drawn down much faster
just to maintain current levels of coal production. Try to replace
oil with coal, using coal-powered technology to do the mining, and
seemingly huge coal reserves run out rapidly.

If other fossil fuels and conventional nuclear power can't take
up the slack, what about exotic technologies such as breeder reactors and nuclear fusion? There has been a great deal of hype about
these high-tech methods, but a flotilla of challenges still has to
be met before any of them contributes even a single kilowatt to
the electricity grid. Most of the handful of breeder reactors built
around the world in the last few decades have been shut down due
to massive technical problems. Fusion has never even gotten that
far despite billions of dollars in research funds. Only Nature has

been able to construct a working fusion reactor that actually produces energy in useable amounts.[12] Even if one or more of these technologies could be made to work, retooling the modern energy economy to make use of them would demand immense and increasingly scarce amounts of money, resources, and time. Proponents of these exotic technologies have never addressed — much less answered — the question of how much *net* energy could be produced.

All of this leaves only renewable resources such as solar power, wind, and biofuels to supply our energy. Some of these have net energies in the single figures, others are close to breakeven, and still others fall well below the breakeven point, making them useless once the energy subsidy from oil runs out. Those that yield positive net energy have a valuable part to play in the world's energy future, but crippling problems of scale make it impossible to replace more than a small fraction of fossil fuels with renewable energy. It's worth taking a moment to see how this works.

Let's imagine, for example, that the United States decided to replace its current gasoline consumption (a large sector of its fossil fuel use, though not the largest) with ethanol derived from corn. The United States uses about 146 billion gallons of gasoline a year; since ethanol only yields three-quarters as much energy per gallon as gasoline, it would take a bit over 194 billion gallons of ethanol to keep the present American automobile fleet on the road for a year. According to US government figures, there are about 302 million acres of arable land in the United States; corn yields about 146 bushels an acre on average, and you can get 2.5 gallons of pure ethanol out of a bushel of corn.[13] This means that if every square inch of American farmland were put to work filling our gas tanks — with none left over to grow food or anything else — the total yield of ethanol would only be a little over 110 billion gallons, which is just a bit more than half of our current gasoline consumption.

Still, this is only the first half of the equation, because oil has more net energy than ethanol. Drilling for oil is relatively cheap in

energy terms, and refining it from crude oil uses 5% or less of the
energy value of the crude oil it comes from.[14] By contrast, it takes
a great deal of energy to produce 146 bushels of corn an acre, and
it takes a good deal more to process and ferment the corn on an
industrial scale. The exact energy costs to grow corn and turn it
into ethanol vary widely depending on details as complex as the
terrain of farmland, the sugar content of the variety of corn, and
the amount of rainfall in the months prior to harvest. It's possible to provide this additional energy in different ways, too — in
terms of growing costs, for example, you can divert a large share
of the ethanol to power tractors and combines, or you can divert
a large share of the corn to feed horses and farmhands — but one
way or another, you have to factor in the extra energy needed to
get from seed and soil to ethanol fuel. Even if all the arable land
in the United States were devoted to replacing gasoline consumption, the amount of energy produced would fall drastically short of
current needs.

The same thing is true of every other form of renewable energy. Today, the world gets much of its energy supply almost free
of charge by drilling a hole in the ground and piping the results
somewhere. Getting the same amount of energy in any other way
requires much more energy to be fed back into the energy production process. Nowhere does the energy subsidy for cheap oil have a
greater effect than on renewables. Making a solar cell, for instance,
requires large infusions of diesel fuel first to mine the raw materials and then to ship them to the factory. Even larger doses of natural gas or coal are needed to generate the electricity that powers
the complex process of turning the raw materials into a cell that
will make electricity out of sunlight. The complexity of the process
makes net energy calculations challenging, but estimates range
from a very optimistic 10:1 yield to more pessimistic, and arguably
more realistic, 1:1 net energy yield.[15] Not even the most optimistic
calculations show solar cells yielding anything in the same ballpark
as the net energy routinely produced by all but the poorest fossil

fuels. The same, as it turns out, is true of every other alternative resource.

Fossil fuels are so much more valuable than other energy resources because they get a double energy subsidy from Nature herself. The first half of the subsidy arrived in the prehistoric past via photosynthesis, the process by which plants absorb and concentrate solar energy. All the fossil fuels, in energy terms, are stored sunlight heaped up over geologic time long before our ancestors strayed out of the shrinking tropical forests of the late Pliocene and launched themselves on the trajectory that led to us. No human being had to put a single day's work or a single gallon of diesel fuel into growing the tree ferns of the Carboniferous period that turned into Pennsylvanian coal beds, nor did they have to raise the Jurassic sea life that became the oil fields of Texas.

The second half of Nature's energy subsidy took the form of extreme temperatures and pressures deep within the Earth. Over millions of years more, these transformed the remains of prehistoric living things into coal, oil, and natural gas and, in the process, concentrated the energy they originally contained into a tiny fraction of their original size. A layer of anthracite coal bed an inch thick, for example, was originally a layer of dead plants several yards thick when it sank below the surface of a swamp 300 million years ago; despite the change in size, it still contains nearly all the flammable carbon of the original biomass. The result is fossil fuel that packs a huge amount of energy into a very small space.

Thus it's important to recognize the crucial distinction between a concentrated energy source and a diffuse one. If you had a handful of burning coal in one cupped palm, and a handful of sunshine in the other, you would certainly notice the difference. In the one hand is a resource that can conceivably support the intensive energy demands of an industrial society, and in the other is a resource that cannot.

All these factors play a part in setting the stage for the energy crisis emerging around us today, making it clear that the predictions of *The Limits to Growth* have stood up to the test of time rather better than the claims circulated by its detractors. Just as the study's authors predicted, industrial civilization finds itself squeezed by resource depletion. Peak oil is the poster child for this unwelcome change, but it's not the only resource likely to be in short supply in the near future. The waves of climate change and freak weather driven by CO_2 emissions from the industrial world's tailpipes and smokestacks provide a sharp reminder that the other side of the Club of Rome's prediction — the menace of rising costs from pollution — is also present and accounted for. Unfortunately the three decades it took to prove the study's thesis were also the three decades in which the first crucial steps in the transition toward sustainability might have been made.

Problems and Predicaments

Plenty of pundits and ordinary people alike insist there still must be some constructive way out of the current situation. First in line are those who insist that replacing the rascals in power with some other set of rascals more to their liking would solve the problems facing industrial civilization. Next come those who argue that if only the right technological fix gets put in place, business as usual can continue. Further down the line are radicals of various stripes who insist that the best solution to the present crisis is to let industrial civilization crash and burn, in the firm belief that it would be replaced by some way of life they consider more appealing. Still others envisage the construction of lifeboat communities that have their own localized sustainable economies, created in an effort to get the basics of an alternative, sustainable economy in place before the existing one falls apart completely. All of these proposals approach the situation as a problem in need of a solution. This may seem like common sense, but it's not. A historical parallel may help point up what's going on here.

Imagine that some ancestor of mine shows up in a prosperous farming village in the English Midlands on a bright autumn

day around 1700. It's a peaceful scene perched on the edge of catastrophic change, courtesy of the imminent arrival of the Industrial
Revolution. Within a century, every building in the village will be
torn down, its fields turned into pasture for sheep, and the farmers and cottagers driven off their land by enclosure acts passed by
a distant Parliament to provide wool for England's cloth industry
and profits for a new class of industrial magnates. For the young
men of the village, England's transformation into a worldwide empire constantly warring with European rivals and indigenous peoples overseas prophesies a future of press gangs, military service,
and death on battlefields around the globe. For a majority of the
other residents, the future offers a forced choice between a life of
factory labor at starvation wages in bleak urban slums and emigra-
tion to an uncertain fate in the American colonies. A lucky few will
prosper spectacularly by betting on ways of making a living that
nobody present on that autumn day has even imagined yet.

Imagine that, improbably enough, my ancestor figured all this
out in advance, and has come to warn the villagers of what is in
store for them. There, on the village green in the shade of an old
oak, with everyone from the squire and the parson to the swine-
herds and day laborers gathered around him, he tells them that
their way of life will be utterly destroyed, and tries to sketch out
for them how the coming of industrial society will impact them,
their children, and the land and life they love. Imagine that, even
more improbably, they take the warning seriously. As the afternoon passes, the villagers agree that this is a serious problem indeed. What, they ask my imaginary ancestor, does he think they
should do about it? What solutions does he have to offer?

What could he say in response? From today's perspective, it's
clear that nothing the villagers could have done would have de-
flected the course of the Industrial Revolution even slightly. Events
far beyond their control — geological events millions of years in
the past that laid down huge coal deposits in the shallow seas that
would someday become England, economic patterns going back

most of the way to the fall of Rome, political shifts that had been shaking all of Europe for two centuries — drove England toward its industrial transformation. If by asking for a solution, his listeners hoped to find a way to change the whole situation for the better, my imaginary ancestor would have had to say that there was none. At most, he might have been able to give the villagers some general advice on how to cope with the torrent of changes about to break over their heads.

The consequences of the Industrial Revolution were just as complex as its causes. The destruction of England's traditional rural economy and the society that depended on it drove waves of change that moved out in all directions. Successful responses to it followed the same divergent paths. Some people prospered by abandoning their old lives and making the crossing to a new continent or a new economy, some by digging in their heels and maintaining their old way of life as long as possible, and others by staying flexible and keeping their options open. Still, none of these options offered a guarantee; many who attempted them found that they led only to impoverishment and an early death.

The question itself is the difficulty. What those English villagers faced in the years after 1700 was a predicament, not a problem. The difference is that a *problem* calls for a solution; the only question is whether a solution can be found and made to work and, once this is done, the problem is solved. A *predicament*, by contrast, has no solution. Faced with a predicament, people come up with responses. Those responses may succeed, they may fail, or they may fall somewhere in between, but none of them "solves" the predicament, in the sense that none of them makes it go away.

For human beings, at least, the archetypal predicament is the imminence of death. Facing it, we come up with responses that range from evasion and denial to some of the greatest creations of the human mind. Since it's a predicament, not a problem, the responses don't make it go away; they don't "solve" it, they simply deal with the reality of it. No one response works for everybody, though some do tend to work better than others. The predicament remains, and it conditions every aspect of life in one way or another.

The difference between a problem and a predicament has particular relevance here and now, because the last three hundred years or so have witnessed a curious shift in the way some of the basic factors of human life have been conceptualized. Since the dawn of industrial civilization, the predicaments that define what used to be called "the human condition" have been reframed as a set of problems to be solved. Death itself falls into this category. On the one hand, we've got transhumanists such as Alan Harrington in *The Immortalist* proclaiming that death is "an unacceptable imposition on the human race;"[16] on the other hand we've got a medical industry willing to inflict almost any amount of indignity and pain in order to preserve bare biological life a little longer at all costs. Our culture's mythology of progress envisions the goal of civilization as a utopian state in which poverty, illness, death, and every other aspect of the human predicament has been converted into problems and solved by technology.

The difficulty with all this is that predicaments don't stop being predicaments just because we decide to treat them as problems. There are still plenty of challenges we can't solve and be done with; we have to respond to them and live with them. Death, for example, is not an "imposition;" it's an inescapable part of the human condition. A good case could be made, and indeed has been made, that it's also one of the prime driving forces behind human art, culture, spirituality, and wisdom, and that the confrontation with the inevitability of one's own death is an unavoidable step on the path to human maturity.

The irony of the current crisis is that a civilization that tried to turn all its predicaments into problems has ended up confronted with problems that, after being ignored too long, turned into predicaments. A controlled, creative transition to sustainability might have been possible if the promising beginnings of the 1970s had been followed up in the 1980s and 1990s. That didn't happen, and now we have to live with the consequences. One of the best ways to gauge the shape of those consequences is to look at older civilizations that have encountered the limits to growth, and draw tentative conclusions based on their experiences.

The Lessons of History

It's unpopular these days to suggest that we have anything to learn from the past. Possibly this is because history holds up an unflattering mirror to our follies. Those who recall the 1929 stock market bubble, for example, can find every detail repeated in the tech market frenzy of the late 1990s. The same claims that a "new economy" and new technology made the business cycle obsolete, the same proliferation of investment vehicles (investment trusts then, mutual funds today), the same airy confidence that stock values would go up forever and fundamentals didn't matter: fast forward seventy years and you saw the follies of 1929 replayed in 1999, cheered on by economists who, of all people, should have known better.

The rise and fall of civilizations offer the same embarrassment on a grander scale. We know what happens to societies that outrun their resource base: they go under. Dozens of past cultures ended up in history's wrecking yard for exactly this reason. Civilizations collapse; as Joseph Tainter pointed out in his useful book *The Collapse of Complex Societies*, it's one of the most predictable things about them. From this perspective, our industrial civilization may not be all that different from the scores of earlier civilizations that overshot their natural resource base and crashed to ruin as a result. The collapse of civilizations is a natural process. It doesn't follow exactly the same course in every situation, but like most natural processes, some things about it can be predicted by comparison with past examples.

One highly relevant example is the ancient Maya, who flourished on the Yucatan Peninsula of Central America while Europe struggled through the Dark Ages. Using only a Neolithic stone

technology, the Maya built an extraordinary, literate civilization
with fine art, architecture, astronomy, and mathematics, and a calendar more accurate than the one we use today. None of that saved
it from the common fate of civilizations. In a "rolling collapse"
spanning the years from 750–900 CE, Mayan civilization disinte-
grated, cities were abandoned to the jungle, and the population of
the lowland Maya heartland dropped by 90%.

The causes of the Maya collapse have been debated for well
over a century, but the latest archeological research supports the
long-held consensus among scholars that agricultural failure was
the central cause.[17] Like modern industrial society, the Maya built
their civilization on a nonrenewable resource base. In their case
it was the fertility of fragile tropical soils, which couldn't support
the Mayan version of intensive corn farming indefinitely. All the
achievements of Mayan civilization rested on the shaky foundation
of swidden agriculture — a system in which fields are allowed to
return to jungle after a few years of cultivation, while new fields are
cleared and enriched with ashes from burnt vegetation. It's a widely
used system in tropical areas around the world, but, like dependence on fossil fuels, it has a hidden vulnerability. Swidden works
extremely well at relatively modest population levels, but it breaks
down disastrously when population growth takes over and farms
can no longer return to jungle long enough to restore soil fertility.

Tropical soils lose most of their fertility after only a few years
of farming, and clearing too much jungle too quickly causes topsoil
erosion. Dust samples taken from cores of lake sediment from the
Yucatan show that both these processes spun out of control during
the Maya zenith and collapse. Soil depletion and erosion combined
with normal cycles of drought in the Yucatan to cause catastrophic
crop failures that sent classic Mayan civilization into a tailspin of
political and military chaos from which it never recovered.

Like modern industrial society, the Maya had plenty of options available as they approached what we might as well call "peak
corn." They knew about crops that give higher yields than corn but

draw less heavily on soil nutrients, such as manioc, sweet potato, or ramon nuts,[18] and they could have switched enough of their farmland to these crops to make a difference. Other ancient peoples managed shifts of this sort easily enough; many of the ancient Greek city-states did exactly that in the eighth century BCE. As a way of dealing with the stark ecological limitations of their rocky peninsula, the Greeks gave up an economy based on grain and cattle in favor of olive and grape farming for export.[19] Among the Maya, though, a switch of this sort was apparently never considered. Archeologists have been able to analyze the ancient Mayan diet by testing skeletons, and they found that corn provided more than 50% of the calories in the Maya diet before, during, and after the collapse.[20]

The reasons behind the failure to switch from corn to other crops is relevant to our own time because corn farming was central to Maya political ideology. The power of the *ahauob*, "divine lords" who ruled the Maya city-states, depended directly on control of the corn crop and indirectly on a religious ideology that made corn farming a core metaphor for government — Maya ceremonial art often showed the ahauob of great cities as farmers planting and cultivating corn fields. Because corn was a central cultural metaphor and a key resource of political power, abandoning it for other crops was unthinkable. Instead, the ahauob responded to the collapse of their agricultural base by going to war to seize fields and food supplies from other city-states, making their decline and fall far more brutal than it had to be.

Even so, the Maya decline wasn't a fast process. Maya cities weren't abandoned overnight, as archeologists of two generations ago mistakenly thought; most of them took a century and a half to go under. Outside the Maya heartland, the process took even longer. Chichen Itza far to the north still flourished long after cities such as Tikal and Bonampak had become overgrown ruins. Some small Mayan city-states survived in various corners of the Yucatan right up to the Spanish conquest.

Map the Maya collapse onto human lifespans and the real scale of the process comes through. A Lowland Maya woman born around 730 would have seen the crisis dawn, but the *ahauob* and their cities still flourished when she died of old age seventy years later. Her great-grandson, born around 800, grew up amid a disintegrating society, and the wars and crop failures of his time would have seemed ordinary to him. His great-granddaughter, born around 870, never knew anything but ruins sinking back into the jungle. When she and her family finally set out for a distant village, leaving an empty city behind them, it likely never occurred to her that their quiet footsteps on the dirt path marked the end of a civilization.

This same pattern repeats over and over again in history. Gradual disintegration, not sudden catastrophic collapse, is the way civilizations end. On average, it takes about 250 years for a civilization to complete the process of decline and fall.[21] This casts a startling light on the crises we face as we collide with the limits to growth. It took the Western world more than two centuries of incremental change to transform itself from an agrarian society to its current status. Now, with its resource base failing and the consequences of its maltreatment of nature piling up around it, it faces the common fate of civilizations. Yet if that fate follows its usual timeline, it could easily take two more centuries of incremental change to transform the industrial world to an agrarian society again.

Startling as this seems, it's supported by telling evidence. Consider our dwindling oil resources. The Hubbert curve we examined at the beginning of this chapter tracks production over time for any scale of oil reserve from a single oil well up to a planet. It's a bell shaped curve: oil comes slowly at first, rises to peak production, then falls gradually to zero. The peak arrives when roughly half the oil is gone. The crucial point here is that after the peak, oil production declines at about the same rate it rose before. If peak comes around 2010, production in 2040 will likely equal something not far from production in 1980 (about 20 billion barrels).

The oil produced in 2040 will have to meet the needs of a much larger global population and a world in crisis, but 20 billion barrels is still a lot of oil. In the same way, as reserves are depleted and production continues to slump over the decades that follow, the available oil will fall further and further below the levels needed to maintain a modern industrial society, but for a long time to come there will still be some petroleum available.

To misquote T. S. Eliot: this is the way the oil ends, not with a bang but a trickle. Other fossil fuels and uranium are headed the same way, but all of them can help cushion declining oil production for a while before they hit their own Hubbert peaks. Renewable energy sources can provide only a small fraction of the energy we now get from fossil fuels, but that fraction can also help cushion the decline and stretch dwindling fossil fuel reserves. The dilemma we face isn't having no energy at all. It's having to make do with less and less each year, until finally we get down to levels that can be sustained indefinitely.

The Olduvai Theory

The logic of the Hubbert curve provides the framework for the Olduvai Theory, an uncompromising look at the future in the aftermath of peak oil proposed by Dr. Richard Duncan, a professor emeritus of electrical engineering, who was also one of the most influential voices in the first days of the peak oil community.[22] Duncan's theory (named for the Olduval Gorge, the famous archeological site where Duncan first conceived the theory's central concepts) starts with White's Law, a widely accepted rule in human ecology that takes energy use per capita as the primary measure of economic development. Globally, energy per capita stood at very modest levels until 1800, when fossil fuels sent it skyrocketing to its all-time peak in 1979. At that point, Duncan's figures show, two centuries of explosive progress began to unravel.

After 1979, global energy use per capita declined as rising population outstripped modest increases in energy production. Once the Hubbert curve reaches its peak and energy production begins to decline, the downward arc of energy per capita will accelerate. Follow the curve, and by 2030 global energy per capita will be where it was in 1930, about a third of its 1979 peak. Duncan argues that the industrial age is a *pulse waveform*, a single, bell-shaped, nonrepeating curve centered on 1979. Since no renewable energy resource can provide more than a small fraction of the immense amounts of fossil fuel energy we've squandered in the recent past, he predicts that the millennia of low tech cultures preceding the industrial pulse — before the fantastic treasure of fossil fuel was discovered and unlocked — will be balanced by millennia of low tech cultures after the industrial pulse — when the treasure will be gone forever.

Such ideas are unthinkable to most people, especially in North America, where the industrial system has arguably achieved more than anywhere else. From the first years of European settlement, the faith that the New World would avoid the mistakes and follies of the old helped drive a dizzying range of social and political experiments. What French president Jacques Chirac mocked as the United States' "almost messianic sense of national mission" has deep roots in our national psyche. Perhaps the most potent of these roots is the rarely expressed but widely held conviction that the United States is exempt from history. The idea that North America's gleaming industrial cities might someday become crumbling ruins no different from the remains of other civilizations is outside the realm of the imaginable for most people today.

A glance at earlier civilizations on the North American continent offers a useful corrective to our delusion of invulnerability. Huge urban centers existed here long before the first European explorers blundered their way to the Atlantic coast. From Copan in the Yucatan jungles to Cahokia on the plains of the Midwest, urban civilizations in America rose, flourished, and fell in the same slow rhythm that defines the history of the Old World. The fact of the matter is that civilizations don't last forever. For all practical

purposes, they have a life cycle like that of other living things, and
when it's over, they die. That doesn't make the project of civilization pointless, as some people suggest, any more than the fact that
every one of us will die someday makes life not worth living. That
latter fact does mean, of course, that someone who insists he's going to live forever, and makes plans for his future based on that
premise, may not be quite as clever as he thinks he is. The same
thing is just as true of civilizations — including our own.

The conviction that history's cycles don't apply to us is especially counterproductive in our present circumstances. Imagine
that someone, confronted with a diagnosis of a life-threatening illness, insisted instead that he would live forever. For that reason,
he refused either to treat the illness or make sure his family would
have some means of support in the event of his death. He would
be considered completely irresponsible by most people — and for
good reason. This is exactly the collective situation we're in right
now. For more than three decades we've known exactly what factors are pushing industrial society toward its own collapse, and it's
no secret what has to be done to make the transition to sustainability, but the vast majority of people in the industrial world remain
unwilling to embrace the necessary changes — and nothing currently suggests that they are interested in thinking about the generations in the future who will grow up in the ruins of our society.

At this point it's almost certainly too late to manage a transition to sustainability on a global or national scale, even if the political will to attempt it existed — which it clearly does not. It's not
too late, though, for individuals, groups, and communities to make
that transition themselves, and to do what they can to preserve essential cultural and practical knowledge for the future. The chance
that today's political and business interests will do anything useful in our present situation is small enough that it's probably not
worth considering. Oil is to modern industrial nations what corn
was to the ancient Maya. The *ahauob* of Washington and Wall
Street, "liberal" as well as "conservative," have turned to the suicidal

strategy of war just as their Mayan equivalents did. Fortunately, their participation in the process of transition isn't needed.

Our civilization is in the early stages of the same curve of decline and fall that so many others have followed before it, and the crises of the present — peak oil, global warming and the like — are the current versions of the historical patterns of ecological dysfunction. To judge by prior examples, we can't count on the future to bring us a better and brighter world — or even a continuation of the status quo. Instead, what most likely lies in wait for us is a long, uneven decline into a new Dark Age from which, centuries from now, the civilizations of the future will gradually emerge.

The Long Descent

Map the likely results of current trends onto a scale of human lifespans and a compelling image of the future emerges. Imagine an American woman born in 1960. She sees the gas lines of the 1970s, the short-term political gimmicks that papered over the crisis in the 1980s and 1990s, and the renewed trouble in the following decades. Periods of economic and political crisis, broken by intervals of partial recovery, shape the rest of her life. By the time she turns 70, she lives in a beleaguered, malfunctioning city where nearly half the population has no reliable access to clean water, electricity, or health care. Shantytowns spread in the shadow of skyscrapers while political and economic leaders keep insisting that things are getting better.

Her great-grandson, born in 2040, manages to avoid the smorgasbord of diseases, the pervasive violence, and the pandemic alcohol and drug abuse that claim a quarter of his generation before age 30. A lucky break gets him into a technical career, safe from military service in endless overseas wars or "pacification actions" against separatist guerrillas at home. His technical knowledge consists mostly of rules of thumb for effective scavenging. Cars and refrigerators are luxury items he will never own, his home lacks electricity and central heating, and his health care comes from an old woman whose grandmother was a doctor and who knows something about wound care and herbs. By the time his hair turns gray the squabbling regions that were once the United States have split apart. All remaining fuel and electrical power have been commandeered by new regional governments, and coastal cities have been abandoned to the rising oceans.

For his great-granddaughter, born in 2120, the great crises are mostly things of the past. She grows up amid a ring of villages that were once suburbs, but now they surround an abandoned core of rusting skyscrapers that are visited only by salvage crews who mine them for raw materials. Local wars sputter, the oceans are still rising, and famines and epidemics come through every decade or so, but with global population less than half what it was in 2000 and still declining, humanity and nature are moving toward balance. The great-granddaughter learns to read and write, a skill most of her neighbors don't have, and a few old books are among her prized possessions, but the days when men walked on the moon are fading into legend. When she and her family finally set out for a village in the countryside, leaving the husk of the old city to the salvage crews, it likely never occurs to her that her quiet footsteps on a crumbling asphalt road mark the end of a civilization.

This is the process I've named the Long Descent — the declining arc of industrial civilization's trajectory through time. Like the vanished civilizations of the past, ours will likely face a gradual decline, punctuated by sudden crises and periods of partial recovery. The fall of a civilization is like tumbling down a slope, not like falling off a cliff. It's not a single massive catastrophe, or even a series of lesser disasters, but a gradual slide down statistical curves that will ease modern industrial civilization into history's dumpster.

Track the impact of decline on public health and you have a model that can be applied to many other dimensions of the process. As domestic heating and air conditioning become too expensive for most, for example, deaths from pneumonia and influenza on the one hand, and heat stroke and insect-borne tropical diseases on the other, will steadily climb. So will infant mortality, while rates of live birth per capita will plunge. Russia is a good model here; since the collapse of Communism, it's seen rising death rates and falling birth rates to such an extent that the population will be cut in half by 2100, and yet there hasn't been any massive catastrophe to account for this — simply shifts in statistics driven by economic and political failure.[23] Those same statistical shifts become inevitable when the ecological basis for a civilization crumbles away as a result of its own mismanagement.

The last few decades have already seen substantial decline in the real standard of living for most Americans and many people elsewhere in the industrialized world. We will likely see quite a bit more in the next few years, especially if the economic juggling act that props up trillions of dollars of paper debt in America and elsewhere gives way. Declining standards of living equate to declining public health. Declining public health impacts population levels. As people become poorer, they become sicker; childhood mortality goes up — the United States is already approaching parity with the nonindustrial world in that department[24] — and other vulnerable groups suffer as well.

There will be crises and disasters in economic, political, social, and military spheres. At certain points along the curve of disintegration, systems become unstable and sudden breakdowns happen. These are the things people will remember afterwards: the day the electric power grid finally went down for good, the winter that the big epidemic took a third of the people in their town, the year that civil war broke out down south, and the decade in which the last shreds of national government dissolved. Ordinary disasters such as hurricanes and massive floods will take on a new role as the resources to rebuild will be less and less available. The lessons of Hurricane Katrina in 2005 are likely to be repeated many times over in the years to come. These sudden events will punctuate the decline, not cause it, and attempts to respond to them without dealing with the broader issues will simply transfer stresses to other aspects of a society in decline.

Sooner or later in the process, we'll see the breakdown of existing social, political, and economic forms and the rise of transitional structures. At some point, continental governments such as the United States and Canada will come apart, in fact if not in name, to be replaced by regional and local governments cobbled together on an ad hoc basis; the global corporate economy will be replaced by jerry-built local exchange systems, and so on. The more sustainable, stable, and effective these transitional structures are, the more people, technology, knowledge, and culture will make it through the couple of centuries that this whole process will take.

That last is the detail that has to be remembered. Nobody now alive will see the end of the process that's now under way. The challenge we face in the short term is how to weather the next round of crises when it arrives. In the long term, the challenge is to get through the Long Descent with as much useful information and resources as possible, and to transmit them to the successor cultures that, to judge by past models, will begin coalescing sometime in the 23rd and 24th centuries. That means making sure that people right now have the information and connections they need to adapt constructively to the changes brought by the decline of our civilization, rather than backing themselves into one blind alley or another. It also means taking a hard look at some of the most fundamental ways people in today's industrial societies think about the world.

The Stories
We Tell
Ourselves

By this point even those of my readers who haven't yet thrown this book at the nearest wall will likely be appalled by the image of the future presented in the last few pages. What I find most interesting about this very common reaction is that it can have its roots in two completely different, and in fact opposite, sets of assumptions and beliefs about the future. On the one hand, many people insist that no matter what problems crop up before us, modern science, technology, and raw human ingenuity will inevitably win out and make the world of the future better than the world of today. On the other hand, some people insist that no matter what we do, some overwhelming catastrophe will soon bring civilization suddenly crashing down into mass death and a Road Warrior future.

Discussions about peak oil and the predicament of industrial society constantly revolve around these two alternatives, as though they were the only possibilities. Many believers in either option don't seem to be able to wrap their minds around the possibility of a third alternative. It's a remarkable situation. If two meteorologists on a weather program were to get into a debate about the weather to be expected on a fall day, and one insisted the only possibility was clear skies and temperatures in the 90s, while the other claimed a sudden blizzard was about to happen, most viewers would probably suspect that something was out of kilter. Too many of today's discussions about the future of industrial society impose an equally strange distortion on the likely shape of the world our children and grandchildren will face.

Blind spots of this sort show the hidden presence of myth. Many people nowadays think only primitive people believe in myths, but myths dominate the thinking of every society, including our own. Myths are the stories we tell ourselves to make sense of our world. Human beings think with stories as inevitably as they see with eyes and walk with feet, and the most important of those stories — the ones that define the nature of the world for those who tell them — are myths.

Most ancient cultures took their myths directly from their religious ideas, using traditional stories about the gods and goddesses to make sense of their world. Our society does the same thing in a hole-and-corner way, dressing up an assortment of old religious ideas in the more fashionable garments of scientific theory or political ideology. Still, scratch the most up-to-date modern worldview or the most casually held popular opinion, and anyone with a nodding acquaintance with traditional myths will recognize the underlying story at a glance.

Progress and Apocalypse

The two competing visions of the future just mentioned are no exception. You don't need to know anything about traditional mythology to recognize them. Unless you've been sleeping in a cave for the last three hundred years, you know them inside and out.

The first is the *myth of progress*. According to this story, all of human history is a grand tale of human improvement. From the primitive ignorance and savagery of our cave-dwelling ancestors, according to this myth, people climbed step by step up the ladder of progress, following in the wake of the evolutionary drive that raised us up from primeval slime and brought us to the threshold of human intelligence. Ever since our ancestors first became fully human, knowledge gathered over the generations made it possible for each culture to go further, become wiser, and accomplish more than the ones that came before it. With the coming of the Scientific Revolution three hundred years ago, the slow triumph of reason over nature shifted into overdrive and has been accelerating ever since. Eventually, once the last vestiges of primitive superstition and ignorance are cast aside, our species will leap upward from the surface of its home planet and embrace its destiny among the stars.

The second myth is the *myth of apocalypse*. According to this story, all of human history is a tragic blind alley. At one time people lived in harmony with their world, each other, and themselves, but that golden age ended with a disastrous wrong turn and things have gone downhill ever since. The rise of vast, unnatural cities, governed by bloated governmental bureaucracies and inhabited by people who have abandoned spiritual values for a wholly material existence, marks the point of no return. Sometime soon the whole rickety structure will come crashing down, overwhelmed by sudden catastrophe, and billions of people will die as civilization comes apart and rampaging hordes scour the landscape. Only those who abandon a corrupt and doomed society and return to the old, true ways of living will survive to build a better world.

Both these myths have deep roots in the collective imagination of the modern world, and very few people nowadays seem to be able to think about the future at all without following one narrative or the other. It would be hard to find any two narratives less appropriate, though, for the future we are actually likely to encounter. Both of them rely on assumptions about the world that don't stand up to any sort of critical examination.

The faith in progress, for example, rests on the unstated assumption that limits don't apply to us because the forward momentum of human progress automatically trumps everything else. If we want limitless supplies of energy badly enough, the logic seems to be, the world will give it to us. Of course the world *did* give it to us — in the form of unimaginably huge deposits of fossil fuels storing hundreds of millions of years' worth of photosynthesis — and we wasted it in a few centuries of fantastic extravagance. The lifestyles we've grown up treating as normal are entirely the products of that extravagance. This puts us in the position of a lottery winner who's spent millions of dollars in a few short years and is running out of money. The odds of hitting another million-dollar jackpot are minute, and no amount of wishful thinking will enable us to keep up our current lifestyle by getting a job at the local hamburger stand.

Nor is the past quite so much of a linear story of progress as the folklore of the industrial age would have it. Look back over the millennia that came before the start of the industrial age, straight back to the emergence of agriculture, and one of the most striking things you'll notice is how little human life changed over that time. The lives of peasants, priests, soldiers, and aristocrats in Sumer in 3000 BCE, say, differed only in relatively minor details from those of their equivalents in the Chou dynasty in China 15 centuries later, Roman North Africa 15 centuries after that, or medieval Spain another 15 centuries closer to our time. Tools gradually changed from stone to bronze to iron, and their shapes evolved with changes in technique, but the requirements of the agricultural cycle and the limited energy available from wind, water, biomass, and muscle imposed a common framework on human societies.

While plenty of new technologies emerged over the millennia, the process of technological change was not a one-way street; many technologies invented in periods of high innovation in the past were lost in later periods of regression. To this day, for example, nobody knows how the Egyptians cut, moved, and fitted the immense stone blocks of the Pyramids.[1] In the same way, the ingenious clockwork technology used in the Antikythera device — an ancient Greek machine for tracking planetary movements — was lost by the time Rome fell and had to be reinvented from scratch in the Renaissance.[2] Before the harnessing of fossil fuels, technological advances were vulnerable to loss because they had only the most limited place in everyday life; without cheap, abundant energy to power them, it was more efficient and economical for premodern societies to rely on human labor with hand tools for nearly all their economic activities.

This stable pattern changed only when the first steam engines allowed people to begin tapping the fantastic amounts of energy hidden away within the Earth. The torrent of nearly free energy that followed those first discoveries played the crucial role in bringing the industrial world into being. For thousands of years before that time, everything else necessary for an industrial society had been part of the cultural heritage of most civilizations. Renewable energy sources? Wind power, water power, biomass, and muscle power were all used extensively in the preindustrial past without launching an industrial society. Scientific knowledge? The laws of mechanics were worked out in ancient times, and a Greek scientist even invented the steam turbine two centuries before the birth of Christ; without fossil fuels it was a useless curiosity.[3] Human resourcefulness and ingenuity? It's as arrogant as it is silly to insist that people in past ages weren't as resourceful and ingenious as we are.

Fossil fuel energy — *and only fossil fuel energy* — made it possible to break with the old agrarian pattern and construct the industrial world. Unless some new and equally abundant energy source comes on line fast enough to make up for fossil fuel depletion, we will find ourselves back in the same world our ancestors knew, with the additional burdens of a huge surplus population and an impoverished planetary biosphere to contend with. Combine these constraints with the plain, hard reality of vanishing fossil fuels, and the myth of perpetual progress becomes a mirage.

Believers in apocalypse, for their part, insist that the end of industrial civilization will be sudden, catastrophic, and total. That claim is just as hard to square with the realities of our predicament as the argument for perpetual progress. Every previous civilization that has fallen has taken centuries to collapse, and there's no reason to think the present case will be any different. The resource base of industrial society is shrinking but it's far from exhausted. The impact of global warming and other ecological disruptions build slowly over time, and governments and ordinary citizens alike have every reason to hold things together as long as possible.

The history of the last century — think of the Great Depression, the Second World War, and the brutal excesses of Communism and Nazism, just for starters — shows that industrial societies can endure tremendous disruption without dissolving into a Hobbesian war of all against all. People in hard times are far more likely to follow orders and hope for the best than to turn into the rampaging, mindless mobs that play so large a role in survivalist fantasies these days. The sorry history of the Y2K noncrisis a few years ago — a subject we'll be discussing in more detail in the next chapter — offers a useful reminder that claims of catastrophe can be overstated.

But fantasy is often more appealing than reality, and most of the apocalyptic notions in circulation these days draw very heavily on popular fantasies. The idea (common just now among some Christians) that all good Christians will be raptured away to heaven just as the rest of the world goes to hell in a handbasket is a case in point. It's a lightly disguised fantasy of mass suicide — when you tell the kids that Grandma went to heaven to be with Jesus, most people understand what that means — and it also serves as a way for people to pretend to themselves that God will rescue them from the consequences of their own actions. That's one of history's all time bad bets, but it's certainly been a popular one.

The Hollywood notion of an overnight collapse is just as much of a fantasy. It makes for great screenplays but has nothing to do with the realities of how civilizations fall. In the aftermath of Hubbert's peak, fossil fuel production will decline gradually, not simply come to a screeching halt, and so the likely course of things is gradual descent rather than freefall, following the same trajectory marked out by so many civilizations in the past. Nor does decline necessarily proceed at a steady pace; between sudden crises come intervals of relative stability, even moderate improvement. Different regions decline at different paces; existing social, economic, and political structures are replaced, not with complete chaos, but with transitional structures that may themselves develop pretty fair institutional strength.

Does this model of punctuated decline apply to the current situation? Almost certainly. As oil and natural gas run short, economies will come unglued and political systems disintegrate under the strain. Nonetheless, there will still be oil to be had — the Hubbert curve is a bell-shaped curve, after all, and if the peak comes in 2010, the world in 2040 will be producing about as much oil as it was producing in 1980. With other fossil fuels well along their own Hubbert curves, nearly twice as many people to provide for, and a global economy dependent on cheap, abundant energy in serious trouble, the gap between production and demand will become a potent source driving poverty, spiraling shortages, rising death rates, plummeting birth rates, and epidemic violence and warfare. Granted, this is not a pretty picture, but it's not an instant reversion to the Stone Age either.

It's reasonable, of course, to consider sudden catastrophe and continued progress as possibilities for the future, but both of these narratives have to be weighed against the realities of our present situation and the evidence of history. In our present context, both possibilities require a *deus ex machina* on a grand scale to change the course of events: ordinary catastrophes aren't enough to bring industrial society down overnight, just as ordinary technological progress isn't enough to get industrial society out of the mess it's made for itself. Without some extraordinary event, our civilization is headed down the well-trodden path of decline. If there's a point in planning for the future at all, it makes sense to plan for the one we're most likely to get.

Both the myth of progress and the myth of apocalypse, on the other hand, have a great deal of emotional power; that's why they're popular. Faith in perpetual progress comforts those people who have made their peace with society as it is and want to believe that the frustrations and compromises of their lives are part of a process that will eventually lead to better things. Faith in imminent apocalypse comforts those people who cannot accept society as it is; they long for a catastrophe massive enough to topple the proud towers of a civilization they loathe. Still, the fact that a belief is emotionally powerful and comforting doesn't make it true.

Secondhand Theologies

The central theme of both these myths, the narrative of progress just as much as the narrative of apocalypse, is a process the philosopher Eric Voegelin called "immanentizing the eschaton."[4] This process underlies a remarkable amount of popular thought these days, and it's worth taking the time to understand what it means and how it works.

The word "eschaton" comes from an old Greek word for "end" or "border." In Christian theological jargon it refers to the process by which the fallen world we experience today will someday give way to the eternal blessedness of the Kingdom of God. An entire branch of theology, called eschatology — literally, the science of the end — evolved over the last two thousand years or so in an attempt to piece together a coherent vision of the future out of the hints and visions provided by scripture and tradition. It's a lively field full of fierce disputes, and no consensus about the End Times has yet found general acceptance among Christian theologians or ordinary believers. Central to nearly all Christian accounts of the eschaton, however, is the idea that it's something completely outside the realm of history as we know it. When the trumpet sounds, the sky tears open and something wholly other comes through.

There's a long and complicated history behind this belief, reaching back half a dozen centuries before the Common Era, when religions across much of the Old World started offering believers the promise of a way out of the cycles of time and the world of suffering — and a way into an eternal realm of perfection. For the most part, the escape hatch from time was sized only for individuals; the Buddhist pursuit of Nirvana and the Gnostic quest to return to the aeonic world of light are good examples of the theme. In a handful of traditions, though, this mutated into the idea that the whole world would enter eternity at a specific point in the future: ordinary history would stop and be replaced by something wholly other. The Jewish vision of the coming Messianic Age is among the oldest of these. Adapted by Christianity, it became the prophecy of the Second Coming, and in this latter form it remains a potent myth through much of the Western world.

In theologian's language the quality of "otherness" that pervades visions of the Second Coming and its equivalents is called transcendence. Its opposite is immanence. One of the great quarrels in theology is whether God or the gods are transcendent — that is, outside nature and free of its limitations — or immanent — that is, part of nature and subject to its laws. Like most such divisions, this one admits of several kinds of middle ground, but the basic distinction is relevant. People who have mystical experiences — which are, after all, common among human beings — very often comment on a difference between the ordinary reality of their lives, and the non-ordinary reality that surges into their consciousness. Did the non-ordinary reality come from someone, something, or somewhere outside ordinary existence? Or was it right here, unnoticed, all the time? That's the difference between transcendence and immanence.

Most religions that put a great deal of attention into eschatology also have a transcendent concept of the divine; the whole point of the eschaton is that ordinary reality dissolves into the wholly other. Most religions that have an immanent concept of the divine, in turn, either have no eschatology at all, or make the end of the world a recurring event in an endlessly repeated cycle of time. Judaism, Christianity, and Islam, with their transcendent god and richly detailed eschatologies, fall on one side of the divide. Religions such as Hinduism, with its universes that bud, blossom, and fall through infinite cycles of time, and Shinto, which has no eschatology at all, fall on the other. So does the Druid spirituality I practice, which recognizes the presence of spirit throughout the world of nature and sees spiritual awakening as something that comes to each soul in its own proper time.[5]

Now and then, though, the two patterns collide and cross-fertilize, and the resulting belief systems locate the eschaton as a possibility to be realized within ordinary history, or even the inevitable result of the working out of historical patterns. The Scientific Revolution of the 17th century, more than anything else, was responsible for putting this new wrinkle in the old myth. To the founders and early propagandists of modern science, human beings didn't need to wait for God to bring on the New Jerusalem; it could be built here and now by harnessing the power of human reason to dominate the world of nature.[6] As a newfound faith in progress redefined the past as a tale of the slow triumph of reason over nature, the Western world embraced a paradoxical vision in which history itself brought about an end to history. Focused through thinkers as different as Hegel and Terence McKenna, this way of thinking about history still remains welded into place in the conventional wisdom throughout our society. For people at all points on the cultural spectrum, as a result, the perfect society remains firmly parked in the near future, accessible once the right set of political, social, or spiritual policies are put into place.

Marxism offers an example familiar to most people nowadays.

In Marxist theory, history is determined by changes in the mode of production that unfold in a fixed order, from primitive communism through slavery, feudalism, and capitalism to the proletarian revolution and the everlasting communist Utopia of the future. While all this is wrapped in the jargon of 19th century materialist science, it's not hard to see the religious underpinnings of the theory, because every element of Marxist theory has an exact equivalent in Christian eschatology. Primitive communism is Eden, the invention of private property is the original sin that causes the Fall. The stages of slavery, feudalism, and capitalism are the various dispensations of sacred history, and so on, right up to the Second Coming of the proletariat, the millennial state of socialism, and the final arrival of communism as a New Jerusalem descending from some dialectical-materialist heaven. Point for point, it's a rephrasing of Christian myth that replaces the transcendent dimension with forces immanent in ordinary history.

Over the last three centuries or so, Christianity's influence on the Western intellect has crumpled beneath the assaults of scientific materialism, but no mythology has yet succeeded in ousting it from its place in the Western imagination. The result has been a flurry of attempts to rehash Christian myth under other, more materialistic names. The mythology of progress itself is one example of this sort of secondhand theology. Marxism is another, and most of the more recent myths of apocalypse reworked the Christian narrative along the same lines that Marx did, swapping out the economic concepts Marx imported to the myth for some other set of ideas more appealing to them or more marketable to the public.

Neoprimitive theorists such as John Zerzan and Daniel Quinn, for example, replace Marxist economics with anthropology. For them, the hunter-gatherer societies of the prehistoric past are Eden, the invention of agriculture is the original sin that led to the Fall, and so on, with the imminent collapse of civilization filling the role of the apocalyptic transformation, after which the righteous remnant enters the New Jerusalem of the hunter-gatherer lifestyle.

In exactly the same way, the reworked liberalism of David Korten's *The Great Turning* fills Eden's role with a set of hypothetical prehistoric matriarchies: the Fall with the emergence of the principle of Empire; and so forth, right up to the "Great Turning" toward a liberal ideology that stands in the place of the Second Coming. In these and many other examples of the same type, ideologies presented as radical new visions turn out on closer inspection to be Christian apocalyptic myth with the serial numbers filed off, with new actors in new costumes filling the same old roles.

Now I'm no great fan of mainstream Christianity myself. To me, all its myths and symbols put together don't carry the spiritual impact of one blue heron flying through dawn mists or a single autumn sunset seen through old growth cedars; that's why I follow a Druid path. Still, it seems to me that if people insist on thinking in terms of Christian myth, they might as well go the rest of the way and embrace Christianity as a whole. That way, at least, they would have the benefit of two millennia worth of Christian philosophy and theology, rather than having to make do with hand-me-downs from Marx, say, or the modern pundits mentioned above.

They might also be able to learn a few lessons from Christian history, or any other kind of history for that matter, about the problems that follow when people try to immanentize the eschaton. It's one thing to try to sense the shape of the future in advance, and to make constructive changes in your life to prepare for its rougher possibilities. It's quite another to become convinced that you know where history is headed, and to insist that the kind of society you like best is also the inevitable result of the historical process. When the course you've marked out for history simply projects the trajectory of a too-familiar myth onto the inkblot patterns of the future, immanentizing the eschaton can all too easily become a recipe for self-induced disaster.

History is littered with the wreckage of movements that convinced themselves that the world was about to be transformed into what they wanted it to be. Not uncommonly, such wreckage

includes a tumbled heap of human lives. The trajectory of Marxism — from the bright dreams for a better future of 19th century
intellectuals to the 20th century nightmares of Stalin's purges, the
Cultural Revolution, and the killing fields of Cambodia — is a
route followed all too often by those who believe they know which
way history is headed.

Myths of Utopia

Each of the modern ideologies that immanentize the eschaton
have recast Christian theology in apparently secular forms, then,
but complex transformations shaped the way they manhandled
their borrowed myths. In its original form, the Christian narrative
of sacred history includes some features close to the myth of progress and others much closer to modern apocalypticism. As sociologist Philip Lamy showed in a useful study,[7] though, the old myth
has been shattered into fragmentary versions over the last century
or two. Many people nowadays, including many Christians, have
abandoned the complexity of traditional sacred history for a "frac-
tured" myth that focuses on some small part of the whole.

The contemporary myths of progress and apocalypse are good
examples, the former stressing the hope of future bliss, the latter the threat of catastrophe. The myth of progress, in effect, fast-
forwards Christian sacred history to the thousand years that are
supposed to come between the Second Coming and the arrival of
the New Jerusalem. The redeeming revelation has already happened in the form of the Scientific Revolution, the allegedly primitive past has been stretched and lopped to make it look like a Vale
of Tears, and today's scientists fill the role of the Church Expect-
ant waiting for the great god Progress to bring Utopia in its own
good time. By contrast, the myth of apocalypse fast-forwards the
Christian myth to the last days of the Tribulation, and proclaims
that some version of the Second Coming is about to overthrow
capitalism, civilization, the Republican Party, or whatever other
surrogate fills Satan's role in their mythology.

There's some complicated cultural history behind the split between progressive and apocalyptic myth. A little over four centuries ago, at the time of the Reformation, mainstream Christianity
effectively capitulated to rational-materialist philosophy and redefined the deeply mythic narratives of the Bible as secular history.
Before then, most theologians discussed what the events described
in Book of Revelations meant as mystical symbols and analogies;
afterward, most of them argued instead about when and how
the same events would happen as historical events in the everyday world. Out of the resulting debates came two main schools of
thought.[8] The first, the premillennialist position, held that Jesus
would return and bring about the Millennium, a thousand-year
period of bliss when Christians would rule the world. The other
party, the postmillennialists, argued instead that Christians would
rule the world for a thousand years of bliss, and after that, Jesus
would return.

The difference may seem about as relevant as the number of
angels that can dance on the head of the late Jerry Falwell, but
each viewpoint has sweeping implications. If the postmillennialists are right, history is on their side, since they're destined to rule
the world for a thousand years before Jesus gets here. Thus postmillennialists tend to believe that things are on the right track and
will get better over time until the Millennium arrives. If the premillennialists are right, on the other hand, history is on Satan's
side, since it will take nothing less than the personal interven-
tion of Jesus himself to give the Christians their thousand years
of world rule. Accordingly, premillennialists tend to believe that
things are on the wrong track and will get worse over time until,
when everything is as bad as it can get, Jesus shows up, beats the
stuffing out of the devil and his minions, and brings on the Millennium.

Drop the theological fine print from these two viewpoints and
you've got the myth of progress and the myth of apocalypse in
their contemporary forms. Believers in progress argue that indus-

trial civilization is better than any other in history and destined to get better still, so long as we just put enough money into scientific research, or get government out of the way of industry, or whatever else they believe will keep history on its course. Believers in apocalypse argue that industrial civilization is worse than any other in history, and its present difficulties will end in an overnight catastrophe that will destroy it and usher in whatever better world their mythology promises them — a better world in which they will inevitably have the privileged place denied them in this one.

Both these mythic narratives, in other words, are myths of Utopia. Both promise that the future will bring a much better world than the present; their only disagreements are about how to get there and how closely the Utopia to come resembles the society we've got now. Thus it's not surprising that believers in progress tend to be those who feel they benefit from the current social order, and believers in apocalypse tend to be those who feel marginalized by the current social order and excluded from its benefits. Either way, the lure of Utopia is a potent force, one that has deep roots in our culture and our collective psyche.

It's also one of the primary obstacles that stand in the way of a constructive response to the crisis of industrial society. The lesson of the limits to growth — a lesson most people have been doing their best to avoid learning, with increasing desperation, since the early 1970s — is that the age of cheap, abundant energy is passing, and nothing we or anyone else can do will keep it here or bring it back. We can't count on the future to bring us a better world, via progress, apocalyptic collapse, or any combination of the two. Rather, we can count on it to bring us a world of hard ecological limits, restricted opportunities, and lowered expectations, in which many of our fondest dreams will have to be set aside for the foreseeable future — or forever. It's a world where hopes can still be realized, dreams can still be pursued, and the experience of being human can still be contemplated and celebrated, but all these things will have to be on a much more modest scale than the experience of the recent past or the utopian dreams that either the progressive or the apocalyptic myth have prepared us to consider.

During the three centuries of industrial expansion, utopian thinking was adaptive, to use ecologists' jargon: it encouraged people to think big at a time when the soaring availability of fossil fuel energy made explosive growth pay off. As the industrial age peaks and begins to decline, the equation is reversing. In a world where energy and all other nonrenewable resources are likely to get progressively more scarce and expensive, it's time to learn again how to think small — and that process will be much easier if we say farewell to Utopia and focus on the things we can actually achieve in the stark limits of time and resources we still have left.

Knowing Only One Story

One of the things that makes our culture's reliance on the utopian myths of progress and apocalypse so problematic as we approach the end of the age of cheap energy is that both narratives claim to explain the entire universe. Universal claims of this sort have become popular in recent centuries, but from a wider historical perspective, stories that claim to be the answer to everything are something of a novelty. Traditional cultures around the world, in fact, have a very large number of stories, and much of the education received by young people in those cultures consists of sharing, learning, and thinking about those stories.

The stories handed down in oral cultures aren't simply entertainment, any more than are the stories we tell ourselves about the universe today. Stories are probably the oldest and most important of all human tools. Human beings think with stories, fitting what William James called the "blooming, buzzing confusion" of the universe around us into narrative patterns that make the world make sense. We use stories to tell us who we are, what the world is like, and what we can and can't do with our lives. Every culture has its stories, and if you pay careful attention to the stories a culture tells, you can grasp things about the culture that nothing else will teach you.

One of the most striking things about old stories — stories of traditional cultures — is that no two of them have the same moral. If you were born in an English-speaking culture, for example, you likely grew up with the last remnant of England's old stories in the form of fairy tales that put different people in different situations, with very different results. Sometimes violating a prohibition brought success (think "Jack and the Beanstalk"), but sometimes it brought disaster ("Sleeping Beauty"). Sometimes victory went to the humble and patient ("Cinderella"), but sometimes it went to the one who had the chutzpah to dare the impossible ("Puss in Boots"). Common themes run through the old stories, of course, but they never take the same shape twice. Those differences are a source of great power. If you have a wealth of different stories to think with, odds are that whatever the world throws at you, you'll be able to find a narrative pattern that makes sense of it.

Over the last few centuries, though, the multiple-narrative approach of traditional cultures has given way, especially in the industrial West, to a way of thinking that privileges a single story above all others. Think of any currently popular political or religious ideology, and you'll likely find at its center the claim that one and only one story explains everything in the world. For fundamentalist Christians, it's the story of Fall and Redemption ending with the Second Coming of Christ. For Marxists, it's the story of dialectical materialism ending with the dictatorship of the proletariat. For believers in any of the flotilla of apocalyptic ideologies cruising the waterways of the modern imagination, it's another version of the same story, with different falls from grace ending in redemption through different catastrophes. For rationalists, neoconservatives, most scientists, and many other people in the developed world, the one true story is the story of progress. The political left and right each has its own story; and the list goes on. From the perspective of traditional cultures, believers in these ideologies are woefully undereducated, since for all practical purposes, they know only one story.

This modern habit of knowing only one story has certain predictable results. One of these is that the story itself becomes invisible to those who believe in it. From their perspective, their story isn't a story, it's simply the way things are, and the fact that it copies other versions of the same story is irrelevant, since their story is true and the others aren't. Often the story becomes so much a part of everyday thinking that it vanishes from sight entirely, becoming a presupposition that may never be stated or even noticed by those who build their lives around it. The myth of progress, a sterling example, has become so pervasive nowadays that few people notice how completely it dominates current thinking about the future. Speaking about historians of his own time who embraced the mythology of progress, the great 20th century historian Arnold Toynbee wrote:

> The difference between these post-Christian Western historians and their Christian predecessors is that the moderns do not allow themselves to be aware of the pattern in their minds, whereas Bossuet, Eusebius, and Saint Augustine were fully conscious of it. If one cannot think without mental patterns — and, in my belief, one cannot — it is better to know what they are; for a pattern of which one is unconscious is a pattern that holds one at its mercy.[9]

While the story itself may become invisible, its implications are anything but, and this leads to the second symptom of knowing only one story: the certainty that whatever problem comes up, it has one and only one solution. For fundamentalist Christians, no matter what the problem, the solution is surrendering your will to Jesus (or, more to the point, to the guy who claims to be able to tell you who Jesus wants you to vote for). For Marxists, the one solution for all problems is proletarian revolution. For neoconservatives, it's the free market. For scientists, it's more scientific research and education. For Democrats, it's electing Democrats; for Republicans, it's electing Republicans, and so on.

What makes this fixation on a single solution so problematic is that the universe is what ecologists call a complex system. In a complex system, feedback loops with unexpected consequences make a mockery of simplistic attempts to predict effects from causes. No one solution will effectively respond to more than a small portion of the challenges the system can throw at you. This leads to the third symptom of knowing only one story: repeated failure. .

Recent economic history offers a good example. For the last two decades, free-market advocates in the World Bank and the International Monetary Fund (IMF) have been pushing a particular set of economic policies on governments and economies around the world, insisting that these are the one and only solution to every economic ill. Everywhere those policies have been fully implemented, the result has been economic and social disaster — think East Asia in the late 1980s, or Russia and Latin America in the 1990s — and every one of the countries devastated by the results has returned to prosperity only after junking the policies in question.[10] None of this has stopped the free market's true believers from continuing to press forward toward the imaginary Utopia their story promises them.

For those who know plenty of stories, and know how to think with them, the complexity of the universe is easier to deal with, because they have a much better chance of being able to recognize what story the universe seems to be following, and act accordingly. Those who don't know any stories at all — if such improbable beings actually exist — may still get by; even though they don't have the resources of story-wisdom to draw on, they may still be able to judge the situation on its own merits and act accordingly, because a lack of stories at least offers some hope of flexibility.

Those who only know one story, though, and are committed to the idea that the world makes sense if and only if it's interpreted through the filter of that one story, are stuck in a rigid stance with no options for change. Much more often than not, they fail, since the complexity of the universe is such that no single story makes a useful tool for understanding more than a very small part of it. If they can recognize this and let go of their story, they can begin to learn. If you've gotten your ego wrapped up in the idea that you know the one and only true story, on the other hand, and you try to force the world to fit your story rather than allowing your story to change to fit the world, the results will not be good.

This leads to the fourth symptom of knowing only one story: rage. The third symptom, failure, can be a gift because it offers the opportunity for learning, but if the gift is too emotionally difficult to accept, the easy way out is to take refuge in anger. When we get angry with people who disagree with us about politics or religion, I'm coming to think, very often what really angers us is the fact that our preferred story doesn't fit the universe everywhere and always, and those who disagree with us simply remind us of that uncomfortable fact.

Plenty of pundits, and many others as well, have commented on the extraordinary level of anger that surges through America these days. From talk radio to political debates to everyday conversations, dialogue has given way to diatribe across the political spectrum. It's unlikely to be a coincidence that this has happened over a quarter century when the grand narratives of both major American political parties failed the test of reality. The 1960s and 1970s saw the Democrats get the chance to enact the reforms they wanted; the 1980s and the first decade of the 21st century saw the Republicans get the same opportunity. Both parties found themselves stymied by a universe that obstinately refused to play along with their stories, and both sides turned to anger and scapegoating as a way to avoid having to rethink their ideas.

That habit of rage isn't going to help us, or anyone, as we move toward a future that promises to leave most of our culture's familiar stories in tatters. As we face the unwelcome realities of the limits to growth, clinging to whatever single story appeals to us may be emotionally comforting in the short term, but it leads to a dead end familiar to those who study the history of extinct civilizations. Learning other stories, and learning that it's possible to see the world in many ways, is a more viable path — but it can be a challenging one that many people can't or won't take.

Faustus and the Monkey Trap

The modern habit of trying to fit all of reality into a single story — whether that's the myth of progress, the myth of apocalypse, or any other — forms one of the mainsprings behind industrial society's failure to deal with the limits to growth. Albert Einstein commented that it's impossible to solve a problem with the same sort of thinking that created it, and this dictum has rarely been so relevant as it is today. In particular, many of today's attempts to do something about peak oil rely on the same thinking, and derive from the same story, that got us into our present predicament. These habits of thought turn out "solutions" guaranteed to make our situation worse than it is already.

Of the dozens of good examples in the daily news, the one that seems most worth noting right now is the economic blowback set in motion by the US government's attempt to bolster its faltering petroleum-driven economy with ethanol. As corn and other grains get diverted from grocery stores to gas tanks, commodity prices spike, inflation ripples outward through the economic food chain, and poor people around the world face the prospect of starvation. More than twenty years ago, William Catton pointed out in his seminal classic *Overshoot* that the downslope of industrial society would force human beings to compete against their own machines for dwindling resource stocks.[11] His prediction has become today's reality.

It's all very reminiscent of an old metaphor much used in cognitive psychology. Many centuries ago in southeast Asia, some clever soul figured out how to use the thinking patterns of monkeys to make a highly effective monkey trap. The trap is a gourd with a hole in one end just big enough for a monkey's hand to fit in, and a stout rope connected to the other end, which is fastened to a stake in the ground. Into the gourd goes a piece of some food prized by monkeys, large and solid enough that it can't be shaken out of the gourd. You set the trap in a place monkeys frequent, and wait.

Sooner or later, a monkey comes along, smells the food, and puts its hand into the gourd to grab it. The hole is too small to allow the monkey to extract hand and food together, though, and the rope and stake keeps the monkey from hauling it away, so the monkey keeps trying to get the food out in its hand. Meanwhile you come out of hiding and head toward the monkey with a net (if there's a market for live monkeys), or with something more deadly (if there isn't). Instead of dropping the food and scampering toward the safety of the nearest tree, most monkeys will frantically keep trying to wrestle the food out of the gourd until the net snares it or the club comes whistling down.

The trap works because monkeys, like the rest of us, tend to become so focused on pursuing immediate goals by familiar means that they lose track of the wider context of priorities that make those goals and means meaningful in the first place. In the terms used earlier in this chapter, the monkey gets stuck in a single story, failing to notice that there may be more options than the obvious one. Once the monkey smells the food in the gourd, it defines the problem as how to get the food out, and it tries to solve the problem in a familiar way, by manipulating the food and the gourd. When the hunter appears, that simply adds a note of urgency, and makes the problem appear to be how to get the food out before the hunter arrives. Phrased in either of these terms, the problem is impossible to solve. Only if the monkey remembers that food is of no value to a dead monkey, and it redefines the problem as primarily a matter of getting away from the hunter, will it let go of the food, get its hand out of the trap, and run for the nearest tree.

The monkey trap may not look like a theme for great literature, but exactly the same dilemma forms the main plot engine of Christopher Marlowe's classic play *Doctor Faustus*. In Marlowe's vision, Faustus is an intellectual *manqué* who has mastered all the scholarship of his time and dismisses it as worthless because he can't cash it in for power. So he conjures the devil Mephistopheles, who offers him twenty-four years of power over the world of appearances, in exchange for his immortal soul. Faustus gladly makes the bargain and proceeds to run riot for the better part of nine scenes, with the ever-obsequious Mephistopheles always ready to fulfill his every wish but one. Finally, the twenty-four years are up, and at the stroke of midnight a crew of devils swoops down on Faustus and hauls him off to Hell.

All this came to Marlowe out of the folk literature that gave him the raw materials for his play. What makes Marlowe's retelling of the story one of Elizabethan England's great dramas, though, is his insight into the psychology of Faustus' damnation. Faustus spends nearly the entire play a heartbeat away from escaping the devil's pact that ultimately drags him to his doom. All he has to do is renounce the pact and all the powers and pleasures it brings him, and salvation is his — but this is exactly what he cannot do. He becomes so focused on his sorcerer's powers, so used to getting what he wants by ordering Mephistopheles around, that the possibility of getting anything any other way slips out of his grasp. Even at the very end, as the devils drag him away, the last words that burst from his lips are a cry for Mephistopheles to save him.

The logic of the monkey trap underlies the entire scenario, because the monkey and Faustus trap themselves in essentially the same way. Both have a proven track record of solving problems using a specific method — the monkey, by manipulating things with its hands; Faustus, by summoning Mephistopheles and having him take care of it. Both keep on trying to use their familiar set of problem-solving tools even when they clearly don't work.

Even when the real shape of the problem becomes clear and breaking out of the old way of thinking becomes a question of immediate survival, they keep on struggling to make the problem fit their choice of solutions, rather than adjusting their solution to the actual problem.

Mephistopheles and the monkey hunter have a crucial ally here, and its name is stress. It's one thing to step back and take stock of a situation when there seems to be plenty of time and no sign of danger. It's quite another to do it in the presence of an imminent threat to survival. Once the true shape of the situation appears, stress reactions hardwired into the nervous systems of men and monkeys alike cut in, making it very difficult indeed to reassess the situation and consider alternative ways of dealing with it. The final scene of Marlowe's drama expresses this dilemma with shattering intensity: as midnight approaches, Faustus tries every means of escaping his fate except the one that can actually save him.

The same dilemma on a larger scale underlies current efforts to deal with the imminent decline of world oil production by finding something else to pour into our gas tanks: ethanol, biodiesel, hydrogen, you name it. Our petroleum-powered vehicles — not just cars, but the trucks, trains, ships, and aircraft that make our current way of life possible — are the food in the monkey's hand and the pact that binds Mephistopheles to Faustus' service. Even in the peak oil community, the problem of peak oil is too often framed as how to find some other way to keep the fuel tanks topped up. This seems like common sense, but that's what the monkey thinks about getting the food out of the gourd, too.

Approached as a question of finding something to fill our gluttonous appetite for highly concentrated energy, the problem of peak oil is just as insoluble as the monkey trap when that's approached as a question of getting food. The discovery and exploitation of the Earth's petroleum reserves gave human beings a fantastic windfall of essentially free energy, and we proceeded to burn through it at an astonishing pace. Now that the supply of petroleum is beginning to falter, the question before us is not how to keep burning something else at the same pace, or how to find some other way to power a civilization of a sort that can only survive by burning extravagant amounts of energy, but how to scale back our expectations and our technology enough to make them work within the limits of the same renewable sources our ancestors had four hundred years ago.

I've suggested earlier in this book that expecting some other energy resource to provide energy on the same scale and level of concentration that petroleum does — just because we happen to want one — is a little like responding to one huge lottery win by assuming that when that money starts running out, another equally large win can be had for the cost of a few more tickets. This is close enough to today's consumer psychology that it's easy to imagine somebody in this position pouring all the money he has left into lottery tickets, throwing away his chances of avoiding bankruptcy because the only solution he can imagine is winning the lottery again. And this, again, is exactly the mentality of current attempts to fuel industrial society by pouring our food supply into our gas tanks.

Faustus may be a better model for the emerging crisis than the monkey because the predicament we face, like his, is precisely the result of what we're best at. Faustus became so dependent on his attendant devils that he lost track of the possibility that he could do something without them. Replace "devils" with "machines" and the parallel is exact. We have become so used to solving problems by throwing energy-intensive technologies at them that when technologies themselves become the crux of a predicament, we have no idea what to do. If any of the achievements of the last three hundred years are to be salvaged from the approaching spiral of crises, we need to rethink this now, before the social, economic, and political stresses become so pressing that clear thought becomes impossible and fossil-fueled spirits appear, on schedule, to drag us off to a close equivalent of the Hell of Marlowe's play.

Distracting Ourselves

The problem of the monkey trap is already a potent factor in contemporary society. Watch the way that pundits and politicians keep trying to solve today's crises with yesterday's solutions — no matter how counterproductive the results — and it's hard not to see a reflection of the poor monkey trying to get its hand out of the trap without letting go of the food that keeps it stuck there. The old saying, "When you realize that you're in a hole, the first thing to do is stop digging," has relevance here. Easy to say, this can be hard to put into practice, especially when digging has been so successful and so profitable for so long that it's the only thing you really know how to do any more.

Yet the monkey trap fastened to the hand of modern industrial society has implications not often recognized. It's best to come at this one in a roundabout way, so I'll begin from an unlikely starting point and talk a bit about the history of the New Age movement.[12]

It's common these days for people to roll their eyes when the New Age or any of the movements of thought associated with it come up for discussion. This fashionable scorn, though, leads many of us to miss the chance to watch a crucial barometer of social trends. In any civilization, it's the cults, fads, and passions of the fringe that point out roads that the rest of society will presently take.

If some prescient Roman scholar of the reign of Nero or Claudius, say, wanted to catch some whisper of the world that would supplant his own, he'd have been wasting his time listening to speeches in the Forum or lectures in the fashionable academies of the day. Instead, he would have had to search out the cultural underbelly of his age, where strange cults from distant lands bid for the loyalties of those long since alienated from the worship of Jupiter Optimus Maximus. The Middle Ages already existed there in larval form, long before anyone in Rome had ever heard of Goths or Huns, or thought of Jesus of Nazareth as anything but a footnote in the history of a minor province somewhere back east.

The New Age movement is unlikely to become for the coming deindustrial age what Christianity became during and after Rome's collapse. If it had an equivalent in the classical scene, it would be the Gnostic movement. Like the New Age, Gnosticism was a diffuse and wildly diverse phenomenon that was popular among the privileged classes of its time, and reflected the attitudes and interests of those classes far too closely to survive the collapse of the society that gave them their status. Gnosticism's Achilles' heel was its intense spiritual elitism — its rigid distinction between the few who had the capacity for *gnosis* (redeeming knowledge) and the many who did not. The New Age movement formulates its notions of privilege in a different way, but those notions are still central to the movement.

Like the Gnostics, the New Age movement drew heavily on older traditions; despite its name there was never that much new about it. Nearly all its ingredients were first assembled by the Spiritualist movement of the mid-19th century: channeling (they called it "mediumship" back then); alternative health systems; positive-thinking psychology; an intense reverence for the wisdom of the East that never quite stooped to learn much about Asian spiritual teachings; and other key elements. By the 1950s, when the New Age movement began to coalesce, this package was the common property of a dizzying range of alternative spiritualities in the Western world, many of which had apocalyptic mythologies of the sort already discussed in this chapter.

Like other apocalyptic faiths, these belief systems made the trip from grand announcements of the imminent arrival of a new world to embarrassed excuses for its failure to appear. One of the classics of modern sociology, *When Prophecy Fails*, came out of a prime example of this sort of apocalyptic embarrassment from the 1950s.[13] Against this backdrop of repeated failure, though, some of the leading figures of the nascent New Age community came up with a novel gambit. They proposed that believers should live their lives in the ordinary world as if the new age had already arrived.

By making the prophesied great change a reality in their own lives here and now, they hoped to catalyze it in the world as a whole.

It's a brilliant strategy, for more than one reason. To begin with, making changes in your own life is the necessary first step toward making them at any other level of human society. Gandhi's comment, "You must be the change you hope to see in the world," is as much a guide to effective tactics as anything else. Yet there's more going on here than clever politics; another factor at work is a very old but very potent technique for shaping consciousness. Put the ideal and the real cheek by jowl and learn to live with the cognitive dissonance between them, and the paradox itself can become a source of creativity and insight. It's been a core technique in the toolkit of initiatory schools since ancient times. Whether the original New Age communities got the idea from the old initiatory traditions or stumbled across it on their own, it quickly caught fire and spread across alternative scenes throughout the industrial world.

The strategy of paradox has a vulnerability, though. There's always the risk of losing track of the "as if" — the gap between the ideal world and the real one where creative paradox lives — and starting to believe that the ideal world is the one that actually exists. That way lies the futile heroics of Don Quixote, who maps the ideal world of chivalric romance onto the prosaic realities of the Spanish countryside with such abandon that he tries to assault windmills under the delusion that they're wicked giants. Of course the windmills fail to play their assigned parts in the romance, and clobber him. Something similar happened to the New Age movement as it became less visionary and more marketable, and the subtle discipline of "live as though you're creating the reality you experience" got dumbed down into "you create the reality you experience."

Of course each of us does play a part in creating the reality we experience; subtle factors such as expectations and assumptions have a much more powerful role in the way our lives turn out than most people realize. In the first stages of their training programs, the old initiatory schools taught simple methods for redefining expectations and assumptions to give neophytes the confidence to tackle the much subtler and more demanding work ahead of them. As the New Age movement gained members and lost focus, though, gimmicks of this sort became the basis for a philosophy of cosmic consumerism that claims the universe is supposedly set up to give people whatever they happen to want, so long as they ask for it in the right way.

It's a popular philosophy that sells exceedingly well, as its latest rehash — the current book and video phenomenon titled *The Secret*[14] — shows clearly enough. The problem is that beyond a certain point, the philosophy doesn't work in practice. You can try as hard as you like to convince yourself that the universe wants to give you whatever you want, but that doesn't mean you will get it. At that point, the monkey trap closes tight around your hand, because if the ideology you've embraced tells you that you have to believe completely in it to make it work, any awareness that it's not working gets shoved aside as an obstacle to success.

Responses to this predicament in the New Age scene have covered the entire range of monkey antics, but one in particular bears noticing: the dramatic increase in the popularity of conspiracy theories in the New Age community over the last few years.

Conspiracy theories start from the recognition that connections aren't always visible, that what looks random and disconnected often has a thread of purpose and meaning tying it together beneath the surface. That recognition is far from useless. In particular, it's a crucial tool for making sense of today's global predicament, not to mention a necessary first step toward the ecological awareness that's our best hope of moving toward a more sustainable way of life. It's also a fundamental element in spirituality; mystics and poets have been pointing out for thousands of years that everything is connected to everything else — as Wordsworth put it, "thou canst not pluck a flower without troubling of a star."

Here, as so often, though, the devil's in the details. While everything's connected to everything else, in any given context some connections are more relevant than others. Some series of subtle links
connects the peanut butter sandwich you ate last Tuesday with the
state of your career, no doubt, but if you got turned down for a promotion on Friday, the peanut butter sandwich probably doesn't belong very high up on the list of the reasons why. If you don't want to
discuss the more important reasons, though, the sandwich might
just make a good way to talk about your career troubles instead of
factors you'd rather not mention.

Quite a bit of the conversation about fossil fuel depletion,
global warming, and other aspects of our current predicament uses
exactly this strategy. While I was writing this chapter, five minutes
on an online search engine turned up websites making diametri-
cally opposed but equally sweeping claims about the "peak oil conspiracy." One website claimed that peak oil is a conspiracy being
perpetrated by left-wing extremists who are trying to bring down
the status quo by foisting a fake crisis on the world. Another website claimed that peak oil is a conspiracy being perpetrated by financiers who are trying to shore up the status quo by foisting a
fake crisis on the world. Now it's certainly true that some political
activists have done their level best to hijack the oil depletion issue
for partisan purposes, and it is possible that the recent run-up in
oil prices was pushed in an attempt to pump more financial liquid-
ity into a faltering world economy. Those are, however, secondary
factors. The driving forces behind peak oil are these:

+ The world's oil reserves are finite.
+ We've already used close to half the total recoverable oil on the
  planet.
+ Every year since 1964 we've pumped more oil than we've dis-
  covered.
+ Production at most producing oil fields is declining.
+ New fields and alternative sources such as tar sands are barely
  filling the gap.

◆ The situation is more likely to get worse than better in coming decades.

These hard physical realities provide the context within which activists, financiers, and everyone else make their decisions and pursue their goals. If liberals are manipulating peak oil to support a partisan agenda, or if the big investment banks are encouraging speculation in the oil markets, that's worth noting, and arguably worth criticizing as well. But neither the liberals nor the bankers can change the reality of peak oil. Still, if you don't want to talk about the reasons that you got passed over for promotion, that peanut butter sandwich makes a good distraction.

Listening to the Space Lizards

You can often make sense of a phenomenon by watching it in an extreme form, and I've had the opportunity to do that with the rise of conspiracy thinking over the last few years. In the small southern Oregon town where I live, quite a few residents participate in the New Age movement, and a fair number of them are into the baroque conspiracy theory launched a few years back by a soccer player turned New Age guru named David Icke.[15]

Icke's theory claims that all the world's political, economic, and cultural leaders are actually evil lizards from another planet. This is admittedly only one of many popular flavors of New Age paranoia these days. Older and potentially more dangerous theories have also begun to surface. It's not precisely a comforting sign that Icke and several other New Age conspiracy gurus have written books that include the complete text of the *Protocols of the Elders of Zion*, the hoary anti-Semitic forgery that helped inspire National Socialism. Still, Icke's version of contemporary conspiracy theory will do as well as any, particularly since it has a wide circulation these days in the New Age scene we've been discussing.

The conjunction between Icke's brand of cosmic paranoia and the New Age movement may seem odd, since one of the core elements of the current New Age credo is "you create your own reality." Why, you might well wonder, would people who believe they create their own reality want to create one in which the world is ruled by evil lizards from outer space? Like most questions, this one contains its own answer, because there are at least three reasons why a world ruled by evil space lizards is more comforting than the one we actually inhabit.

First, *it's not your fault*. If evil space lizards dominate our planet, it doesn't matter that your comfortable lifestyle depends on Third World sweatshops and environmental devastation, or that the choices you make are helping to guarantee your grandchildren a poorer life on a more barren world. Because the lizards run the world and you don't, they're to blame, not you.

Second, *the world does what it's told*. If evil space lizards control the world, that means the world is under control, and thus at least potentially under *your* control. The world around you loses its independence and becomes an object to be pushed around at will. You don't have to confront a universe governed by its own laws and momentum, in which you, your desires, and your opinions aren't important.

Third, *you don't have to change your life*. If evil space lizards are responsible for all the world's problems, then opposing the lizards is far more important than solving the problems. It's also much easier, since it doesn't require you to give up unsustainable lifestyle choices.

These advantages go a long way toward explaining why Icke's lizard mythology has become so popular on the far edges of today's zeitgeist. The same three ideas, though, play at least as large a role in the far less exotic versions of conspiracy theory that surround the current predicament of industrial society. Far too often, talk about the various manifestations of that predicament focuses exclusively on who's to blame. Whether the target du jour is liberal activists, financiers, oil companies, or George W. Bush, the assumption seems to be that if only the right scapegoat can be found and punished, the problem will be solved.

It won't, though. Criticism has its place in any healthy society. When it turns into a replacement for constructive action, on the other hand, it becomes wasted breath, and when it becomes a way for people to avoid dealing with their own complicity in the situation, it can easily become part of the problem it claims to address. That's true even if some of the potential scapegoats helped make the situation worse than it had to be.

The shift from visionary mysticism to paranoiac conspiracy culture makes sense when read in the context of psychologist Carl Jung's theory of "projecting the shadow." The shadow, in Jung's psychology, is the sum total of everything we don't accept about ourselves.[16] We try any number of psychological tricks to keep from becoming aware of our shadows, but one of the standard methods is to project it onto someone else. Instead of owning up to the fact that we have characteristics we claim to despise, we see those characteristics in *Them* — whether "them" is an ethnic group, a religious community, a political party, or what have you. The more intense our hypocrisy, the more forcefully we project our own negative characteristics on somebody else, and the more savagely we hate the target for mirroring back to us, at least in our own minds, the things we project onto them.

This process of projection is exactly what's going on in large parts of the New Age community today, with a twist. The shadow of the New Age is the reality of limitation — the hard fact that you can't always get what you want, no matter how much you want it. Projecting that shadow, as Jung pointed out, is one effective way to deal with it, and conspiracy theories allow the faithful to project the shadow of their failure onto a fantasy of ultimate evil. In David Icke's theories, for example, the evil space lizards aren't just to blame for everything wrong with the world, they deliberately created and maintain the "illusion" of a material reality with real, inflexible limits. Thus believers in Icke's worldview can maintain their faith in their ability to create their own reality; if it doesn't work in practice, that's because the space lizards are slithering around behind the scenes messing things up.

The Religion of Progress

Now all this may seem to have little to do with the themes of peak oil and societal decline discussed in this book, but there's a direct connection. The myth of progress, like the belief that everyone creates their own reality, raises expectations that the real world simply isn't able to meet in an age of diminishing resources. As the gap between expectation and experience grows, so, too, does the potential for paranoia and hatred. Those who cling to faith in progress, like those who believe they create their own reality, are all too likely to go looking for scapegoats when the future fails to deliver the better world they expect.

The emotional power of the myth of progress makes the quest for scapegoats a difficult trap to avoid. The claim that progress is inevitable and good has become so deeply woven into our collective thinking that many people nowadays simply can't get their minds around the implications of fossil fuel depletion, or for that matter any of the other factors driving the contemporary crisis of industrial civilization. All these factors promise a future in which energy, raw materials, and their products — including nearly all of our present high technology — will all be subject to ever-tightening limits that will make them less and less available over time. Thus we face a future of regress, not progress.

The problem here is that regress is an unthinkable concept these days. Suggest to most people nowadays that progress will soon shift into reverse, and that their great-great-grandchildren will make do with technologies not that different from the ones their great-great-grandparents used, and you might as well be trying to tell a medieval peasant that heaven with all its saints and angels isn't there any more. In words made famous a few years ago by Christopher Lasch, progress is our "true and only heaven;"[17] it's where most modern people put their dreams of a better world — and to be deprived of it cuts to the core of many people's view of reality.

Even those who reject the myth of progress in favor of the myth of apocalypse draw most of their ideas from the faith they

think they've abandoned. Like Satanists who accept all the presup-
positions of Christian theology but root for the other side, or like
that minority of feminists who argue that gender discrimination
is bad when it privileges men but good when it works the other
way around, most of today's believers in apocalypse swallow whole
the mythic claim that progress is as inevitable as a steamroller;
it's simply that they believe the steamroller is about to roll its way
off a cliff. The suggestion that the steamroller is in the process of
shifting into reverse, and will presently start rolling patiently back
the way it came, is just as foreign to them as it is to believers in
progress.

It's not going too far, I think, to call belief in progress the established religion of the modern industrial world. In the same way
that Christians have traditionally looked to heaven and Buddhists
to nirvana, most people nowadays look to progress for their salvation and their explanation for why the world is the way it is. To
believers in the religion of progress, all other human societies are
steps on a ladder that lead to modern industrial civilization. From
the standpoint of the myth, the things our civilization happens to
be good at are the things that matter, and the things our civilization has never been able to master don't count; our kind of progress
is the only kind there is, and the road to the future thus inevitably
leads through us to future societies that will be like ours, but even
more so. All of these claims are taken for granted as self-evident
truths by most people in today's industrial societies. Not one of
them has a basis in logic or evidence; like the doctrine of the Trin-
ity or the Four Noble Truths, they are statements of faith.

The religion of progress has a central role in driving the predicament of industrial civilization because the dead end of dependence
on rapidly depleting fossil fuels can't be escaped by continuing on
the path we've been following for the last three centuries or so. Almost without exception, the technological progress of the industrial age will have to shift into reverse as its foundation — cheap,
abundant energy — goes away, and most of the social and cultural

phenomena that grew out of fossil fuel-powered technology will go away as well. The peak and decline of the world's oil reserves is the first step in this process, and the slower exhaustion of coal and other nonrenewable fuels will complete it, setting the industrial world on a trajectory that will most likely lead to something like the technology and society it had before the industrial revolution began in the first place.

What will happen to the faith in progress in an age of obvious technological regress, when cars and computers and footsteps on the Moon all belong to the departed glories of the past? No doubt some diehard believers will claim that whatever changes come as we slide down the far side of Hubbert's peak are further evidence of progress. We've already seen the first wave of that among green-tech proponents who argue that their technologies are "more advanced" and therefore more progressive than the competition alternatives. Still, it seems unlikely that many people will keep the faith. The religion of progress has maintained its hold for the last three centuries because it has delivered on its promises, filling our lives with technological marvels wondrous enough to distract us from the cost to our world, our communities, and ourselves.

When the parade of wonders grinds to a halt, then, the impact on deindustrializing cultures may be immense. If, as I've suggested, progress is the unrecognized religion of the industrial world, the failure of its priests to produce miracles on cue could plunge many people into a crisis of faith with no easy way out. The recent vogue for conspiracy theories and apocalyptic visions of the future strike me as two clear signs that people are beginning to turn their back on the religion of progress and seek their salvation from other gods. Neither pursuing scapegoats nor waiting for redemption through catastrophe are productive as ways of dealing with the transition to the deindustrial age, but both of them offer a great deal of emotional consolation, and it's likely to take more than the usual amount of clearheadedness to avoid them in the difficult times we are likely to encounter in the near future.

Peoples of the past, when stripped of their traditional faith in one way or another, have responded in many ways. Some launched revitalization movements to renew the old faith or to revive some older vision of destiny, some embraced newly minted belief systems or traditions imported from distant lands, and some simply huddled down into themselves and died. We have begun to see examples of each of these reactions in the modern industrial world. Which of them turns out to be most common may have drastic effects on the way the twilight of the industrial age works out, because the stories we tell ourselves will have an immense impact on the world we create at the end of the industrial age.

Briefing
for the
Descent

In the wide space between the myth of perpetual progress and the myth of imminent apocalypse, we can begin seeking a clearer and more nuanced sense of the possible futures open to industrial civilization as the age of cheap, abundant energy comes to an end. Any such exploration has to start from a sense of the possibilities of civilization — the form of human society that includes such things as cities, schools, market economies, and the combination of literacy and book distribution that makes it possible for you to encounter my ideas in the first place — because those possibilities define crucial limits on what can be achieved as the deindustrial age begins.

It's long been fashionable to claim that civilized societies are better by definition than the less complex tribal societies from which civilizations emerge and to which, in times of decline and disintegration, they tend to revert. In recent years, it's become just as fashionable in some circles to stand the equation on its head and insist that civilized societies are by definition worse than tribal societies. Both these claims reduce history to a morality play in which all human cultures, in their richness and moral complexity, are forced into two-dimensional roles as good guys or bad guys. This sort of moralizing is fine if your goal is cultivating self-righteous indignation, but it's a good deal less useful in the quest for understanding.

It's clear from the historical record that some civilizations have, on the whole, been good places for human beings to live, and others have been much less so. It's also clear that civilization can flourish indefinitely with minimal ecological damage in certain bioregions, and equally clear that in other bioregions civilization is a mayfly phenomenon that flits past and vanishes in a blink of ecological time. Visit eastern China, where the same rice paddies, villages, and cities have been in use for five thousand years, and the potential continuity of civilization is hard to dispute; visit the ruins of Tikal in the Yucatan jungle, where classic Maya civilization crashed and burned a thousand years ago, and the potential fragility of civilization is just as obvious. Trying to force both these examples to fit the Procrustean bed of a single story requires so much stretching and lopping that the results have much more to do with the prejudices of the storyteller than the facts on the ground.

One of the keynotes of history, though, is that a long rhythm of rise and fall seems to shape the lives of civilizations. Over the five thousand years they have witnessed so far, for instance, the cities and villages of eastern China have seen Chinese civilization expand and contract numerous times. Periods of economic growth and cultural creativity have been followed by periods of economic contraction and social disintegration. The same rhythm appears in other civilizations around the world with astonishing regularity. On average, civilizations take between five hundred and one thousand years to rise out of the ruins of some past civilization, then decline and fall in their turn over a period of one to three centuries, and give way to a new cycle that follows the same trajectory.

This rhythm offers little support to either the progressive or the apocalyptic faith. Fortunately, there are other options. The rise and fall of civilizations has been a central preoccupation of historians since not long after history first emerged as a distinct form of scholarship. Many of the greatest historians of the past, from Polybius (c. 200–118 BCE) through ibn Khaldun (1332–1406) to Giambattista Vico (1688–1744), focused much of their efforts on the question of why civilizations rise and fall. These three historians were among those who pointed out that wildly different societies followed very similar trajectories, and they tried to tease out general laws that defined the expansion and contraction of civilizations.

Their lead was taken up by two of the leading figures in 20th century historical studies, Oswald Spengler (1880–1936) and Arnold Toynbee (1889–1975).[1] Spengler, surveying the casualty list of past societies, concluded that civilizations were organic entities with lifespans like any other living thing. He has been roundly condemned for that, but as an observation of facts rather than a theory about causes it has much to recommend it. Toynbee, building on Spengler's insights while rejecting his biological metaphor, took the argument one step further and proposed that what drives the cycle is a factor he called "the nemesis of success."[2] Each human society faces challenges; when a society meets its challenges with successful responses, it opens up a space of possibility that allows for growth. The greater the success won by any given response, though, the greater the chance that the society will become locked into that response and will keep on trying to solve new challenges with old methods. To use terms introduced in Chapter 2, the society gets stuck in a single story and enters a spiral of repeated failure that ends in collapse.

More recently, in *The Collapse of Complex Societies*, (1988), Joseph Tainter critiqued Spengler and Toynbee harshly but argued for what, in many ways, is simply a more precisely worked out version of Toynbee's theory. To Tainter, the rising costs and dwindling payoffs of social complexity form the two jaws of the nemesis of success. Each civilization starts out at a low level of social complexity and, as it develops, adds complexity to respond to challenges and take advantage of the results of its success. Like everything else, though, complexity taken too far reaches the point of diminishing returns; the cost/payoff ratio goes negative, and each additional layer of complexity costs the civilization more than it produces. Since increasing complexity has always worked in the past, though, most civilizations keep on adding new layers of complexity to deal with problems that are caused by complexity itself. Finally the sheer cost of maintaining complexity outruns the available resources, and the result is collapse.

Around the same time Tainter's book saw print, environmental historians began to point out that the nemesis of success could easily take the shape of a head-on crash between a civilization and the limits of its environment. Clive Ponting's *A Green History of the World* (1992) and Jared Diamond's *Collapse* (2005) (among many other books) present a strong case that many past societies committed suicide by wrecking the ecological systems on which they depended for their survival. The collapse of the Maya civilization, as outlined back in Chapter 1, is the poster child for this theory, and the close resonance between the Maya collapse and our own predicament make it particularly relevant here.

Tainter's theory and the environmental hypothesis can easily be combined into a single narrative of how civilizations fall. My attempt to frame that narrative is the theory of catabolic collapse.

Catabolic Collapse

The word "catabolism" comes from the Greek, by way of the life sciences. In today's biology it refers to processes by which a living thing feeds on itself. One of the most striking features of the dead civilizations of the past is that they go through precisely this process as they move through the stages of decline and fall. In the course of the Maya collapse, for example, a complex, literate society with an abundance of practical, scientific, and religious knowledge reduced itself step by step to scattered villages in a jungle dotted with ruins. In some cases, the process of collapse has erased the vast majority of a civilization's legacy, leaving only sparse fragments for later peoples to puzzle over.

At the same time, there are other examples where collapse stopped short of this point, and a new civilization picked up where its predecessor left off. The Maya heartland went through this cycle at least once before the final collapse, and Mayan successor states in the northern Yucatan managed the same thing on a smaller scale after the classic Maya collapse.[3] China is perhaps the most remarkable example of this less disastrous form of collapse on record; from the Hsia dynasty's origins well before 2000 BCE right up to the present, a slow drumbeat of collapse and recovery has given Chinese civilization its measure, without impairing cultural continuity.[4] The theory of catabolic collapse started off as an attempt to understand the difference between these two possible outcomes of the cycle of rise and fall.

My original essay on catabolic collapse[5] bristles with equations, footnotes, and all the other impedimenta of the modern academic paper. Still, the basic idea is simple enough, and it's best communicated through a metaphor: imagine that, instead of the fate of civilizations, we're discussing home ownership. Until recently, when people went shopping for a home, most of them were sensible about it and bought one within their means. The housing bubble of the last few years, though, encouraged many people to buy much more house than they could afford, on the assumption that appreciating real estate values and the other advantages of home ownership would make up the difference.

Too many of these people, however, didn't take the time to work out just how much their new McMansion would cost to own, maintain, and repair, and soaring real estate prices made it very difficult to remember that every boom sooner or later ends in a bust. Once these realities began to sink in, many people who expected to get rich off their houses found themselves in an awkward predicament as their monthly paychecks no longer covered their

monthly expenses. Home equity loans offered one popular way to
cover the gap, but once housing prices began to slump and banks
cut back on easy credit, that option shut down. From that point
on the possibilities narrowed sharply, and every option — taking
on more debt, deferring repairs and maintenance, leaving bills un-
paid — eventually adds to the total due each month. Sooner or
later, the rising tide of expenses overwhelms available income, and
the result is foreclosure.

That's catabolic collapse in a nutshell. Like suburban man-
sions, civilizations are complex, expensive, fragile things. To keep
one going, you have to maintain and replace a whole series of capital stocks: physical (such as buildings); human (such as trained
workers); informational (such as agricultural knowledge); social
(such as market systems); and more. If you can do this within the
"monthly budget" of resources provided by the natural world and
the efforts of your labor force, your civilization can last a very long
time. Over time, though, civilizations tend to build their capital stocks up to levels that can't be maintained; each king (or industrial magnate) wants to build a bigger palace (or skyscraper)
than the one before him, and so on. That puts a civilization into
the same bind as the homeowner with the oversized house. In the
terms used in the original paper, production falls short of the level
needed to maintain capital stocks, and those stocks are converted
to waste: buildings become ruins, populations decrease, knowledge is lost, social networks disintegrate, and so on.

What happens then depends on whether the civilization's
most important resources are being used at a sustainable rate or
not. Resources used at a sustainable rate are like a monthly paycheck; in the long run, you've got to live within it, but as long as
you can keep expenses on average at or below your paycheck, you
know you can get by. If a civilization gets most of its raw materials
from ecologically sound agriculture, for example, the annual harvest puts a floor under the collapse process. Even if things fall apart
completely — if the homeowner goes bankrupt and has her house

Diagram 3.1. How Catabolic Collapse Works

(a) A growing or stable society

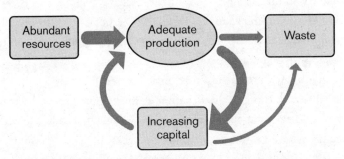

In a growing or stable society, the resource base is abundant enough that production can stay ahead of the maintenance costs of society's capital – that is, the physical structures, trained people, information, and organizational systems that constitute the society. Capital used up in production or turned into waste can easily be replaced.

(b) A society in catabolic collapse

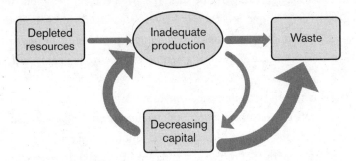

In a society in catabolic collapse, resources have become so depleted that not enough is available for production to meet the maintenance costs of capital. As production falters, more and more of society's capital becomes waste, or is turned into raw material for production via salvage. If resource depletion can be stopped, the loss of capital brings maintenance costs back down below what production can meet, and the catabolic process ends; if resource depletion continues, the catabolic process continues until all capital becomes waste.

foreclosed on, to continue the metaphor — that monthly paycheck will allow her to rent a smaller house or an apartment and start picking up the pieces. Civilizations such as imperial China, which were based on sustainable resources, cycled through this process many times, from expansion through overshoot to a self-limiting collapse that bottomed out when capital stocks got low enough to be supported by the stable resource base.

If the civilization depends on using resources at an unsustainable rate, though, the situation becomes much more serious. In terms of the metaphor, our homeowner bought the house with lottery winnings, not a monthly paycheck; his income is only a fraction of the amount he spends each month. In the first flush of prosperity, it's all too easy for our lottery winner to commit to far bigger monthly expenses than his income can cover. By the time the problem becomes clear, very little can be done about it. The money is gone, our homeowner is faced with bills his monthly income won't even begin to cover, and by the time the collection agencies get through with him he may very well end up living on the street. Civilizations such as the Maya, which used vital resources at an unsustainable rate, went through this process; the "collection agencies" of nature left nothing behind but crumbling ruins in the Yucatan jungle.

This is not good news for our modern industrial civilization because its capital stocks are supported by winnings from the geological lottery that laid down fantastic amounts of fossilized solar energy in the form of coal, oil, and natural gas. Even the very small fraction of our resource base that comes from the "paycheck" of agriculture, forestry, and fishing depends on fossil fuels. Since the late 1950s, scientists have been warning that what's left of our fossil fuel resources won't sustain our current industrial system indefinitely, much less support the Utopia of perpetual economic growth we have grown up expecting. For the most part, these warnings have been roundly ignored. If they continue to be ignored until actual shortages begin, we may be in for a very ugly future.

That future may be closer than most people like to think. The collapse of New Orleans after Hurricane Katrina drew attention from around the world, but few people seem to have noticed the implications of the Big Easy's fate. The United States suffers catastrophic hurricanes every decade or so. In the past, the destruction was followed by massive rebuilding programs — but not this time. The French Quarter and a few other mostly undamaged portions of the city have reestablished a rough equivalent of their former lives, but much of the rest of the city has been bulldozed or simply abandoned to the elements. The ruins of the Ninth Ward, like the hundreds of abandoned farm towns that dot the Great Plains states and the gutted cities of America's Rust belt, may be a harbinger of changes most Americans will find it acutely uncomfortable to face.

The housing metaphor breaks down in two places, though. First, even in societies dependent on unsustainable resource use, catabolic collapse unfolds gradually, in a distinctive rhythm of crisis followed by partial recovery. It's similar to a homeowner who, facing financial ruin, sells his existing house and uses the proceeds to buy a smaller one; when he can no longer afford that, he repeats the process, until eventually he either moves into a home he can afford, or he ends up in a cardboard box on the street. In terms of the model, the mismatch between production and the maintenance costs of capital causes a certain fraction of a civilization's capital stock to be turned to waste. Since that fraction no longer has to be maintained, and because some of it can be recycled into raw materials, each wave of collapse is followed by a respite, as costs drop far enough to give the declining civilization breathing room. The result is the stairstep pattern of decline found in the histories of nearly every dead civilization.

Second, a civilization has a fractal structure — that is, the same patterns that define it at the topmost level also appear on smaller scales. The cities of eastern China that were mentioned at the beginning of this chapter maintained urban life through the fall of empires precisely because of this fractal structure; a single city and its agricultural hinterland can survive even if the larger system comes apart. The recent spread of peak oil resolutions and projects by cities and towns across America is thus a very hopeful sign. It's going to take drastic changes and a great deal of economic rebuilding before these communities can get by on the more limited resources of a deindustrial future, but the crucial first steps toward sustainability are at least on the table now. If our future is to be anything but a desperate attempt to keep our balance as we skid down the slope of collapse and decline, these projects may well point the way.

Four Facets of Catabolic Collapse

How will the process of catabolic collapse work itself out in the present situation? Prophecy is among the chanciest of arts, but a careful eye on current trends allows some educated guesses to be made about the way the near future is likely to unfold. Though the future we face is far from apocalyptic, four horsemen still define the most likely scenario.

First out of the starting gate is *declining energy availability*. Around 2010, according to the best current estimates, world petroleum production will peak, falter, and begin an uneven but irreversible descent. North American natural gas supplies are predicted to start their terminal decline around the same time. Some of the slack can be taken up by coal, wind and other renewables, nuclear power, and conservation — but not all. As oil depletion accelerates, and other resources such as uranium and Eurasian natural gas hit their own production peaks, the shortfall widens, and many lifestyles and business models that depend on cheap energy become nonviable.

The second horseman, hard on the hooves of the first, is *economic contraction*. Energy prices are already beginning to skyrocket as nations, regions, and individuals engage in bidding wars driven to extremes by rampant speculation. The global economy, which made economic sense only in the context of the politically driven low oil prices of the 1990s, will proceed to come apart at the seams, driving many import- and export-based industries onto the ropes, and setting off a wave of bankruptcies and business failures. Shortages of many consumer products will follow, including even such essentials as food and clothing. Soaring energy prices will have the same effect more directly in many areas of the domestic economy. Unemployment will likely climb to Great Depression levels, and poverty will become widespread even in what are now wealthy nations.

The third horseman, following the second by a length or two, is *collapsing public health*. As poverty rates spiral upward, shortages and energy costs impact the food supply chain; energy-intensive health care becomes unaffordable for all but the obscenely rich; global warming and ecosystem disruption drive the spread of tropical and emerging diseases; malnutrition and disease become major burdens. People begin to die of what were once minor, treatable conditions. Chronic illnesses such as diabetes become death sentences as the cost of health care climbs out of reach for most people. Death rates soar as rates of live birth slump, launching the first wave of population contraction.

The fourth horseman, galloping along in the wake of the first three, is *political turmoil*. What political scientists call "liberal democracy" is really a system in which competing factions of the political class buy the loyalty of sectors of the electorate by handing out economic largesse. That system depends on abundant fossil fuels and the industrial economy they make possible. Many of today's political institutions will not survive the end of cheap energy, and the changeover to new political arrangements will likely involve violence. International affairs face similar realignments as nations whose power and influence depend on access to abundant, cheap energy fall from their present positions of strength. Today's supposedly "backward" nations may well find that their less energy-dependent economies turn into a source of strength rather than weakness in world affairs. If history is any guide, these power shifts will work themselves out on the battlefield.

The most important thing to remember about all four of these factors is that they're self-limiting in the near term. As energy prices soar, economies contract, and the demand for energy decreases, bringing prices back down. Even as the global economy comes apart, human needs remain, so local economies take up the slack as best they can with the resources on hand, producing new opportunities and breathing new life into moribund sectors of the economy. As public health fails, populations decline, taking pressure off other sectors of the economy. As existing political arrangements collapse, new regimes take their place, and, like all new regimes, these can be counted on to put stability at the top of their agendas.

Thus in the near future, at least, we're most likely facing a period of crisis, followed by a period of renewed stability, with another round of crises waiting in the wings. That's how the process of catabolic collapse unfolds, in a stair-step process alternating periods of crisis with breathing spaces at progressively lower levels of economic and political integration. If past examples are anything to go by, the approaching period of crisis will likely last around 25 years, with the breathing space following it around the same scale or a little longer. The great challenge of the present, then, is to deal with the immediate crisis in each of its manifestations.

The Energy Predicament

Of all the many aspects of the predicament of industrial society, the peak of world petroleum production will likely have the most drastic impact in the short and middle term. Now it's true, as *The Limits to Growth* pointed out, that unlimited growth on a limited planet bids fair to run into many shortages, not just one. On cue, plenty of other resources are also running short worldwide, from fertile topsoil and fresh water to dozens of minor but economically important minerals.[6] In the latter days of industrial civilization, shortages are inevitable, but no other globally traded commodity is as central to the world's industrial economies as oil — and no other commodity faces so imminent and irreversible a decline.

Thus the end of the age of cheap oil promises a sea change in the world's economies and societies as significant as the beginning of the fossil fuel age some three hundred years ago. Its impact can easily be overstated, though, and indeed it has been overstated by quite a few writers on the survivalist end of the peak oil community. Many of these writers insist that the inevitable result of declining petroleum production will be the rapid collapse of civilization in an uncontrollable spiral of violence, anarchy, and mass death.

This is as mistaken as it is counterproductive. It's certainly possible to dream up worst case scenarios that result in sudden collapse, but these scenarios run headlong into an awkward historical fact: declines in petroleum use equal to the ones we face on the downslope of Hubbert's peak have occurred many times in recent history, without producing anything like the consequences the survivalist theory predicts. In America, World War II saw gasoline rationing and sharp reductions in the use of oil throughout the civilian economy; the energy crises of the 1970s set in motion a 15% decline in petroleum use worldwide that lasted for most of a decade. Unlike the future we face today, those periods of declining petroleum use proved to be temporary, but they show that American society can use less oil without collapsing.

Overseas, far more drastic reductions in petroleum supplies and energy use have often been made. The results included hard times and human suffering, but the collapse of civilization? Hardly. Two world wars, the greatest depression in modern history, and plenty of less global but no less severe crises have forced individuals and economies to make do with much less for extended periods. Except in a few exceptional and very short-term situations, social order has remained intact and economies have adapted to extreme conditions, shedding energy- and resource-intensive sectors and establishing new networks to get food and other necessities to those who need them. This, rather than the total social collapse of the survivalist fantasy, is what we face in the next few decades.

Here in North America, the end of cheap oil will be made more complex by another factor: a large fraction of electricity and home heating nowadays comes from natural gas, and North American natural gas reserves are depleting fast.[7] Over the next decade or so, as the inevitable shortages hit, the rising prices and dwindling availability of natural gas will make both these uses unaffordable for most people. Some writers have claimed that this will lead to the total collapse of electric power grids nationwide, but this hardly follows. As the supply of electricity decreases, prices rise, and demand goes down as people cut their usage or are disconnected for failure to pay their bills. As shortages become more severe, grid operators and governments have plenty of options varying from mandatory conservation programs to rationing schemes to cutting entire sectors out of the grid so that power can be saved for other uses. None of these will allow current rates of energy use to be maintained, but all of them will cushion the descent into a deindustrial world.

Where electrical power is concerned, in fact, the 21st century may well look like a film of the 20th century run in reverse. As the 1930s were the decade of rural electrification in America, when electricity finally made its way to farm families nationwide, the 2030s may turn out to be the decade of rural de-electrification, when rural America goes off the grid for good. Well before 2100, electricity will be what it was in 1900, an urban amenity generated by hydroelectric, wind, and coal-fired plants — and used mostly by the wealthy. Not long after that most of the coal will be gone and other fossil fuels will be a fading memory, but wind and running water will remain, and cities will likely have their own sustainably powered electrical grids providing modest amounts of light and power to the homes and businesses of the well-to-do.

Transportation is a more complex matter. A transportation network of the sort we have today requires not only fuel and vehicles, but a sprawling and energy-intensive infrastructure of highways, bridges, gas stations, tanker truck fleets, storage depots, highway police, and more, all demanding constant investment — and all vulnerable to the impact of catabolic collapse. As costs soar and resources run short, expect to see that network come gradually unraveled. Rural areas far from major routes are already seeing infrastructure disintegrate as roads are no longer repaired and gas stations far from the freeways go out of business. As this process speeds up, resources will most likely be concentrated on a network of critical freeway corridors and urban regions. This network will then contract over a period of several decades until resource availability drops below a critical value and truck transport stops being economically viable.

The private car never did make much sense, except as a way to maximize employment in the manufacturing and construction sectors of the economy,[8] and the complex of industries centered on the automobile can be counted on to go the way of the dodo in short order. Soaring gas prices will render most of American human geography worse than useless, as people no longer can afford to shuttle among retail cores, employment centers, and suburban bedroom communities that are many miles from one another. The "doughnut geography" common to so many North American urban centers, with decaying urban cores surrounded by prosperous suburbs, has already begun to reverse in many areas as middle-class families move to gentrifying urban neighborhoods, while their former suburban homes are relegated to the lower classes. Expect this trend to accelerate over the next few decades, as today's suburbs become slum districts like those surrounding Third World cities today, and the suburban tract housing spawned by the now-deflating housing bubble turns into raw materials for the shantytowns of the permanently poor.

Trains, which require a much simpler infrastructure and use much less energy than trucks to move cargo, will potentially be viable much longer. Those countries that have maintained their rail networks will have a massive advantage as the automobile age comes to an end. In North America, by contrast, the railroad network has undergone many decades of malign neglect, and unless significant resources go into maintaining and upgrading it soon, it will likely disintegrate as resources run short. Even if the railroads get the emergency investment they need, it's an open question whether rail travel can keep going over the long term without fossil fuels. If the railroad network unravels in the same way as the highways, the social and political consequences will be immense. Lacking cheap transcontinental transport, for example, it's unlikely that the United States or Canada will maintain political unity for long.

The transportation network of last resort depends on water. North America's navigable waterways have suffered at least as much neglect as the railroads, but they can be maintained and rebuilt at a much lower level of technology; several crucial links — above all the Erie Canal and St. Lawrence Seaway, connecting the Great Lakes with the eastern seaboard — remain intact. If the railways fail, the economically viable region of North America will contract by more than half because the inland West will lose any effective way to import goods or export its own produce. Still, waterways weave together the Atlantic seaboard, the Great Lakes states and provinces, and the Mississippi valley. The harsher topography of the west coast offers far fewer options for water travel; the Columbia and Sacramento watersheds connect agricultural regions in the far west to coastal ports, but a regional waterway network is out of reach even with today's machinery, so regional and local devolution will be hard to prevent.

The end of cheap energy thus promises to remake the human geography of North America and reshape the lifestyles of almost everyone living on the continent. The transition to the new deindustrial society, though, will take place over decades, not overnight, as governments, businesses, and individuals scramble to deal with shrinking supplies of fossil fuel energy. So much time has been wasted, and so little has been done to prepare for the inevitable, that a great deal of human suffering and deprivation is inevitable at this point.

Avoiding the Y2K Fallacy

In all probability, the most sweeping dimension of the change we face is economic. For the last three hundred years, the key to prosperity has been the replacement of human skill with mechanical energy. The steam-powered factories of 18th century England heralded the arrival of a new economic order in which technological progress and fossil fuel extraction went hand in hand, and success went to those who pushed mechanical energy into new economic sectors — replacing sails with steam, farm horses with tractors, local theaters with movies and TV, folk culture with mass-produced pop culture, and so on.

Hubbert's peak marks the limit of this process. If the last three hundred years funneled wealth to those who exploited fossil fuels to the fullest, and allowed them to build centralized, technologically driven economic structures, then the next three hundred years will see exactly the opposite. Success will go to those who get ahead of depletion curves by reducing their reliance on fossil fuels further than others, and by relying instead on human skills and sustainable, low-intensity energy inputs.

These changes won't take place overnight, though, and the most likely future ahead of us is a long and uneven period of economic contraction and technological decline. There will be plenty of bumps and potholes in the course of the Long Descent, to be sure. Systems failures will likely play a significant role. The aftermath of Hurricane Katrina in 2005, which reduced large portions of coastal Louisiana and Mississippi to a deindustrial condition from which they show few signs of recovering as of this writing, offers an example of the sort of thing that can be expected in the future. Still, systems failures don't automatically spiral out into total collapse.

This point has been notably lacking in many discussions about the economic impact of peak oil. It's been argued, for example, that the financial shock imposed by rising energy costs will cause the entire global economy to come apart at the seams, leaving people unable to get food and other necessities, and turning them into the marauding hordes of survivalist fantasies. This is a classic example of what might as well be called the Y2K fallacy; revisiting the Y2K fiasco will cast some light on where current speculations about peak oil have run off the rails.[9]

In the late 1990s, as my readers will doubtless remember, computer experts began to warn that many older computer systems had no way to process year-numbers beginning with a 2 rather than a 1, so they could crash when the calendar rolled over from 1999 to 2000. Early surveys of the problem showed that a very large number of systems could be affected, especially in banking, telecommunications, and government. By the beginning of 1998 or so, it was clear that a major mess was in the making unless something was done.

This real and serious problem, though, quickly got blown out of proportion by believers in the myth of apocalypse. By early 1999, survivalist visions of social collapse and mass death via Y2K spilled out of this subculture and percolated through American society. I knew many people who confidently expected the end of civilization as we knew it on New Year's Eve of 1999; they waited all night in their basements for the blackouts, systems failures, and rampaging mobs that never came.

Some pundits have used these failed predictions to argue that the whole Y2K crisis wasn't real in the first place, but this misstates the whole lesson of the experience. The threat was real; believers in apocalypse simply missed the four most important words in the prediction — "unless something was done." Faced with a credible threat, a hard deadline, and a clear course of action, people responded predictably by doing something about the situation. Sales of Y2K-compliant computers and software soared off the charts (powering a boomtime in high-tech industries that deflated dramatically once the crisis was over). Software jockeys made money hand over fist reprogramming old machines. Some of us used simpler fixes; I simply reset the calendar on my old and non-compliant computer to December 31, 1949, and went through the rollover to January 1, 1950 with no trouble at all.

The fallacy that bedeviled the Y2K survivalists was the belief that government, business, and citizens, faced with an imminent threat and presented with a clear, constructive response to it, would sit on their hands and do nothing until catastrophe overwhelmed them. This same odd belief can be found throughout current discussions about peak oil. As oil plateaus and then declines, energy prices will rise sharply; that's the threat. The obvious response, which succeeded brilliantly in the 1970s, is to reduce energy use through conservation and increased efficiency.

The collision between declining fossil fuel production and increasing demand is far more likely to cause drastic swings in the price of energy than the sort of sustained rise imagined by some peak oil theorists. As energy prices rise, speculators dive into the market, driving up prices further than actual shortfalls in production capacity would justify. Many energy consumers respond by cutting back on their energy use by means of lifestyle changes and conservation technologies, while others are simply priced out of the market. The result is that demand drops, stockpiles rise, and prices start to slide. The speculators dive out of the market, driving down prices further than actual declines in demand would justify, and the cycle begins again. These whipsaw movements in the price of energy can cause plenty of economic damage all by themselves, but there again it's possible to respond to volatility constructively — for example, by stockpiling fuel when it's cheap and drawing down those stockpiles when prices spike.

The same logic needs to be applied to other aspects of our economic situation. The United States today, as many people have pointed out, is a spendthrift debtor nation. We borrow more than

$2 billion a day from overseas to pay for imports that far exceed our
exports, and for a standard of living that can't be supported by our
anemic manufacturing and resource-extraction base. Major shifts
in the world economic order are inevitable as the resulting imbal-
ances work themselves out. Those who claim that the result will
inevitably be social collapse and a Road Warrior future, though,
haven't been paying attention to world economic affairs. Over the
last fifty years or so, quite a few nations have borrowed and spent
their way into fiscal crisis. Some responded with austerity and periods of recession; some inflated their currencies, went into hyperinflation, and came back out of it; some repudiated their foreign
debts and weathered the international reaction; others simply
muddled through. All of them survived the crisis and rebuilt afterward, and so will the United States.

Many people nowadays, it has to be said, underestimate the re-
siliency of the modern nation-state. A US government faced with
a severe economic crisis has plenty of options. It can respond to a
market crash by flooding the economy with cheap credit, as Japan
did after the 1990 stock debacle. It can respond to currency collapse by abandoning its old currency and issuing a new one with
solid backing, as Germany did in the 1920s to end its bout of
hyperinflation. It can manipulate markets, nationalize industries,
enact wage and price controls, levy punitive tariffs and embargoes,
subsidize basic necessities for the population, and impose rationing of fuel and food. If necessary, it can declare martial law and use
the military and National Guard to restore civil order. In the last
half century or so, all of these tactics have been used by other governments around the world as they faced the possibility of chaos.
Any or all of them could readily be employed here — and for that
matter, some already have.

There are still very rough times ahead, to be sure. After a quarter century of reckless borrowing and waste fueled by absurdly
extravagant use of the world's finite energy resources, the United
States is likely to face a period of contraction as bad as the Great

Depression; an economic breakdown on the scale of the one that engulfed Russia after the collapse of the Soviet Union is far from impossible. Still, the United States continued to exist after the Depression, Russia still exists today, and millions of people came through each of these economic crises with their lives, families, homes, and livelihoods intact.

Thus we can expect the next few decades to see a great deal of economic volatility and wrenching change. Energy costs will be impossible to predict; prices will spike and crash, following a slow but very uneven upward trend. Economic sectors dependent on stable access to energy will face a very rough road indeed. On average, those people and industries that require more energy will do worse than those that can make do with less, and those professions that meet actual needs will do much better than those devoted to the mass production of the unnecessary. To make sense of these changes, though, it's necessary to take a second look at the economy and draw some rarely noticed distinctions between the real economy of goods and services and the fictive economy that currently dominates the way goods and services are produced, distributed, and sold.

Hallucinated Wealth

I have no idea if kids still do this, but in my elementary school days in the late 1960s it was common practice to write IOUs for "a million billion trillion dollars" or some equally precise sum, and use those as the stakes in card games like Old Maid and Go Fish. Some of those IOUs passed from hand to hand dozens of times before they were accidentally left in a pocket and met their fate in the wash. Kids who were good card players amassed portfolios with very impressive face values, especially compared to the 25 cents a week that was the standard allowance in my neighborhood just then. If I recall correctly, though, nobody ever tried to convert their IOU holdings into anything more substantial than cookies from a classmate's lunchbox. Apparently that's the one thing that kept me and my friends from becoming pioneers of modern finance.

It surprises me how many people still seem to think that the main business of a modern economy is the production and distribution of goods and services. Far and away the majority of economic activity nowadays consists of the production and exchange of IOUs. The United States has the world's largest economy not because it produces more goods and services than anyone else — it hasn't done that for decades — but because it produces more IOUs than anyone else, and it sells those IOUs to the rest of the world in exchange for goods and services.

An IOU, after all, is simply a promise to pay a given amount at some future time. That describes nearly every instrument of exchange in today's economy, from bonds and treasury bills through bank deposits and government-issued currency to credit swaps and derivatives. All these share three things in common with the IOUs my schoolmates staked on card games. First, they cost almost nothing to issue. Second, their face value needn't have any relationship to the issuer's ability to pay up. Third, they can be exchanged for goods and services — like the cookies in my example — but their main role is in exchanges where nothing passes from hand to hand except IOUs.

It's harsh but not, I think, unfair to call the result an economy of hallucinated wealth. Like the face value of those schoolroom IOUs, most "wealth" nowadays exists only because everyone agrees it does. Outside the social game of the market economy, financial instruments have no value at all, and the game continues only because the players — all of them, from the very rich to the ones with scarcely a million billion trillion dollars to their name — keep playing. They have to keep playing, because access to goods and services, not to mention privilege, perks, and power, depend on participation in the game.

The resulting IOU economy is highly unstable because hallucinated wealth has value only as long as people believe it does.

The history of modern economics is thus a chronicle of booms and busts, as tidal shifts in opinion send various classes of IOUs zooming up in value and then crashing back down to Earth. Crashes, far from being signs of breakdown, are a necessary and normal part of the process. They serve the same role as laundry day did in the schoolroom IOU economy: by paring down the total number of IOUs, they maintain the fiction that the ones left still have value.

All this leaves us in a historically unprecedented situation. Economies based purely on hallucinated wealth existed before the 20th century, but only for brief periods in the midst of speculative frenzies — the Dutch tulip mania, the South Sea bubble, and so on.[10] Today's hallucinated wealth, by contrast, has maintained its place as the mainspring of the global economy for more than half a century. Social critics who point to the housing bubble, the derivatives bubble, or the like and predict imminent disaster when these bubbles pop, are missing the wider picture: the great majority of the global economy rests on the same foundations of empty air.

Those who have noticed this wider picture, on the other hand, are fond of suggesting that sometime soon, given a suitable shock, the entire structure will come cascading down. Those of you who were reading the alternative press at the time of the 1987 stock market crash will recall predictions of economic collapse in the wake of that vertiginous plunge; I made some myself, within my circle of friends, and I ended up with egg on my face when nothing of the sort happened. Similar predictions have accompanied each of the notable fiscal crises since then — the Japanese stock market debacle of 1990, the Mexican debt crisis of 1995, the Asian currency crash of 1998, the tech-stock crash of 2000, and so on. Similar claims are now being made about the housing bubble, the US trade and credit deficit, and of course about peak oil as well.

Plausible as these claims of imminent disaster seem, I suspect they're missing the core of the situation, as well as the lessons taught by twenty years of violent economic gyrations. It's a mistake to expect hallucinations to obey the laws of gravity. It's doubly a mistake when the institutions charged with keeping them in midair — the Federal Reserve Board in the United States and its equivalents in other industrial nations — have proven adept at manipulating markets, flooding the economy with cheap credit (that is, more IOUs) to minimize the effects of a crash, and inflating some other sector of the economy to take up the slack of a deflating bubble. It's triply a mistake when the North American middle classes and, to a lesser extent, their equivalents in other industrial countries, display a faith in speculation so invulnerable to reality that their response to a crash in one market is to go looking for a new speculative bubble somewhere else.

To say that the economic empire of hallucinated wealth will continue to exist, though, does not imply that it will continue to produce the goods and services or the jobs that people need. Arguably, it doesn't do that very well right now. The "jobless recovery" of recent years saw most economic statistics rise well into positive territory, while most people saw their expenses rise and their incomes shrink. Things could go much further in the same direction. It requires no great suspension of disbelief to imagine a future in which the stock market hits new heights daily and other measures of economic activity remain in positive territory, while most of the population is starving in the streets.

Partly, as Bernard Gross predicted decades ago,[11] economic indicators have morphed into "economic vindicators" that promote a political agenda rather than reflecting economic realities. The statistical gamesmanship inflicted on the consumer price index and the official unemployment rate in the United States show this with a good deal of clarity.[12] Partly, though, most of the common measures of economic well-being only track hallucinated wealth. The markets that keep the financial news agog with their antics are IOU markets disconnected from what remains of the real economy, where real people produce and consume real goods and services. Thus, trying to track the economic impact of peak oil, global warming, and other aspects of our predicament by watching markets and financial statistics may turn out to be as misleading as trying to track the supply of cookies in a schoolroom by watching the exchange of IOUs in card games.

In today's world of hallucinated wealth, the theory that a massive market crash triggered by peak oil will bring down the real economy of goods and services is implausible at best. Crashes there will certainly be, and some of them may be monumental, since volatility in the energy markets tends to play crack-the-whip with the rest of the hallucinatory economy. Crashes aren't threats to the system, though; crashes — and the recessions and economic turmoil that follow them — are part of the system.

The economy of markets and statistics has aptly been compared to a circus and, like any other circus, it serves mostly to distract. While interest rates wow the crowd with their high-wire act, and clowns pile into and out of various speculative vehicles, the real process of economic decline will unfold elsewhere — all but invisible behind a veil of massaged numbers, and discreetly unmentioned by the mainstream media — in the non-hallucinated economy of goods and services, jobs, and personal income.

As the boom and bust cycle accelerates on the downside of the Hubbert curve, we can expect each recession to push more people into poverty and each recovery to lift fewer out of it. As industries dependent on cheap, abundant energy fold, we'll see jobs evaporate, lines form at the doors of soup kitchens, and today's posh suburbs mutate into tomorrow's shantytowns. Rising transport costs and sinking median incomes will squeeze the global trade in consumer goods until it implodes; shortages and ad hoc distribution networks will be the order of the day, and wild gyrations in currency markets could easily make barter and local scrip worth a good deal more than a million billion trillion dollars of hyperinflated IOU-money. Poverty, malnutrition, and desperation will be among the few things not in short supply. Until waves of change rock the political systems that keep the IOU economy in place, though, it seems most likely that the circus of hallucinated wealth will continue performing.

Slow-Motion Disaster

Ironically, while economic failures are likely to prove less drastic than some recent predictions have made them appear, declining public health will likely turn out much worse than most people nowadays suspect. Though it's all but unnoticed so far — outside of a small cadre of worried professionals — the coming disintegration of public health in coming decades promises a disaster in slow motion.[13]

It's not surprising that this crisis has gotten so little air time. Public health is one of the least regarded — though it's among the most necessary — of the basic services industrial society provides its citizens. It's not exciting stuff. Sanitation, pest control, water treatment, food safety regulations, and the like are exactly the sort of humdrum bureaucratic activities that today's popular culture ignores most readily. Even infectious disease control rarely achieves the level of intensity chronicled, say, in Randy Shilts' history of the AIDS epidemic, *And The Band Played On*; more often it's a matter of collecting statistics, tracing contacts, and sending local officials and hospitals e-mails that are easily and often ignored. On these pedestrian activities, though, rests the industrial world's relative freedom from the plagues that visited previous societies so regularly and killed so many of our ancestors.

The impending collapse of public health, like most aspects of our current predicament, has an abundance of causes. One is the failure of government at all levels to maintain even the very modest financial support public health received through most of the 20th century. Lacking an influential constituency in the political class, public health departments came out the losers in the tax and budget struggles that dominated American state and local politics in the aftermath of the 1970s. Worse, food safety regulations were among the consumer protections gutted by business-friendly politicians, with results that often make headlines these days.

A second factor in collapsing public health is the end of the antibiotic age.[14] Starting in the early years of the 20th century, when penicillin revolutionized the treatment of bacterial infections, antibiotics transformed medical practice. Dozens of once-lethal diseases — diphtheria, tuberculosis, bubonic plague, and many others — became treatable conditions. A few prescient researchers cautioned that microbes could evolve resistance to the new "wonder drugs" if the latter were used too indiscriminately, but their warnings went unheard amid the cheerleading of a pharmaceutical industry concerned only with increasing sales and profits and a medical system that had become little more than the pharmaceutical industry's marketing arm. The result has been an explosion of antibiotic-resistant microbes. As current news stories report the rapid spread of lethal antibiotic-resistant organisms such as methicillin-resistant *Staphylococcus aureus* (MRSA) and extreme drug-resistant (XDR) tuberculosis, epidemiologists worry what the microbial biosphere will throw at humanity next.

A third and even more worrisome factor is the impact of ecological disruption on patterns of disease.[15] As the number of people on an already overcrowded globe spirals upward and more and more of the Earth's wild lands come under pressure, microbes that have filled stable ecological niches since long before our species arrived on the scene end up coming into contact with new hosts and vectors. HIV, the virus that apparently causes AIDS, seems to have reached the human population that way; Ebola and a dozen other lethal hemorrhagic fevers certainly did, along with many others. At the same time, global warming driven by our smokestacks and tailpipes has changed distribution patterns of mosquitoes and other disease vectors, with the result that malaria, dengue fever, and other tropical diseases are starting to show up on the edges of today's temperate zones.

Loss of adequate government support, the end of the antibiotic age, and the ecological shifts bringing dangerous organisms into contact with human populations pose serious challenges to public health all by themselves. Add the impact of fossil fuel depletion and the results are unwelcome in the extreme. In a future of soaring energy costs and crumbling economies, public health is guaranteed less support from local government budgets than it has now, meaning that even the most basic public health services are likely to go by the boards. The same factors make it unlikely at best that pharmaceutical companies will be able to afford the expensive and resource-intensive process of developing new antibiotics that has thus far kept physicians one step ahead of most of the antibiotic-resistant microbes. Finally, ecological disruption will only increase as a world population dependent on petroleum-based agriculture scrambles to survive the end of cheap oil; many countries will likely switch to coal, putting global warming into overdrive in the next few decades.

The inevitable result is the return of the health conditions of the 18th and 19th centuries, when deadly epidemics were routine events, childhood mortality was common, and most people could expect to die from infectious diseases rather than the chronic conditions that fill the "cause of death" slot on most death certificates these days. If you factor in soaring rates of alcohol and drug abuse, violence, and malnutrition — all inevitable consequences of hard economic contraction — you have a situation where the number of people on the planet will take a sharp downward turn. Statistics from Russia, where a similar scenario played out in the aftermath of the Soviet Union's collapse, suggest that population levels could be halved within this century.[16] This doesn't require massive epidemics or the like; all it takes is a death rate in excess of the birth rate — and that's something we will certainly have as the deindustrial age begins.

Imperial Sunset

The cascade of consequences that will follow the peaking and decline of world petroleum production can't be understood outside
the context of politics. One dimension of that context is likely to
become the preeminent political fact of the age of peak oil: the impending decline — and, at least potentially, the catastrophic collapse — of America's world empire.

Empires are unfashionable these days, which is why those who
support the American empire generally start by claiming that it
doesn't exist, while those who oppose it seem to think that the simple fact of its existence makes it automatically worse than any alternative. Both these views deserve serious questioning. When the
United States maintains military garrisons in more than a hundred nations, supporting a state of affairs that allows the five percent of humanity who are American citizens to monopolize a third
of the world's natural resources and industrial production, it's difficult to discuss the international situation honestly without words
like "empire" creeping in. It requires a breathtaking suspension of
disbelief to redefine American foreign policy as the disinterested
pursuit of worldwide democracy for its own sake.

Still, portraying today's American empire as the worst of all
possible worlds (a popular sport on the left for the last fifty years
or so) requires just as much of a leap of faith. If Nazi Germany,
say, or the Soviet Union had come out on top in the scramble for
global power that followed the implosion of the British Empire,
the results would certainly have been a good deal worse: those who
currently exercise their freedom to criticize the present empire
would face gulags or gas chambers. The lack of any empire at all
may be a desirable state of affairs, of course, but until our species
evolves efficient ways to checkmate the ambitions of one nation to
exploit another, that state of affairs is unlikely to obtain this side
of Neverland.

Ever since transport technology evolved enough to permit one
nation to have a significant impact on another, there have been

empires; since the rise of effective maritime transport in the 15th
century, those empires have had global reach; and since 1945, when
it finished off two of its rivals and successfully contained the third,
the United States has maintained a global empire. That empire
was as much the result of opportunism, accident, and necessity as
of any deliberate plan, but it exists, and if it did not exist, some
other nation would fill a similar role. So, like it or not, America
rules the dominant world empire today — and that will likely become a source of tremendous misfortune for Americans in decades
to come.

In part, the downside of empire is built into the nature of
imperial systems themselves, because the pursuit of empire is as
self-destructive an addiction as anything you'll find on the mean
streets of today's inner cities. The systematic economic imbal-
ances imposed on client states by empires, while hugely profitable
for the empire's political class, wreck the economy of the imperial
state by flooding its markets with cheap imported goods and loading its financial system with tribute. Those outside the political
class become what Arnold Toynbee has called an internal proletariat: the people who are alienated from an imperial system that
yields them few benefits and many burdens. Meanwhile, members
of the external proletariat — the people of the client states whose
labor supports the imperial economy but who gain little or nothing in return — eventually respond to their exploitation with a
rising spiral of violence that moves from crime through terrorism
to open warfare.[17] To counter the twin threats of internal dissi-
dence and external insurgency, the imperial state must divert ever
larger fractions of its resources to its military and security forces.
Economic decline, popular disaffection, and growing pressures
on the borders hollow out the imperial state into a brittle shell
of soldiers, spies, and bureaucrats surrounding a society in free-
fall. When the shell finally cracks — as it always does, sooner or
later — nothing is left inside to resist change, and the result is implosion.

It's possible to halt this process, but only by deliberately step-
ping back from empire before the unraveling has gone too far.
Britain's response to its own imperial sunset is instructive; instead
of clinging to its empire and being dragged down by it, Britain
allied with the rising power of the United States, allowed its colonial holdings to slip away, and managed to keep its economic
and political system more or less intact. Compare that to Spain,
which had the largest empire on Earth in the 16th and 17th centuries. By the 19th century it was one of the poorest countries in
Europe, two centuries behind the times economically, racked by
civil wars and foreign invasions, and utterly incapable of influ-
encing the European politics of the age. The main factor in this
precipitous decline was the long-term impact of empire. It's no accident that Spain's national recovery only really began after its last
overseas colonies were seized by the United States in the Spanish-
American war.

In this light, the last quarter century of American policy has
been suicidally counterproductive in its attempt to maintain the
glory days of empire. That empire rested on three foundations: the
immense resource base of the American land, especially its once-
huge oil reserves; the vast industrial capacity of what was once
America's manufacturing hinterland and now, tellingly, is known
as the Rust Belt; and a canny foreign policy, codified in the early
19th century under the Monroe Doctrine, that distanced itself
from Old World disputes and focused on maintaining exclusive
economic and military influence over Latin America. With these
foundations solidly in place, America could intervene decisively in
European affairs in 1917 and 1942 and launch an imperial expansion after 1945 that gave it effective dominance over most of the
world.

By 1980, though, the economic impacts of empire had already
gutted the American industrial economy — a process that has
only accelerated since then — and the new and decisive factor of
oil depletion added substantially to the pressures toward decline.

A sane national policy in this context would have withdrawn from imperial commitments, shifted the burdens of empire onto a resurgent western Europe, and pursued military and economic alliances with rising powers such as China and Brazil. The economic and social turmoil set in motion by the energy crises of the 1970s could have been used as an opportunity to downshift to less affluent and energy-intensive lifestyles, reinvigorate the nation's industrial and agricultural economy, and renew the frayed social covenants that united the political class with other sectors of the population in a recognition of common goals.

The realities of American politics, however, kept such a plan out of reach. In a society where competing factions of the political class buy power by handing out economic largesse to sectors of the electorate (which, as mentioned before, is what "liberal democracy" amounts to in practice), the possibility of a retreat from empire was held hostage by a classic "prisoner's dilemma." Any elite group willing to put its own short-term advantage ahead of national survival could take and hold power (as Reagan's Republicans did in 1980) by reaffirming the imperial project and restoring access to the payoffs of the tribute economy. For that reason, especially since 2000, the American political class — very much including its "liberal" as well as its "conservative" factions — has backed the survival of America's global empire using all available means.

This would be disastrous even without the factor of peak oil. No empire, even in its prime, can afford to pursue policies that estrange its allies, increase its overseas commitments, make its enemies forget their mutual quarrels and form alliances with one another, and destabilize the world political order, all at the same time. American foreign policy in recent years has accomplished every one of these things, at a time when America's effective ability to deal with the consequences is steadily declining as its resource base dwindles and the last of its industrial economy fizzles out. To call this a recipe for disaster is to understate the case considerably.

Peak oil, though, is the wild card in the deck, and at this point in the game it's a card that can only be played to America's detriment. To an extent few people realize, every aspect of American empire — from the trade networks that extract wealth from America's client states to the military arsenal that projects its power worldwide — depends on cheap, abundant petroleum. As the first nation to systematically exploit its petroleum reserves on a large scale, the United States floated to victory in two world wars on a sea of oil, learning the lesson that the way to win wars was to use more energy than the other side. That was possible in the first half of the 20th century, when America was the world's largest oil producer and exporter. It became problematic in the 1970s, when domestic oil production peaked and began to decline while consumption failed to decline in step, making America dependent on imports. The arrival of worldwide peak oil completes the process by making America's energy-intensive model of empire utterly unsustainable.

How this process will play out is anyone's guess at this point. What worries me most, though, is the possibility that it could have a very substantial military dimension. The US military's total dependence on energy-intensive high technology could easily become a double-edged sword if the resources needed to sustain the technology run short or become suddenly unavailable. At the same time, its investment — economic as well as intellectual — in a previously successful model of warfare could turn into a fatal distraction if new conditions make that model an anachronism.

Any student of history knows that people tend to overestimate the solidity of the familiar and are commonly taken by surprise when the foundations of an established order crumble away from beneath them. The possibility that the global political scene could change out of all recognition in the aftermath of military catastrophe is hard to dismiss. If that happens, those of us who live in today's United States and its remaining allies could be facing a very rough road indeed.

The Slow Train To The Future

It bears repeating that the predicament outlined in this chapter is
not primarily a set of technical problems. Rather, it is a social and
intellectual challenge; I might even risk using an utterly unfashionable word and call it a spiritual challenge as well. There are massive
technical issues involved in downshifting from an energy-wasting
economy and society based on fossil fuels to an energy-conserving
economy and society based on renewable energy resources, but
those issues could potentially have been solved if they had been
tackled in earnest starting in the 1970s.

Even today, though it's almost certainly too late to manage the
transition without wrenching social disruptions and immense
human cost, it might still be possible to deal with those challenges
and make the leap to sustainability given the social and political
will to do so. Every one of the challenges reviewed in this chapter
could be mitigated substantially by responses that are well within
the power of the leaders and citizens of today's industrial societies.
Yet it's precisely the social and political will to deal with the crisis
that is nowhere to be found. We need to talk more about why this
has happened, and one place to start is precisely with what happened at the end of the 1970s, when the industrial world turned
its back on the signs of crisis, and a great many promising steps toward sustainability went into the dumpster.

Part of that sea change in industrial society was political, of
course. "Conservative" parties (the word belongs in quotation
marks, since today's conservatives have forgotten how to conserve
just as thoroughly as their liberal counterparts have forgotten how
to liberate) in most of the industrial world realized that they could
cut their opponents off at the knees by proclaiming that limits
to growth didn't exist and by papering over the energy crises of
the previous decade with short-term political and economic gimmicks. Part of the change, though, was a reflection of the success of
the sustainability movement of the 1970s. In the aftermath of that
movement, defying nearly all predictions, petroleum consumption

and energy use per capita throughout the developed world went down and stayed down for much of a decade.

This movement toward sustainability, as much as anything else, made it possible for politicians in the United States and Britain to force down the price of oil to levels that, in constant dollars, were lower than ever before. When oil hit $10 a barrel, alternative energy and conservation technologies that had been profitable at higher energy prices became a quick ticket to bankruptcy. To the extent that the push for energy efficiency in the 1970s helped drive down the demand for oil, the sustainability movement of that decade dropped dead from the consequences of its own success.

It's a useful experience to read through publications on energy issues from the 1970s and compare their confident predictions that permanent limits to growth had arrived with the very different realities of the decades that followed. One of the bits of 1970s nostalgia on my shelves is a thoughtful little book titled *The Rise of the Welsh Republic* by Derrick Hearne; it's an attempt to imagine the first decade of the history of an independent Wales in the imminent Age of Scarcity.[18] Hearne did not invent the idea of an Age of Scarcity; it was seen as the logical consequence of the emerging limits to growth by many other thinkers of the same period, and Hearne's proposals mirrored those being discussed in now-forgotten periodicals such as *Rain* and *Seriatim*, where appropriate technology and organic agriculture rubbed elbows with social criticism amid the last hurrah of the idealism of the 1960s.

Fast forward from these mostly forgotten visions to today's peak oil debates and you might be forgiven a strong sense of déjà vu. Part of the received wisdom in the peak oil community these days is that once worldwide petroleum production peaks and begins its permanent decline, the mismatch between production and demand will cause exactly the same sort of Age of Scarcity that Hearne and so many other thinkers imagined in the 1970s. Now as then, the major issue under debate is whether the changeover to sustainability can be done quickly and thoroughly enough to prevent a crash.

There are good reasons to think that the effort put into this debate will turn out to be just as misplaced as it was in the 1970s — and for much the same reasons. Prophecy is risky business, but it's a risk worth taking on occasion, so I would like to offer the following seemingly unlikely prediction: twenty years after the definite arrival of a peak in oil production, the price of crude oil in Euros will be no higher than it is today, and it may actually be quite a bit lower.

The time frame is more important here than it may seem at first glance. The likely immediate aftermath of a significant decline in world oil production, of course, is skyrocketing prices for oil and everything made or transported with it; the possibility that oil could hit €200 a barrel or higher (even corrected for inflation) is a real one. Price surges on that scale will be a body blow to the economies of most nations in the developed world. Such astronomical prices would also mean that any method of conserving energy or using alternative energy resources in place of oil will be worth much more than its weight in light sweet crude.

So far, these predictions match the conventional wisdom in the peak oil community, but it's worth looking a step further into the future. If economies across the industrial world contract, the demand for petroleum will soften as people are forced to abandon the lifestyle choices that account for much of today's extravagant energy usage. Especially in the United States, where 5% of the world's people use 25% of its petroleum production, a severe economic contraction could readily cause what economists call "demand destruction," which can be simply defined as the process by which people who can't afford a product stop using it. Meanwhile, in a global market awash with effectively limitless amounts of paper capital, the chance for huge profits in the conservation and alternative energy sectors guarantees that entrepreneurs in these fields will have more money they know what to do with. The most

Diagram 3.2. Cycles of Descent

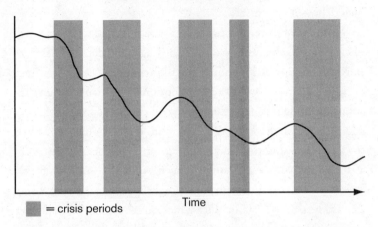

■ = crisis periods   Time

This abstract model of a society in catabolic collapse shows the stairstep process of decline that historically is the most common way for civilizations to break down. Each period of crisis causes losses in infrastructure, social organization, information resources, and population; these losses are partly made up during the times of stability and recovery – but only partly. The industrial world has already experienced one period of mild crisis in the 1970s, and a period of stability and recovery in the following decades; the same process, with more severe crises and briefer pauses, is likely to shape the history of the next two centuries or so.

likely result, as these trends start to bite, is that the price of oil will level off and then begin to decline.

Does this mean that peak oil can be ignored, because it poses no threat to industrial society? Hardly. As oil production worldwide continues to contract, and conservation and alternative energy reach the point of diminishing returns, oil prices will spike upward in turn, rising even higher than before and unleashing another wave of economic and social disruption. Just as the economic contractions of the 1970s and 1980s spawned intractable unemployment in most industrial societies and launched a process of downward mobility from which many families never recovered, each wave of economic contraction will likely force more of the population into a permanent underclass for whom the abstract phrase "demand destruction" plays out in a downward spiral of impoverishment and misery.

In such a future, the periods of apparent recovery that will likely follow each round of energy shortages and demand destruction will provide little room to rebuild what has been lost. Those periods will, however, make it exceptionally difficult for any response to fossil fuel depletion to stay on course, so long as that response relies on market forces or politics for its momentum. Each time oil prices slump, the market forces that support investment in a sustainable future will slump as well, while governments facing calls for limited resources will face real challenges in maintaining a commitment to sustainability which, for the moment, no longer seems necessary. Thus the collapse of public and private funding for the alternative energy sector in the aftermath of the 1970s will likely be repeated over and over again as we stumble down the long downhill side of Hubbert's peak.

Those planning for a future of peak oil, in other words, need to beware of the perils of linear thinking. Much more often than not, history moves in circles rather than straight lines; planning for a future that is like the present, only more so, is a good way to come to grief in the real world. Instead of the express trip to Utopia or oblivion on which so much prophecy and planning has been lavished, we are on board the slow train to the deindustrial future, and the scenery along the route is likely to be a good deal more complex and less predictable than either of our familiar myths have led us to believe.

The upside of this situation, as mentioned earlier in this chapter, is that the crises defined in this chapter will most likely prove self-limiting, at least in the short and middle terms. Energy prices will soar, but not indefinitely and not forever; the economy will come apart and then, slowly and painfully, come back together; public health will slump and then undergo some form of recovery as the economic situation stabilizes; political systems will shatter and then be replaced by others. To judge by past examples, the period of extreme crisis is unlikely to last much more than a quarter century or so. Thus the immediate problem we face isn't how to survive the end of industrial civilization, it's how to get through the next wave of crisis and make it to the period of renewed stability on the other side. This is a much more manageable task, and it makes room for possibilities that fashionably apocalyptic models of our predicament hide from sight.

Facing the
Deindustrial Age

People try to anticipate the shape of the future for many
of the same reasons that drivers pay attention to the road
ahead: it's easier to respond to dangers and opportunities alike
if you can see them at least a little in advance. As we move into
the poorly mapped territory on the far side of Hubbert's peak,
however, differences between the futures we anticipate and the
one we are most likely to get may challenge us to our core. I've already talked about the ways our culture's familiar narratives turn
into obstacles to understanding in the face of a predicament they
fit poorly, if at all. The same factors raise obstacles at least as high
to constructive action and help explain one of the most striking
differences between the energy crisis of the 1970s and the one unfolding around us today: the disconnect between theory and practice and between proposals for change and the willingness to make
change where it counts, in our own lives.

It bears noticing that between 1956, when Hubbert originally
announced the approach of peak oil, and the present moment, a remarkable paradox has unfolded. On the one hand, the evidence for
the imminence and catastrophic potential of peak oil has grown

steadily more convincing. On the other hand, the prospect of any constructive response to peak oil has grown steadily more distant. Despite occasional bursts of lip service, every major political party in every major nation in the industrial world supports economic policies that effectively subsidize increases in fossil fuel use, and thus move the world further away from a transition to sustainability with each passing day. The more imminent and obvious the dangers become, the more stubbornly the world's political and economic systems cling to exactly the policies that guarantee the worst possible outcome in the not very long run.

This astonishing failure of will and vision can be traced to factors already discussed in this book. The mythic narratives and the logic of the monkey trap explored in Chapter 2 have had a potent influence on the way things have worked out over the last three decades. It's crucial to grasp that these are just as much part of our predicament as the petroleum in the ground and the cars on our highways, and they have as potent an influence on what can still be done as do any of the hard, technical facts of the case. The predicament we face is at least as much a social and cultural crisis as a technical one, and its technical side — difficult though that may be — is arguably the least challenging of its dimensions.

Political Action

A failure to grasp this last consideration, or at least to take it seriously, has hobbled the peak oil community since the first loud alarms were sounded in the 1990s. From the start, many people argued that the issue could best be dealt with by alerting the world's governments and getting them to solve the problem. This approach remains popular today, even though the world's governments show no sign of listening, and no significant political party in the developed world has seriously discussed adopting a realistic plan to deal with peak oil.

Another popular activity among people concerned with peak oil has been the drafting of plans to deal with the approaching crisis. Many of these plans are extremely well designed and, even this late in the game, they could do a great deal to cushion the rough path ahead of us. Even the least plausible of them would likely have better results than the industrial world's current policy of sleepwalking toward the abyss. Yet while the books pile up on the shelves of libraries and used book stores, the sleepwalkers continue on their way.

The reason for this disconnect lies in the awkward fit between the demands of a peak oil future and the realities of energy use in the industrial world. While it's popular in some circles to assume that extravagant energy use is purely the fault of the very rich, large corporations, or some other collection of upper-class scapegoats, the fact is that the availability of cheap, abundant fossil fuel energy has changed nearly every aspect of life throughout the world's industrial nations. Most of us, not just a privileged few, benefit every day from the wasteful use of energy that characterizes modern society, and these benefits are among the many things peak oil places in jeopardy.

This has implications few people take the time to think through. Consider a cup of coffee. The energy needed to run the coffee maker is only a tiny portion of the total petroleum-based energy and materials that go into the process. Unless the coffee is organically grown, chemical fertilizers and pesticides derived from oil are used to produce the beans; diesel-driven farm machinery harvests them; trucks, ships, and trains powered by one petroleum product or another move them around the world from producer to middleman to consumer, stopping at various fossil-fuel-heated or -cooled storage facilities and fossil-fuel-powered factories en route; consumers in the industrial world drive to brightly lit and comfortably climate-controlled supermarkets on asphalt roads to bring back plastic-lined containers of ground coffee to their homes. To drink coffee by the cup, we use oil by the barrel.

This is exactly the sort of extravagance that will not be viable much longer as the age of cheap, abundant energy draws to a close.

One implication is that, as fossil fuels stop being cheap and abundant, standards of living throughout the industrial world will sink toward the level of the nonindustrial world. There's no way to sugarcoat that very unpalatable reality. In the last century, oil and other fossil fuels made it possible for a majority of people in the world's industrial nations — and a small minority elsewhere — to embrace lifestyles that don't require constant hard physical labor. Fossil fuels allowed people to wallow in a torrent of consumer goods — cars, exotic foods, expensive health care systems, and much more. As we head into the territory on the far side of Hubbert's peak, all of that will go away. How many people would be willing to listen to such a suggestion? More to the point, how many people would vote for a politician or a party who proposed to bring on these changes deliberately, now, in order to prevent disaster later on?

This isn't simply a rhetorical question; the experiment has been tried. In 1992, the MIT team that did the original *Limits to Growth* study ran their numbers again with updated figures; the resulting study pointed out that the industrial world had frittered away most of its options in two decades of unconscionable delay.[1] The team found that in the previous two decades industrial society had gone into *overshoot* — the term environmental scientists use for a population of living things that is consuming vital resources so extravagantly that the ability of their environment to keep supporting them is at risk. Their new book *Beyond the Limits* urged an emergency program to stave off disaster. They pointed out, however, that the level of cuts in energy and resource use necessary to stave off disaster would require the American people to accept a reduction in their average standard of living that would bring it in line with that of Brazil. No politician or political party anywhere has taken up their suggestion as a platform, for obvious reasons. It's hard to think of a better recipe for political suicide.

Back in 1992, John Kenneth Galbraith wrote a brilliant, mordant book, *The Culture of Contentment*, about the reasons why today's societies have proven to be so incapable of constructive change. He compared today's American political class — the people who have a significant voice in our collective decisions — to the French aristocracy before the Revolution. Starting in the late 17th century, French governments pursued an aggressive imperialist foreign policy supported by the dubious short-term means of deficit spending and pulling resources away from a faltering domestic economy. By the second half of the 18th century, as a result, the kingdom of France teetered on the edge of bankruptcy, with debt service eating up half of all government income by 1770, while most of the French people lived in poverty that was extreme even by the standards of the time.[2]

Reforms were a constant subject of discussion. The problem was that no real change could be put in place without loading serious short-term costs onto the government and the aristocracy. Everybody with access to the levers of power knew the situation was insupportable and that eventually there would be an explosion, but the immediate costs of doing something about it were so unpalatable that the French political class decided simply to do nothing and hope that things would somehow work out. Deficit spending continued in full spate until the fiscal crisis of 1788 and the collapse of government finances that led straight to the French Revolution. In the end, the unwillingness of Louis XVI and his courtiers to deal with the burden of living within their means brought them to the guillotine.

This is an excellent example of what sociologist C. Wright Mills called "fate." Mills argued that the driving force behind most of the unintended changes in society is the power exerted by the countless small decisions made by people in the course of their daily lives.[3] Market economies and democratic governments both rely on fate; both trust in the steady pressure of people making their own small choices to keep society on track. Much of the time this works, but as the example of the French Revolution suggests, fate can also bring about the collapse of a government — or a civilization.

This type of disastrous outcome is most likely when it's hard to see the connection between a short-term benefit and its long-term costs, or when the connection is hidden by ideology. Any sort of collective decision making can suffer from what sociologists call "social traps" when the positive and negative consequences of a course of action sort out differently over time.[4] Political systems of all sorts usually settle on choices with short-term benefits and long-term costs rather than choices with short-term costs and long-term benefits, even if the long-term issues are of far greater importance.

The pressure of fate is among the most important and least recognized forces blocking the way to a solution for the approaching crisis. If we had enough time and resources — and the political and collective will to use them — we might still be able to make the transition to a conserver society based on renewable resources, one with far fewer goods and services per person but with the promise of long-term stability. Neither the leadership of the industrial world nor its citizens show any sign of having the will to make the necessary changes; resources are running short — and so is time. The jaws of the social trap have closed tight around industrial society.

That trap has an important feature in common with Galbraith's example of the French Revolution. The social trap that doomed the French aristocracy in the years leading up to 1789 was especially insidious because its effects, and the costs of change, both built gradually over time. If the political classes of *ancien regime* France had found the courage and foresight to bite the bullet early on, the tax burdens and fiscal limits needed to bring matters back into balance would have been relatively easy to bear. That very fact made it easy for the political class to dismiss the need for change, since the problem seemed so small. By the time it was obvious that something had to be done, the costs of doing anything at all had become monumental — and those costs would have been borne directly and personally by each member of the political class. Thus the crisis built up to its inevitable explosion. Only in the explosion's aftermath did constructive change become possible once again.

The social trap imposed by the limits to growth works the same way. When the necessary changes could have been made easily, the danger was still so far away that it was all too easily ignored; now that the danger is becoming obvious, the costs of change amount to requiring the population of the industrial world to surrender everything they think of as a normal lifestyle. Once the next wave of crises hits industrial society and today's elaborately defended political and economic arrangements are washed away like so many sand castles, political reform may become a viable option, but those reforms will only respond to disaster; they will not prevent it.

The dynamics of our social trap thus put a political solution to the crisis of industrial society effectively out of reach, at least for the time being. Claiming that a political solution is "the only option," to repeat a phrase too often used these days, misses a crucial point: collapse is also an option. The fact that it's not the option we'd prefer does nothing to make it less likely.

Survivalism

Too often nowadays, however, those who understand the futility of a political solution go to the opposite extreme, borrowing the strategy made famous by rats aboard sinking ships. It's become very common for people aware of the imminence of peak oil to embrace the narrative of survivalism — the belief that the only workable response to the decline and fall of industrial civilization is to hole up in a cabin in the woods with stockpiles of food and firearms and live the virtuous frontier life while the world outside goes crashing down in flames.[5]

Much of the discussion of what to do about the aftermath of peak oil has thus focused on steps such as stockpiling gold, silver, and stored food; arranging effective means of defense against the rampaging mobs expected to roam the landscape in the aftermath of collapse; and then finding mates for one's children so that civilization can survive.[6] This sort of thinking is surprisingly common these days. It draws on the myth of apocalypse, of course, but it has deep roots in another common cultural narrative as well.

In the colonial states of the European diaspora, from the 18th century right up to the present, it's been a popular bit of rhetoric to contrast the rich, crowded, and wicked cities of the coasts with the poor, isolated, and allegedly more virtuous back country. Fuse that rhetoric with one version or another of Christian apocalyptic mythology with the serial numbers filed off, and you get the classic survivalist creed. That creed first surfaced in the 1920s in the United States. Since then, survivalists have insisted that theirs is the one viable answer to any crisis you care to imagine — epidemic disease, nuclear holocaust, race war, the advent of Antichrist, the predicted meltdown of the world's computer systems on January 1, 2000, and the list goes on.

From a survivalist point of view, peak oil is simply one more reason to head for the hills until the rubble stops bouncing. All the same, it doesn't fill the bill very well. True, the peaking of world oil production will usher in an age of rising energy costs and dwindling supplies, and that will bring plenty of economic, social, political, and demographic problems in its train, but I have yet to see anyone make a reasonable case that these problems will cause civilization to collapse overnight. We're facing decline, not apocalypse, and in the face of a gradual decline unfolding over several centuries, a strategy relying on canned beans, M-16s, and an isolated cabin in the woods is a distraction at best. It's also among the best pieces of evidence that people nowadays pay no attention to the lessons of history.

One of the more common phenomena of collapse is the breakdown of public order at the rural peripheries and the rise of a brigand culture preying on rural communities and travelers. During the twilight of the Roman Empire in the West, for example, the countryside sank into anarchy long before cities stopped being viable, and bands of raiders made life outside city walls difficult at best. As the industrial world moves into its own decline and poverty shifts from the cities to the rural hinterlands — a process already well under way in North America — the same phenomenon is likely to repeat itself. Isolated survivalist enclaves with stockpiles of food and ammunition would be a tempting prize and could count on being targeted. Towns and small cities surrounded by arable land often do much better than rural areas when civilizations fall, because they can draw on a larger and more diverse labor force and more complex social networks to overcome problems that scattered rural villages or households cannot.

North America is unusually vulnerable to a descent into rural anarchy because of its size, its dependence on automobiles, and its lack of a pre-petroleum infrastructure; Europe will be in much better shape, what with its massive rail system and cities that make sense on foot. The worst of the early phases of the collapse may be focused here in North America as much as anywhere; it doesn't help that the United States, at least, has a citizenry armed to the teeth. Contemporary North America also lacks a social infrastructure of human-scale, local community organizations, so once the mass institutions go under, people have nothing to fall back on — and little experience organizing themselves on a local level. That doesn't mean a Hollywood-style overnight collapse; it does mean we will have an unnecessarily hard time of it.

The same factors also make it hard to support the popular notion that stockpiling precious metals or other valuables will make the stockpilers exempt from the consequences of decline and fall. This strategy has been attempted over and over again in recorded history; the one thing that can be said about it is that it consistently doesn't work. Every few years, for example, archeologists in Britain dig up another cache of gold and silver hidden away by some wealthy landowner in Roman Britain as the empire fell apart.[7] Such caches are usually not far from the ruins of a Roman villa that shows signs of having been sacked and looted by the barbarian raiders that ended Roman civilization in Britain.

As a working rule, if your value consists of what you've stockpiled, you can assume that an unlimited number of other people will be eager to remove you from the stockpile so they can enjoy it themselves. However many you kill, there will always be more — and eventually your ammo will run out. Of course, it's also more than a little relevant that you can't eat gold or silver — or do much else constructive with them. The fetishism that makes precious metals precious in our present society may not survive the sort of prolonged brush with ecological reality that the limits to growth will most likely bring.

The temptation to rely on stockpiles of food, technology, weapons, or precious metals to get through the impact of an age of decline is, among other things, a natural product of modern ways of thinking. For two centuries, as a result of the vast energy resources we've extracted from the Earth, machines and their products have been cheaper than skilled human beings. The result is a habit of valuing things over skills and, ultimately, a "prosthetic society" in which we're taught to neglect our innate abilities and then pay for technological replacements. We use day planners instead of training our memories, buy bread machines instead of learning to bake, watch television instead of using our imaginations. So many people have come to think that the best way to deal with anything is to buy enough of the right product that it's natural that they attempt to deal with the twilight of industrial society in the same way — natural, but fatal.

Once the fragile legal frameworks that give the concept of "ownership" its current meaning break down, stockpiles of wealth or weaponry become an invitation to seizure by governments as well as less officially sanctioned thieves. Those whose value consists of things they can do and teach, on the other hand, give everyone a reason to leave them unharmed. This latter strategy, unrealistic as it looks from the modern world's viewpoint, has worked consistently in the past. The success and survival of Christian monks in Dark Age Europe is paralleled by that of Buddhist monks in the bitter wars of the *Sengoku jidai* period of medieval Japan, Taoist priests and hermits in the repeated disintegrations of imperial China, and many other people who have embraced strategies based on the value of knowledge in past ages of collapse. Even in the pirate havens of the 16th century Caribbean, among the most brutal and lawless societies in recorded history, physicians, shipwrights, and other skilled craftspeople led charmed lives, because everybody knew their own lives might depend on access to those skills at some point in the future.

Finally, even collapse events with extreme depopulation, historically speaking, leave five to ten percent of the former population. To put that in perspective, if you live in a town of 100,000 people, there will be 5,000 to 10,000 people still living there after the dust finally settles two hundred years from now. Your children, their children, and the grandchildren of their grandchildren will have no trouble finding mates of their own. Thus the entire survivalist strategy depends on a mistaken assessment of the challenges ahead, and it directs energy where it's not needed while missing the places where effort can have constructive results.

Lifeboat Communities

One of the ironies of the current predicament of industrial society is that many of the people who recognize the problems with each of the previous approaches turn to a third option that combines most of the problems of both. For decades now, one of the most frequently repeated proposals for doing something about the predicament of industrial society has been building lifeboat communities: isolated, self-sufficient settlements stocked with the resources and technology to survive the end of the industrial age. Such 1970s classics as Roberto Vacca's *The Coming Dark Age* discuss such communities in detail, and these discussions have been picked up and expanded substantially over the last decade or so.

Now, to some extent, this sort of thinking is simply a variety of Survivalism Lite, with more emphasis on organic gardening than automatic weapons. One of the advantages of survivalism, though, is that it can be pursued on a very modest budget. Probably more than half the adults in North America today can afford to fit themselves out with a few firearms, some outdoor gear, a stock of stored food, and a cabin in the woods that can do double duty as a deer camp during hunting season. Plans for lifeboat communities in circulation these days are on a much more grandiose scale. Vacca's book, for example, suggests lifeboat communities on the scale of large villages, with multiple buildings, plenty of arable land for food crops, and stockpiles of useful technology. Others resemble nothing so much as an upper middle class suburb tucked incongruously away in some isolated mountain valley.

The historical model Vacca uses for his communities are the monasteries of the Middle Ages. This is potentially a valuable parallel, because monasteries have accomplished something very like Vacca's prescription in the twilight years of several civilizations.[8] During and long after the fall of the Roman Empire, Christian monasteries served as living time capsules in which many of the treasures of classical culture stayed safe through the centuries. Buddhist monasteries filled the same function in Japan's feudal age, and Buddhist and Taoist monasteries took turns doing the same thing through China's repeated cycles of imperial boom and bust. It's by no means impossible that some similar project could salvage the best of modern civilization as a legacy for future ages.

Yet monasticism accomplished these things because it drew on motivations very different from the ones that drive today's lifeboat community projects. The Christian monasteries that preserved classical culture through the last set of dark ages were not staffed by people trying to maintain some semblance of a middle-class Roman lifestyle while the world fell apart around them. Quite the opposite — the monks and nuns who copied old texts, taught at abbey schools, and kept the lamps of Western civilization burning, voluntarily embraced a lifestyle even more impoverished and re-stricted than that of the peasants among whom they lived. The same point is equally true of the Buddhist and Taoist monastics who accomplished the same vital task in other places and times. Arguably, it's precisely this willingness to embrace extreme poverty for the sake of higher goals that frees up the time and effort needed for the economically unproductive activities needed to keep the heritage of a civilization alive.

While the monastic model is still often cited in talk about life-boat communities, a less challenging set of cultural narratives pro-vides the unstated framework for most of these projects. In North America, from colonial times on, groups of disaffected people from all corners of the religious, political, and intellectual continuum have set out to build communities in the wilderness to prepare for the coming of a new world.[9] A direct line of cultural continu-ity runs from the Rosicrucian communes of colonial Pennsylvania straight through to the Transcendentalists, the Mormons, and ev-ery other band of dreamers who convinced themselves that a bet-ter world could be reached by the simple expedient of following Huck Finn's example of heading out into the Territories and build-ing it themselves.

This model had its most recent workout during the backwash of the 1960s. Many people alive today remember what happened when large numbers of white, middle-class young people left the urban centers where the counterculture had its roots and tried to build a new society in communes scattered across rural North America.[10] It was a grand experiment but, on the whole, a failed one, and the root cause of its failure is instructive.

That root cause in most cases was a fundamental lack of recog-nition that rural life involves a great deal of very hard work. Of the many thousands of young communards who headed back to the land, few understood how much sheer muscular effort it takes to grow one's own food and provide the other necessities of life; even fewer had the most basic skills needed to tackle that technically complex and demanding task. Subsistence farming is a more than a full-time job; it requires firm command of a range of technical skills most middle-class people these days have never encountered, much less had the opportunity to learn. A little pottering around in garden beds with a copy of a half-read book in one hand doesn't even begin to do the trick.

Critiques of industrial society have proliferated in recent years, but few of them deal with the fact that life in an industrial economy powered by abundant fossil fuels really is much easier than subsistence farming in nonindustrial conditions. When this awkward reality collided head on with the 1960s' idyllic fantasies of living the good life in the lap of nature, the fantasies came out much the worse for wear. In the aftermath of the collision, some of the communes of the 1960s figured out ways to batten off the larger society through welfare, drug dealing, or some other sideline, while most simply let out a few bubbles and sank once the first bright rush of idealistic enthusiasm wore off. By the middle years of the 1970s, most of the enthusiastic communards of the previous decade or so had returned to middle-class lives in the world they had once tried to abandon.

Potential lifeboat communities in a world perched unsteadily on the brink of peak oil will have to cope with the same mismatch between popular fantasies of rural life and the laborious realities of subsistence farming. Anyone who seriously wants to pursue the goal of rural self-sufficiency needs to leave any desire for a modern middle-class lifestyle at the door. The highest standard of living one can expect a rural lifeboat community to provide is that of a peasant farmer in the nonindustrial world, and that will be within reach only if the participants are as competent at the art of subsistence farming as farmers in the nonindustrial world generally are.

Given competent training and a high tolerance for hard physical labor, day in and day out, a group of healthy adults can keep themselves and their dependents adequately fed, clothed, housed, and equipped with necessary tools, with a little left over for barter or sale. For thousands of years this has been the standard human lifestyle over most of the world, and once the brief era of fossil-fueled extravagance we call modern industrial civilization is over, it will likely be the standard human lifestyle once again. Compared to the ease, comfort, opportunity, and abundance of a modern middle-class lifestyle, though, it is a very hard life. It has to be remembered, furthermore, that the decline of the industrial world is likely to be a slow and uneven process, with periods up to several decades long when it may well look as though the crisis is over and the warnings inaccurate. When these periods arrive, it will most likely be even harder to keep pursuing a rural subsistence lifestyle when the much easier lifestyles of the industrial world are still available.

As a result, the lifeboat community project faces a miniature version of the same social trap that has paralyzed political responses to peak oil. The land, buildings, and equipment needed to launch a lifeboat community of any size cost money — upward of a million dollars would be a good starting budget for such a project — and the people who commit themselves to the project must be willing to give up their careers in today's world in order to devote their time to building a new society that may not be needed for decades or centuries to come. The costs involved have to be paid up front by the people involved, while the benefits come only later and are shared by all. Thus it's not surprising that, despite all the talk about lifeboat communities, few of them have gotten past the talking stage.

Seeing Other Options

In one sense, the difficulty with all three of the alternatives surveyed so far in this chapter — awakening the political system in time to solve the crisis; holing up with guns and food in a fortified enclave; and building lifeboat communities to weather the fall of the modern world — is that they aren't actually responses to our predicament; they're existing cultural narratives looking for problems to solve. Visit the nearest multiscreen movie theater and you may just find all three of them playing this afternoon. Go through the door on the left and you can watch the movie about the lone visionary who recognizes an imminent crisis that no one else can see and then finally manages to get the authorities to pay attention in time. Through the door on the right, there's the movie about the small band of heavily armed heroes blazing away at mindless, faceless hordes in some apocalyptic setting. Up the stairs in the middle, you can find the movie about the community of plucky survivors thrown together by some world-ending catastrophe who struggle through the aftermath and rebuild a clone of today's society from the ground up. Endlessly repeated in popular entertainment, these narratives have a powerful presence in the collective imagination of the industrial world, and it's important to be aware of the gravitational attraction they exert on our thinking.

The core assumption common to all three proposals is that there's no middle ground between preserving the modern industrial system intact and a rapid descent into primal chaos. Both of the mythic narratives discussed over the last two chapters, the myth of progress just as much as the myth of apocalypse, feed into this assumption. Its popularity, however, doesn't make it anything like as reasonable as it seems. There's a wide middle ground between contemporary society and a Road Warrior struggle of all against all. It's in that middle ground that the most likely futures of the industrial world will take shape, and aiming for a constructive response to the futures of the middle ground is in all probability the best strategy we have.

A metaphor might be useful here. Imagine that you found out today that tomorrow morning you'll be taken up to 10,000 feet in an airplane and tossed out the cabin door. That's a real crisis, and it demands serious thought and action. If you believe that the only two options are either staying in midair at 10,000 feet or falling to your death, though, you may just overlook the action that would be most likely to save your life: wearing a parachute.

The metaphor can be extended a little further. The problem with being thrown out of an airplane at 10,000 feet isn't that you fall; it's that you fall too fast and land too hard. The same is true of the end of the industrial age. If the transition from industrial society to the deindustrial cultures of the future could be made gradually, with plenty of time to scale back our expectations and replace energy-intensive technologies with simpler ones, our predicament would be so mild it would barely merit the name. At this point, however, so many opportunities have been wasted and so many resources depleted that the transition out of the industrial age will likely be a good deal more disruptive, with close parallels to the breakdowns and dark ages that followed other civilizations in the past. This still leaves plenty of room for strategies that, like the parachute in the metaphor, will slow the descent and minimize the shock of landing.

Thus it's one thing to try to find some way to power today's industrial system with renewable sources while leaving intact the structures of everyday life that give our civilization its extravagant appetite for energy. It's quite another thing, and much closer to the realm of the possible, to use renewable energy to meet the far more modest energy requirements of an agrarian society. Especially in North America, restating the question in this way opens up immense possibilities. Very few people who live on this continent, for instance, have noticed that it's only our energy-wasting lifestyles that keep us dependent on imported oil — with all the unwelcome economic and political consequences that brings. Even 35 years after its own Hubbert peak, the United States is still one of the largest producers of oil on Earth.[11] If the average American used only as much energy per year as the average European, America would be exporting oil, not importing it. Only our insistence on clinging to the dysfunctional lifestyles of an age that is passing away keeps such an obviously constructive goal off the table in discussions of national energy policy.

The same logic can be extended much more broadly. Today's

industrial agriculture, for example, will become utterly unsustainable once the huge fossil fuel inputs that go into farm machinery, agricultural chemicals, worldwide transport networks, and the like stop being economically viable. That doesn't mean, as some of the more extreme peak oil theorists argue, that once fossil fuels become too scarce and costly to use for agriculture, we'll all starve. It simply means that the agriculture of the future will have to rely on human and animal muscle, and other locally produced sources, for energy, and turn compost and manure into fertilizer, the way farmers did for millennia before the invention of the tractor. It also means that the sooner we launch the transition back to this more viable way of farming, the better.

There are still people alive today who grew up working horse-drawn combines in the 1920s, when American agriculture was already productive enough to make the Great Plains the world's breadbasket. Converting back to horse-powered agriculture would be a challenge, but one well within the realm of the possible; relatively simple changes in agricultural, taxation, and land use policy could do much to foster that conversion.[12] With severe depopulation setting in across much of America's old agricultural heartland, more dramatic steps such as a renewal of the old Homestead Act,[13] coupled with price guarantees for organically grown grain crops, would make a good deal of sense as well.

If the mythology of progress didn't blind today's policymakers to such options, any number of steps could be taken to ease the transition from industrial to deindustrial society. Those steps are likely to remain outside the realm of the politically thinkable for a long time yet, at least on a large scale, but the same logic can be applied on a local and individual scale. Individuals, groups, and communities, just as much as nations and industrial civilization as a whole, face the challenge of managing the descent from Hubbert's peak. The longer we try to cling to the peak, the harder and faster the fall is going to be, and fewer are the people and cultural resources that are likely to survive it. If we accept that the Long

Descent is inevitable and try to make it in a controlled manner, on the other hand, the way is open not only for bare survival, but for surviving in a humane and creative fashion while preserving as much of value as possible for the future.

Nor are all possible deindustrial societies of the future equal. The future need not be condemned to medieval squalor unless we throw away the opportunity to deal with the realities of our predicament while there is still time. It's entirely possible to have a cultured, literate, humane society with thriving cities and a vigorous exchange economy on a very limited resource basis. During the Tokugawa period (1603–1868), for example, Japan closed its borders to the outside world in a successful bid to stay out of the clutches of the European colonial empires of the day. With a large population and few natural resources, Tokugawa Japan ran almost entirely on human muscle. Yet this was one of the great periods of Japanese art, literature, and philosophy; literacy was so widespread that the three largest cities in Japan had 1,500 bookstores among them, and most people had access to basic education, health care, and the necessities of life.[14] If we get past the distractions of emotionally appealing mythologies, face the future squarely, and start getting ready for it now, future deindustrial societies could achieve as much. That goal is within reach, and it's hard to think of a better gift we can offer the future.

Some people in debates about the future of industrial society have argued that attempting to cushion the decline instead of preventing it is morally wrong because this way of approaching our predicament accepts the unacceptable. This sort of thinking is understandable, but it misses the central point at issue. We don't necessarily have a choice about what we have to accept. All of us, for example, will have to accept the reality and inevitability of death — not only our own deaths, but those of the people we love as well. In the presence of death, we can rail against the inevitable, or we can deal with its reality and do what we can to minimize its negative dimensions.

The same principle applies to the current situation. At this point in history, after decades of wasted opportunities and profligate energy use, preventing the industrial age from ending would most likely be impossible even if our societies were prepared to muster the will and leadership to take the necessary steps — which they clearly are not. As suggested in Chapter 1, this conjunction of events defines the present crisis as a predicament, not a problem. At the same time, prevention isn't the only option that can save lives and salvage at least some of the cultural treasures of the last six thousand years. A parachute, again, won't keep you from being thrown out of that airplane at 10,000 feet, but it's still a very useful thing to have if your efforts at prevention fail. In the present situation, equivalent steps are arguably the only options we've got that make moral or practical sense.

Coping with Catabolic Collapse

Responding to the decline and fall of a civilization, of course, is a good deal more complex than strapping on a parachute. Fortunately, the process of decline is also a good deal slower than falling out of an airplane, and this makes room for options that apocalyptic mythologies hide from view. If, as I've suggested, the decline and fall of industrial civilization will resemble rolling down a bumpy slope more than falling off a cliff, it becomes possible to meet each wave of crises as it comes, using resources that are already on hand. For example, there's no need to flee to the wilderness to build communities to survive the transition to deindustrial society; we already have communities in place — the cities, towns, and rural neighborhoods where we live right now; these can be reshaped to handle the challenges and opportunities of the future.

None of the four horsemen described in Chapter 3 — declining energy availability, economic contraction, collapsing public health, and political turmoil — are new to human experience. Our great-grandparents knew them well, and today they are familiar to the vast majority of our fellow human beings. Only the inhabitants of the world's industrialized societies have had the opportunity to forget about them, and then only during the second half of the 20th century. Before then, most people knew how to deal with them, and most of the strategies that were developed and used in the past will still be viable far into the future. The one hitch is that we have to be ready to put them into practice. Since governments have by and large dropped the ball completely, it's up to individuals, families, groups, and local communities to get ready for the future ahead of us. Each of the four horsemen requires a different response, and so different preparations will be needed for each.

To cope with the first horseman, *reducing energy use* is the core strategy. The less energy you need to keep yourself alive and comfortable, the easier you can cope when energy costs spin out of control. Minor tinkerings aren't going to be enough, though; you need to pursue the sort of comprehensive changes in energy use pioneered so successfully in the 1970s. Plan on cutting your energy use by half, to start with, and be ready to cut it further as needed. That means significant changes in lifestyle for most people, of course. In particular, commuting by car has to become a bad memory, and if this requires you to move, get a new job, or change your lifestyle, that's what it requires. Get rid of your car if you can; if you can't, trade in your gas hog for a light, efficient compact, and keep it in the garage under a tarp except when you actually need it. While you're at it, practice coping with blackouts, brownouts, and other forms of energy shortage; they'll be frequent visitors in the future.

To cope with the second horseman, *choosing a viable profession* forms the essential step. Most of the jobs in America today don't produce necessary goods and services, and most goods and many services used in America today aren't produced here. This mismatch promises massive economic disruptions during the crisis period, as an economy and a work force geared to sales, retail, and information processing collides with a new economic reality that has little room for these but a desperate need for locally produced food, clothing, and tools. Anyone prepared to step into a viable economic role in this new reality has a much better chance of thriving as the old economy goes away. You'll need to choose a craft that requires very modest energy inputs, and produces something people need or want badly enough to buy even in hard times. Think of market gardening, garment sewing, home appliance repair, and beer brewing as examples. You'll need to get your training and tools in advance, of course, and the sooner you hang out your shingle the better, even if it's just a hobby-business patronized by your friends until the next wave of crises hits.

To cope with the third horseman, *taking charge of your own health* is the central task. Modern medicine is one of the most energy- and resource-intensive sectors of the economy; it's already priced itself out of reach of many people in nations that don't have socialized health care, and in many of the nations that do, access to care is being whittled away by budget cuts and service restrictions. It is probably best to assume that by the time the next wave of crises arrives, your only health care will be what you can provide for yourself. Plan on learning about preventive medicine and sanitation, taking advanced first aid classes, and arranging for do-it-yourself health care in any other way you can. Don't neglect alternative health care methods, either; while there's some quackery in the alternative field, there's also much of value, and the denunciations of alternative health care that come from the medical establishment are mostly just attempts to protect market share. Finally, get used to the inevitability of death. You probably won't live as long as you used to expect, and if you need high-tech medical help to stay alive, you'll have to accept that it may stop being available without warning. Death is simply part of the human condition. The stark terror of death that haunts so many people in industrial societies is a luxury that a deindustrializing world can't afford.

To cope with the fourth horseman, *community networking* provides the necessary response. This doesn't mean the sort of utopian projects that were tried and failed so dismally during the 1960s; it means the proven and effective approaches that have been used for hundreds of years by people who learned that working together is an essential tool for survival. If you've participated in a block watch, shopped at a farmers market, or belonged to a community service organization, you've taken part in community networking activities. In the future, local citizens will need to maintain basic community services such as sanitation, dispute resolution, and public safety during times when centralized government isn't functioning. Getting to know your neighbors and participating in local community organizations helps build connections that will make the ad hoc arrangements needed in a crisis achievable.

Energy Possibilities

The shortsighted choices and missed opportunities of the last thirty years have given us a future in which energy will become drastically more expensive when it can be obtained at all. At this point in history, this unwelcome transformation can't be prevented. Today's national and regional governments are so blinkered by the myth of progress and so beholden to the existing economic order that the chance they'll pursue a constructive response to our predicament at this point is minimal at best. The one remaining option is preparation on the personal, family, and community level.

Even in the realm of energy, this option offers more possibilities than a casual glance might suggest. One of the many ironies of our present situation is that today's energy-squandering lifestyles actually bid fair to give us more room for maneuver as energy supplies decline. In North America, in particular, we waste so much energy on nonessentials that a large fraction of our energy use can be conserved without severely impacting our lives. Consider the suburbanite who mows his lawn with a gasoline-powered mower and then hops in a car to drive down to the gym to get the exercise he didn't get mowing his lawn! From Christmas lights and video games to three-hour commutes and Caribbean vacations, most of the absurd extravagance that characterizes energy use in the world's industrial countries only happens because fossil fuel energy has been so cheap for so long.

It's been pointed out many times that the average North American uses about three times as much energy each year as the average European.[15] It's much more rarely noted that the standard of living that Americans buy with this extravagance isn't significantly better than the one Europeans enjoy at a third of the energy cost. This means that North Americans could cut their energy use by two-thirds without seriously affecting their standard of living. Most European countries have infrastructure and urban design that support relatively low-energy lifestyles, while most of North America lacks these, so what is theoretically possible may be difficult for most people to achieve. Major cuts, though, are well within reach.

Mature technologies and proven lifestyle changes already exist that can save half or more of the energy the average North American family uses in the course of a year. Nearly all of them were already on the shelf by the late 1970s, and books from that period on appropriate technology and energy conservation — most of which can be bought on the used book market for a few dollars each — provide detailed instructions.[16] At this point it's simply a matter of putting them to work. Because most of them require modest investment, and prices for many of the materials involved are likely to soar once energy prices shoot up and conservation becomes a matter of economic survival for all but the very rich, getting them in place as soon as possible is essential.

Let's start with transportation, the largest single energy use for most people in North America. Commuting by private car swallows a majority of most people's gasoline budget and a very large fraction of their total energy use. Few aspects of today's lifestyle are as dysfunctional in a deindustrial world as our habit of driving long distances between home, work, stores, and shops. After fifty years of car-centered land-use planning, getting out of the commuting lifestyle will take careful planning and a willingness to do without certain amenities, but it can certainly be done.

If your present job uses local materials and labor to produce goods or services people need — and thus will still be viable in a deindustrializing world — you need to live within walking or, at most, bicycling distance of your workplace. Otherwise you won't have a job once shortages hit and commuting becomes impossible. (You won't be able to rely on public transit, because millions of other people will be trying to use it at the same time you are.) If your present job is like most employment in a modern industrial society, producing nothing people actually need, you need to switch to a career producing necessary goods and services, so you need to live within walking distance of your future workplace and the people who will patronize you. In either case, you need to be within walking distance of other people who can provide you with goods and services you need.

The best way to manage this is to live in an old-fashioned mixed-use neighborhood that includes homes, small businesses, and public facilities such as schools and libraries, all of which are within easy reach of one another. The neighborhood can be in a rural area, a town, or a small or middle-sized city. It can even be in the sort of old-fashioned suburb that surrounds a small business district or retail core. Moving to such a neighborhood can involve giving up amenities that many people want, but to be frank, you'll just have to live with that. A lifeboat is more cramped and less comfortable than an ocean liner, but if the liner's sinking, the lifeboat is still a better option.

Don't let the first wave of crises find you living in a bedroom suburb miles from the nearest shopping or employment. Nor will you want to be in the sort of lone house or cabin in the backwoods that most of today's survivalists fancy, not unless you plan on meeting your own needs for food, fuel, clothing, health care, police protection, and everything else. All these things will still be available during the crisis years. Although supplies will be sporadic and shortages common, the experience of European nations during the wars and depressions of the 20th century shows that local economies will readily emerge as the global economy comes apart. Barter and foreign currencies will come into use if the national currency becomes worthless. In the decaying suburbs and the rural periphery, though, goods and services will be out of reach, and, unless you've thoroughly practiced self-sufficiency and are willing to embrace a primitive lifestyle, trying to get by in isolation is a one-way ticket to starvation, exposure, and death.

Once you can get to essential goods and services on your own feet, other aspects of transportation are easily handled; local economies will generate their own transport networks as supply and demand come back into balance. The great challenge will be getting through the first wave of crises, as the commuter economy grinds to a halt and the transitional economy that will replace it struggles to get going. Preparation is essential. For example, the sooner you start commuting on foot, as well as walking to the grocery store and bringing home your purchases in cloth bags or a backpack, the less difficulty you'll have when these are the only options left.

So much for transportation. Household uses account for most of the remaining energy that people in today's industrial societies actually need, and here the conservation techniques developed in the early 20th century and perfected in the 1970s can be put to use. Few of today's houses have adequate insulation, and little tricks like putting gaskets behind light switch plates and electrical outlets have been all but forgotten since the beginning of the Reagan years. Fixing these things — adding insulation, weatherstripping, storm windows, and the like — can save a great deal of energy with very modest investment. More ambitious steps such as solar hot water heating, passive solar retrofits, earth berms, and the like can also be put to good use. Sweaters, quilts, and other ways of conserving body heat also have their place. While you're at it, learn to be comfortable with changes in temperature; your great-grandparents got along just fine without air conditioning and central heating, and so will you.

Having a backup source of heat for your home is essential in a future where blackouts and fuel shortages will be a common occurrence. In many cases, a wood stove or fireplace insert will be your best option, because the fuel can be produced locally. Coppicing[17] and other methods of producing firewood that don't impact surviving forests will be essential, and — if the pun may be forgiven — will likely become one of the 21st century's growth industries. Using wood as a heating fuel will increase the death rate from asthma, but not doing so will increase the death rate from hypothermia and infectious disease; in the future ahead of us, such bleak tradeoffs will be commonplace.

Other household issues can be dealt with similarly. You'll need to have at least one backup method for cooking food, and you should be prepared to wash your clothes in the bathtub and take care of other necessities when the power goes out or the price of electricity soars out of reach. Assess every appliance and amenity you have, and make sure that you can either do the equivalent by hand, using tools you own and know how to use and maintain, or do without it altogether. The time to do that assessment, of course, is now, while the tools you'll need are readily available.

It's important to recognize that the benefits of doing these things aren't limited to the people who do them. The logic here is the same that makes airlines tell you to put on your own oxygen mask before trying to help anyone else get theirs on; you're not going to be able to help anyone else survive the crises of the approaching deindustrial age unless you've taken care of your own basic needs first. If you've already learned the skills and made the adjustments that the end of abundant energy requires, you can show other people how to make the same changes. The experience of the 1970s shows that, in the presence of the sort of hard economic incentives rising energy prices bring, many more people will embrace necessary lifestyle changes than not.

The same principle works on a wider scale as well. Critics of conservation programs often point to the Jevons Paradox as an argument against trying to save energy. First described by the 19th century economist William Stanley Jevons, this rule of thumb holds that when new technology allows a resource to be used more efficiently, the amount of the resource being used goes up, not down, because the increased efficiency makes it cheaper compared to alternatives.[18] This is only true, however, when the only limit on using the resource is how much it costs. When the resource itself runs short due to physical limits, increases in efficiency blunt the impact of the shortage by making up some of the shortfall; increased levels of efficiency will thus prevent prices from rising as far and as fast as they would otherwise.

In the opening years of the deindustrial age, putting the Jevons Paradox to work will be crucial. The longer the world's remaining fossil fuel reserves can be stretched out and used to cushion the decline of industrial civilization, the less traumatic and chaotic the transition will be. Every gallon of gas and kilowatt of electricity that doesn't have to be spent on household uses will be available for trains that bring grain from farms to cities, factories that build wind turbines and solar panels, and a hundred other desperate necessities. The same factors that made gasoline rationing and victory gardens essential during the Second World War will play at least as vital a role in the forced transition to sustainability ahead of us.

The Sound of Aunt Edna's Knitting

The economic landscape on the far side of Hubbert's peak can be traversed with the same sort of practical steps just outlined. Changes on the larger scale — the scale of whole economies or societies — will be much harder to accomplish, because the noise of volatility can too easily hide the signal of decline. Just as occasional plunges in the price of oil and natural gas encourage people to embrace the comforting delusion that they no longer have to worry about long-term energy availability, the upside of the post-peak economy — the fortunes that will made, the speculative gambles that will pay off, the boomtimes that will come when demand destruction crashes energy prices and all seems right with the world — will make it easy for people to convince themselves that industrial society is still on track.

It's easy to understand this sort of thinking since the alternative is to accept the unacceptable: to admit that the industrial age is ending, and the luxuries, conveniences, and standard of living that define ordinary lifestyles in the modern world are going away — not just for a little while, but forever. That the unacceptable is also inevitable makes it no easier to cope with. Still, accepting the unacceptable is the crucial step in dealing with the economic impact of peak oil. Every assumption about the future has to be reassessed in the light of a contracting economy in which money and other forms of abstract wealth no longer guarantee access to goods and services.

Not that long ago, after all, money played only a minor role in the overall economic picture. Until the 18th century, more than half of all goods and services in the Western world were produced within household and community economies and exchanged in customary networks governed by obligation and reciprocity, not supply and demand. Most households produced the great majority of their own food, clothing, and other necessities, using surpluses to barter for specialty goods with local producers. Cash served as a means of exchange for things produced so far away that transport costs and spoilage made barter unworkable. It took cheap, abundant fossil fuel energy to make transportation so cheap that centralized production and distribution of commodities could take the place of local production for local use.

In the aftermath of peak oil, such local economies will be the wave of the future, and the money economy of the present and recent past will be a self-defeating anachronism. Since fossil fuel depletion is a gradual process, though, the changeover won't happen overnight. This is a good thing, since the vast majority of people in the industrial world today are completely without the skills and tools they will need to function in a local economy. Most jobs — from executives and consultants through salespeople, office staff, and all the other cubicle-shaped pigeonholes in the corporate caste system — serve functions internal to the industrial economy instead of producing goods and services people want or need.

The jobs that matter in a deindustrial economy, by contrast, are the ones that meet human needs directly. Farming is the classic example. If you grow food crops with your own labor, you don't actually need the money economy, except to deal with property taxes and the like. Your labor provides you with value directly because some of your crops end up on your own kitchen table; the rest can be exchanged with other local sources of goods and services you need — the seamstress next door, the blacksmith down the road, the general store in town. Money is a convenient way of facilitating these exchanges, but it's not necessary — you can as well use barter, or local scrip, or any other means of exchanging value that comes to hand. Because what you produce has value to other people, you can trade for the things other people produce, whether or not the money economy is there to mediate the trade.

Compare the farmer to a corporate marketing assistant or a factory worker in an injection-casting plant, and the differences become clear. The marketing assistant provides a service — helping to create and manage marketing plans for a corporation — that has no value outside the money economy. If she wanted to barter with a farmer for food, she probably wouldn't get far offering to help manage his corporate identity via a media campaign! The factory worker is in a slightly better position. If the money economy comes unglued, the factory owners might pay him in castings, and he could then try to barter these for the goods and services he needs (exactly this arrangement was common in the former Soviet Union during the economic collapse of the early 1990s). Still, he depends on the factory and its owners to provide him with a workplace and some form of pay; in a volatile, crumbling economy, his situation is a precarious one.

In the deindustrial age, then, the farmer's economic model is the more viable, because it can do without the mediation of the money economy. Other professions that produce necessary goods and services will be in the same comfortable position because people will continue to need food, clothing, shoes, tools, and the like and will trade for them using whatever means are available. Except in the most difficult times, they will also be willing to trade for other things that aren't quite necessities; someone who can brew good beer, for example, will be able to count on a lively market for his product even in the most apocalyptic times.

Healing arts form another set of essential professions, but they also belong on the list of essential skills everyone needs to master. Access to those skills has an immediate payoff as well, because the medical system we have now does not have to wait for catabolic collapse to go under; it's already broken beyond repair. Especially in the United States, but not only here, economic forces long ago turned the theoretical triumphs of scientific medicine into a real-world fiasco. For many years now, medical care has been the leading cause of death in the United States — add together the annual death toll from iatrogenic (physician-caused) illnesses, nosocomial (hospital-transmitted) infections, drug side effects and interactions, risky but heavily advertised elective surgeries such as stomach stapling, and simple malpractice, and the resulting figure soars well above the annual toll for heart disease, or cancer, or anything else.[19]

Many people are already voting with their feet by abandoning conventional medicine for various alternative and traditional forms of medicine. Even when these don't work — and of course some of them don't — placebos are at least less likely to cause harm than the toxic drugs and invasive surgeries that form the mainstay of today's conventional medicine. Many alternative health care systems, on the other hand, treat common illnesses quite effectively.

Another factor, though, makes alternative methods much better suited to the coming deindustrial age. Today's medical system, with its global supply chains, complex technologies, and centralized facilities, is among industrial civilization's most voracious users of energy and natural resources; almost without exception, alternative medical treatments use much less of both. Many of the most effective alternative systems — herbalism and acupuncture come to mind — evolved long before the industrial system came into being and use very modest amounts of sustainable resources to treat illnesses. In an age of energy scarcity and hard ecological limits, systems like these are the wave of the future.

Still, in the absence of effective public health measures, even the best health care — alternative or otherwise — will have its limits. No medicine can take the place of adequate sanitation, pure water, clean and wholesome food, or the other foundations of public health so many of us take for granted nowadays. All these things will be in short supply in the deindustrial future, and so illness and death will be a constant and familiar presence. Learning to live with that reality will also be an essential skill in the twilight of the industrial age. We will no longer be able to afford the fantasy that death is something that only happens to other people — and in the process of coming to terms with our own mortality, we may just learn something essential about being human.

Since the twilight of the money economy will be a gradual process, it won't necessarily be useful or even possible for individuals to make the transition to a deindustrial career in a single leap. What can and must be tackled right now is the learning curve demanded by any of these skilled trades. It's not enough to line your shelves with books about organic farming, for example; you need to start buying tools, digging garden beds, and growing your own crops, and you need to do this as soon as possible, because mastering the craft of organic farming takes time. The same is true if you decide to take up sewing, brewing, or any other useful trade: you need to get the tools and start learning the craft, so you'll have your Plan B firmly in place as the money economy begins to fold out from under you.

Skilled trades for local exchange are part of the picture, but another part is just as essential — the reinvention of the household economy. Not so long ago, a large fraction of all economic value came from the household sector. Many of us still remember grand-mothers who always had jars of homemade jelly in the cupboard and crochet hooks dancing in their hands, and grandfathers whose garages were as full of tools as their gardens were of ripe toma-toes. The marketing campaigns that squeezed the last traces of the household economy out of existence stigmatized these activities as hobbies (and dowdy hobbies at that) but they were once a good deal more — and in a world on the brink of deindustrialization, they desperately need to be revived.

People have different opportunities and talents, and one size emphatically does not fit all. For those who have access to garden space, though, a household garden is probably the top priority here. It's not necessary to grow all your own food, or even a large propor-tion of it, for a garden to have a significant impact on your quality of life. In North America, at least, bulk crops such as grains and beans will likely be available on the market for many years to come. Fruits, vegetables, and animal foods — that is, sources of vitamins, minerals, and protein — are another matter. A vegetable garden, a couple of fruit trees, and perhaps a rabbit hutch, a chicken coop, or a small aquaculture tank for carp or tilapia may mean the differ-ence between malnutrition and health.

Whether or not you have access to garden space, consider tak-ing up a useful handicraft or two. Aunt Edna's habit of knitting cardigans for all and sundry may have seemed quaint in the heyday of the industrial economy, but when central heating prices itself out of existence and transport costs shatter the supply chain that fills stores in the industrial world with the products of overseas sweatshops, warm clothing you can make with your own hands has obvious value, and it may also be a useful item of barter. The same is true of many other skills, from soapmaking and herbal medicine to the handyman skills that allow plumbing, furniture, and small appliances to be repaired at home.

Another response to human wants and needs outside the money economy will be vital during the deindustrial age, and it needs to be revived and practiced as soon as possible. This is the art of doing without. The industrial economy has trained all of us to think that the only possible thing to do with a desire is fulfill it, preferably by spending money on some consumer product or other. The contracting economy of the deindustrial age will offer very little leeway for this sort of self-indulgent thinking. On the far side of Hubbert's peak, your capacity to survive will largely be measured by the number of things you can do without. It's hardly an accident, either, that the world's spiritual traditions also affirm the value of being unattached to material things.

Among the things we will have to learn to do without — perhaps the most important — is not a material thing at all, but a habit: the deliberate cultivation of uselessness that goes nowadays by the name of "leisure." Only a society flush with cheap energy could convince itself that the highest goal of human life is to sit around doing nothing, and even so, it takes the nonstop blare of the media to distract us from the fact that sitting around doing nothing is the dullest of all human activities. Our grandparents' generation and their ancestors knew as much, which is why the leisure activities of a century ago focused on creative activities rather than indolence, and it's why Aunt Edna knitted all those cardigans long after the industrial economy made home production of clothing unnecessary. The twilight of industrial society, like the fall of other civilizations before it, will doubtless be accompanied by plenty of tumult and shouting, but the real story — the signal behind all that noise — will be a much fainter sound: the soft clatter of Aunt Edna's knitting needles, beginning to knit the fabric of a new and more sustainable world.

Rebuilding Civil Society

The political dimension of catabolic collapse demands a response as well, but the nature of that response is far from political in the usual sense of the word. Over the last half century, the political systems of the United States and its close allies have wedged themselves into the impossible position of trying to sustain two unsustainable things: a global empire, and the extravagant standards of living that the now-departing age of empire fooled North Americans into seeing as their birthright. Like the bread and circuses of ancient Rome, the petroleum-fueled prosperity of the 20th century fostered a culture of entitlement in which most citizens believed that they deserved to get whatever they wanted without having to pay the full price for it. One consequence of this cultural shift has been the collapse of democratic politics in North America.

It's popular these days to blame this consequence on the machinations of some nefarious elite group or other, but the real responsibility lies elsewhere. Democracy takes work. Casting a ballot in elections once every year or so is not enough to keep it going, though even this minimal investment of time and effort is apparently too much for something like three-fifths of adults in the United States. What makes a democratic system operate is personal involvement in the political process on the part of most citizens. Precinct organizations and caucuses, town meetings, and other political activities at the local level formed the indispensable foundation of democratic politics in the days when the United States and Canada were not yet elective oligarchies.[20]

These activities drew on a broader base of local community organizations — churches, civic societies, fraternal orders such as the Freemasons and the Grange, and many others — that rarely engaged in explicit political discussion or activism, but taught skills and made connections that inevitably found their way into a political context. These institutions of civil society created a context in which individuals could orient their lives to the politics of the day and act in ways that could influence policy all the way up to the national level. People who wrestled with the nuts and bolts of the democratic process in community organizations needed no further education when time came for the precinct caucuses that chose candidates and party platforms.

It's often claimed by modern writers that these institutions of civil society thrived as they did because people didn't have anything else to do with their time,[21] but this says more about our own fantasies about the past than it does about historical reality. Most people a century ago worked longer hours than we do today, and the popular media of their time was less technologically complex but no less widely distributed or eagerly sought than ours. The difference lay, rather, in prevailing attitudes. Alexis de Tocqueville famously described early 19th century America as a land of associations, where the needs of society were met, not by government programs or aristocratic largesse, but by voluntary organizations of common people.[22] The civil society of pre-imperial America thrived because people recognized that the social and personal benefits they wanted could only be bought with the coin of their own time and money.

One example worth remembering is the way that fraternal orders, rather than government bureaucracies, provided the social safety net of 19th century North America. The Odd Fellows, a fraternal order founded originally in Britain, launched this practice shortly after its arrival on the American continent in 1819. Odd Fellows lodges in Britain had the useful habit of taking up collections for members in need, especially to cover the living costs of those who had fallen sick — remember, this was long before employers offered sick pay — and to pay the burial costs of those who died. In the North American branch of the order, this quickly evolved into a system of weekly assessments and defined benefits.

The way it worked was simple enough. Each member paid weekly dues — 25 cents a week (roughly the equivalent of $20 a week today) was average — and the money went into a common fund. When a member in good standing became too sick to work, he received regular sick pay and, in most lodges, visits from a physician who received a fixed monthly sum from the lodge in exchange for providing care to all its members. When a member died, his funeral costs were covered by the lodge, and his dependents could count on the support of the lodge in hard cash as well as the less tangible currency of the international Odd Fellows network. By 1900, as a result of this system, Odd Fellowship was the largest fraternal order in the world. In that same year more than two thousand North American fraternal orders had copied this model, and nearly half of all adult Americans and Canadians (counting both genders and all ethnic groups, by the way) belonged to at least one fraternal order.[23]

This effective and sustainable system, though, depended on the willingness of large numbers of people to support their local lodges by attending meetings and paying weekly dues. Equivalent systems throughout civil society had the same requirements, and, with the coming of empire, these turned into a fatal vulnerability. As the profits of empire made it possible for governments to buy the loyalty of the middle class with unearned largesse, the old system of voluntary organizations lost its support base and withered on the vine. With it perished the local politics of precinct caucuses and town meetings. When participation in the political system stopped being seen as an opportunity to be heard, and turned into an annoyance to be shirked, democracy mutated into today's system of elective oligarchy.

What happened, in effect, was that most people in North America made the consumer economy their model for political participation. A consumer's role in the economic process is limited to choosing from a selection of lavishly advertised and colorfully marketed products provided by industry. In the same way, most people in the industrial world embraced political systems in which all they had to do was choose from a selection of lavishly advertised and colorfully marketed candidates provided by the major parties. It's not accidental that when people today complain about the low caliber of candidates offered for their vote, their tone and language often don't differ noticeably from their complaints about the low quality of consumer products offered for their purchase. Absent in both cases, too, is any recognition that there might be an alternative to choosing among products somebody else made for them.

Until this attitude changes, nothing will bring back democracy. No institutional change, however drastic, will create a democratic nation unless the people of that nation are willing to invest the time, effort, forbearance, and resources that a democratic system needs. Nor will throwing one set of rascals out of office, in order to replace them with another set of rascals more to one's taste, have any noticeable effect on the character of the system as a whole. Until people come to the conclusion that the costs of democracy are less burdensome than the costs of doing without it, they will continue to have a government of the people in name only — not because some elite group has taken it away from the people, but because the people themselves have turned their backs on it.

Nor, I think, is there much hope that peak oil, global warming, or any other aspect of our current predicament will induce them to do otherwise. Combine any of these factors with the decline of American empire, and the result you get is a future in which people of all classes must get by with a great deal less wealth and leisure than they think they deserve. It seems unlikely that they will respond by giving up even more of their wealth and leisure to renew a dimly remembered democratic system that, despite its many other virtues, offers no hope of regaining these things.

Instead, my guess is that the focus of the next century or so of North American politics will be attempts to hang onto as much of the prosperity of empire as possible. Not all these attempts may be as hamfisted as current American foreign policy might suggest, and for this reason people of other nations would do well to be wary of proposals for some sort of "world community" emanating from American soil, no matter how apparently liberal the language in which they are phrased. The American people have already faced a choice between democracy and the profits of empire, and we know which one they chose. The fact that they will end up with neither is one of the ironies of history, but I doubt that many will see it that way.

What, though, can those who value democracy do within the constraints of a collapsing empire and a declining industrial civilization? The one workable strategy, it seems to me, is rebuilding the foundations of civil society that made democracy work in the first place. Though it's unfashionable (and politically incorrect) to suggest this, and doubtless new forms will also need to be evolved, I think that much value remains in the old institutions of North American civil society, in particular in the handful of surviving fraternal orders — the Freemasons, the Odd Fellows, the Grange, and their equivalents. Behind lodge doors, all but forgotten even by the retirees who keep the old lodges going, lies a rich history and a wealth of proven methods that weathered every challenge except that of unearned prosperity.

Those approaches could readily be put to use again. Equally, other dimensions of civil society wait to be rebuilt or reinvented. A great many of the common assumptions of our imperial age will have to go by the boards in this process, however. In particular, the notion of entitlement needs to be an early casualty of the approaching changes. The Odd Fellows and their many equivalents did not dispense charity; they provided a means for those willing to contribute to the common welfare to spread out the risks and share the benefits of life in an uncertain world. Those who did nothing to help others did not get help in their own time of need. This may seem harsh, but in a time of unbending ecological limits, it's also necessary.

The 19th century was such a time and, given the realities of peak oil, global warming, and the other elements of the predicament of industrial civilization, the 21st century will be no better — and it may be worse. The one question is whether enough people will embrace the challenge of rebuilding civil society in time to make a difference on a community scale, or whether — as in the declining years of so many past empires — it will be left up to small groups on the fringes of society to embrace a path of mutual aid and preserve today's legacies for the future.

First Steps Toward Sustainability

Many of the strategies just outlined extend well beyond the reach of the individual, and to some extent this cannot be avoided. The community, not the isolated individual, is the basic unit of human survival, and one of the central lessons of the deindustrial age will likely be the value of community connections. Still, there are things that individuals can do by themselves to start down the road to sustainability. For some people the following ideas will be impractical, and for almost everyone they will be at least a little inconvenient. All of them, however, will be an inescapable part of the reality most people will have to live with in the future — and quite possibly the very near future, at that. The sooner people concerned with peak oil and the rest of the predicament of industrial society make changes like these in their own lives, the better able they will be to surf the waves of industrial decline and help other people make the transition toward sustainability.

1. **Replace your incandescent light bulbs with compact fluorescents.**

   If you haven't done this already you haven't been paying attention. Compact fluorescent bulbs last about eight times as long as ordinary light bulbs, producing the same amount of light for a quarter the electricity. The less wattage you use, the less of a burden you put on the electrical grid and the biosphere. Go shopping for compact fluorescent bulbs this week, and notice the impact on your electric bill next month.

2. **Retrofit your home for energy conservation.**

   Most of the lessons of the 1970s energy crises were forgotten long before the recent housing bubble took off, and nearly all recent residential construction leaks heat the way a sieve leaks water — not a good thing in a world of rising energy costs. Fortunately this can be fixed easily for a very modest investment of money and labor. Weatherstripping doors and windows, putting foam gaskets behind light switch and electrical outlet plates, and the like can be done even by apartment dwellers, and more extensive projects such as putting an extra layer of insulation in the attic are within the range of most homeowners and house renters. As energy prices rise, heat will once again be too precious to waste. Over the coming year, learn what you can do to conserve energy at home, and do it; your bank balance will thank you, and so will the planet.

3. **Cut back on your gasoline consumption.**
   Our dependence on cars is as much emotional and psychological as it is practical, but few people are willing to take the step we're all going to have to take sooner or later and actually get rid of their cars. Everyone can cut down on the amount of gas they use, however. Whether you do it by trading in a gas-guzzler for a more modest and more efficient car, cutting back on casual driving, walking or bicycling more, or switching to carpooling or public transit for your commute, each gallon of gas you don't use helps stretch out the downside of the Hubbert curve and buys time for a transition to sustainability. Keep track of how much gas you use each month, and try to make the total go down each month.

4. **Plant an organic vegetable garden.**
   Today's agricultural practices depend on fossil fuels to power equipment, transport produce, and provide fertilizers and pesticides. This makes organic food gardening one of the skills that will be needed most desperately as fossil fuels run short in the decades to come. Pick up a good book on organic gardening and find a patch of soil for your garden, and you're ready to go. Apartment dwellers can often use window boxes or half-barrels full of dirt on a patio or balcony as a micro-garden, arrange to borrow a corner of a house-owning friend's yard, or get a patch in a community garden. It doesn't matter if you can only grow

a few pounds of vegetables over the course of the season — the important thing is getting past the steepest part of the learning curve before you need to rely on your own produce.

5. **Compost your food waste.**
Vegetable waste from your kitchen should go back to the soil, not into a landfill. Composting is a simple technology that does the job quickly, cleanly, and efficiently. Read a good book on composting and go to work. If you have a yard, set up a compost bin and use it for your kitchen and yard waste. If you don't, talk to a friend who gardens — if she composts, she'll likely be grateful for your compostable waste. If you own your home and your local code permits (most do), consider replacing your flush toilet with a composting toilet. In the deindustrial age, survival will depend on understanding nutrient cycles and working with them, not against them. You might as well get started now.

6. **Take up a handicraft.**
The end of the age of cheap energy means, among other things, that economies based on centralized mass production are on their way out. In the future, just as in the past, most goods and services will have to be produced by local craftspeople or the end users themselves. The coming of peak oil requires the recovery of the old handicrafts people once used to preserve food, make clothes, fashion tools, and produce a hundred other things now shipped worldwide from sweatshops in the nonindustrial world. All these crafts require practice to master, so the sooner you learn them, the better off you'll be.

7. **Adopt an "obsolete" technology.**
In recent decades, the social changes we are pleased to call "progress" have replaced many older, sustainable technologies with newer ones that use energy more extravagantly, wear out or break down more frequently, and depend on an ever widening network of other machines. These changes will come

undone in a big way as the end of cheap energy makes most of the 20th century's technological changes unsustainable. As energy supplies peak and begin to decline, a window of opportunity exists for some of the older technologies to be brought back into use before they are forgotten and have to be laboriously reinvented decades or centuries in the future. Many of them work just as well as their more modern replacements — a slide rule can crunch numbers as effectively as a pocket calculator, for example, and a hand-cranked beater will beat eggs just as well as an electric one. Choose an old technology that interests you and make it an everyday part of your life.

8. **Take charge of your own health care.**
Health care in the industrial nations has become a massive industry even more dependent on extravagant energy consumption and international supply chains than most. In the United States, at least, it has already become so costly that almost half of Americans can no longer afford even routine care, and it will likely be among the first economic sectors to break down as energy supplies contract and the global economy fractures. Older, less energy-dependent healing methods, most of them part of today's alternative healing movement, offer one of the few ways of responding to this. Many of them can be learned and practiced, at least in a basic form, without a great deal of training. Choose a method of providing your own health care, learn its strengths and limitations, and use it to maintain your health and treat your minor illnesses.

9. **Help build your local community.**
The Petroleum Age saw the twilight of community across the industrial world and the birth of a mass society of isolated individuals tied to the larger society only by economic interactions. The results have not been good, and they will likely get much worse as the Petroleum Age ends and the economic glue of mass society comes apart. Many of the old institutions

of community still exist, and new networks have begun to take
shape in many communities. More than anything else, such
networks need people willing to invest a modest amount of
time in them. Choose one of them, get involved, and stay ac-
tive in it.

10. **Explore your spirituality.**

At the core of the consumer society — and the fossil fuel-
powered industrial system that spawned it — lies the conviction that the highest goals of human existence can be found
in material consumption. This notion took shape in opposition to an equally dysfunctional belief that despised the material world and grounded all human hopes in an invisible
otherworld on the far side of death. The bitter sibling rivalry
between these twin ideologies has hidden from many people
the fact that many other options exist. In the twilight of the
industrial age, the faith in progress that buoyed the consumer
economy faces extinction, but the hopes once confided to it deserve better homes. In spirituality as well as ecology, diversity is
a positive good, and it's long past time we discard the claim that
every human being can, much less should, approach the great
mysteries of existence in the same way. Whatever your own vision of spirituality may be, then, explore it more deeply, and
study its teachings in the context of the coming deindustrial
age. You may find that, seen in that light, those teachings make
an uncommon amount of sense.

There are a good many other, similar steps that can be taken.
Anything that provides functional alternatives to energy-wasting
lifestyles lays foundations for the transitional societies of the late
21st century and ultimately for the sustainable successor cultures
that will most likely begin to emerge in North America in the 23rd
and 24th centuries. The important point, it seems to me, is to do
something constructive now.

Tools
for the
Transition

It makes a great deal of difference how we come to view
the challenge of the next century. On the one hand, it could
be portrayed as a struggle to keep modern industrial civilization moving along the endless upward curve of progress. On the
other, it could more usefully be envisioned as a matter of managing
the end of the industrial age and coping with the decline to a more
modest and less ecologically suicidal deindustrial society. We're in
much the same situation as family members who have to decide on
medical treatment for an elderly parent who has half a dozen vital
systems on the verge of giving out. If the only outcome we're willing to accept is keeping Dad alive forever, we guarantee ourselves
a desperate, expensive, and futile struggle with the inevitable. People, like civilizations, are mortal; no matter how much money and
technology gets poured into keeping them alive, sooner or later it
won't be enough.

On the other hand, if we accept that Dad is going to die sooner
or later, and we concentrate on giving him the best possible quality of life in the time he has left, there's quite a bit that can be done.

The last part of Dad's life can be made better, and so can the lives of the generations that follow him, because the money that might have been spent paying for exotic medical procedures to keep Dad alive for another three months of misery can go instead to pay college tuition for his grandchildren. The same thing is likely to be true in the twilight years of industrial civilization; the resources we have left can be used either to maintain the industrial system for a few more years, or to cushion the descent into the deindustrial future — but not both.

Now, it's sometimes true that the only way to deal with a hard fact is to take the even harder path of acceptance. In at least one sense, this describes the situation we're in right now. The current predicament can't be dealt with at all if "dealing with it" means finding a way to prevent the decline and fall of the industrial system and the coming of the deindustrial age. That option went out the window around 1980, when the industrial world turned its collective back on a decade of promising movements toward sustainability. At this point we've backed ourselves into the trap predicted by *The Limits to Growth* back in 1972; we no longer have the resources to simultaneously meet our present needs *and* provide for our future. When the future becomes the present, we will no longer have the resources to do either one. At that point, catabolic collapse begins in earnest, and industrial society starts consuming itself.

It bears repeating, though, that this isn't a quick process, nor is it a linear one. Civilizations fall in a stepwise fashion, with periods of crisis and contraction followed by periods of stability and partial recovery. The theory of catabolic collapse explains this as, basically, a matter of supply and demand. Each wave of crises brings about a sharp decrease in the amount of capital (physical, human, social, and intellectual) that has to be maintained, and this frees up enough resources to allow effective crisis management — until resource supplies drop further and the next round of crises hits. This same sequence is likely to repeat itself many times over the next few centuries, as industrial civilization slides down the slope of its own decline and fall.

The Strategy of Salvage

The stepwise decline of industrial civilization can be understood in another way, though, and this points toward possibilities for constructive action that can still be pursued, even this late in the game. Civilizations in full flower typically evolve complex, resource-intensive ways of doing things, because they can, and because the social benefits of extravagance outweigh the resource costs. The infrastructure that serves these functions contains substantial resources that, in a less extravagant time, can be salvaged and put to more prudent uses. As whatever passes for high technology in a given civilization drops out of use, the resources once locked up in high-tech equipment become raw material for simpler and more resource-efficient technologies. People realize that you don't need pyramids to bury a king, or Roman baths to wash your skin; pretty soon, the stone blocks of the pyramid and the plumbing of the Roman baths get salvaged and put to more immediately useful purposes.

This same process bids fair to play a massive role in the twilight of the industrial age. Proponents of the neoprimitivist movement have claimed that as industrial civilization winds down, the survivors will slide all the way back to the stone age, because the last few centuries of mining have stripped the planet of all the metal ores that can be processed by low-tech means.[1] Even if the people of the future had to rely on ores still in the ground, this wouldn't be true because bog iron concentrated by chemosynthetic bacteria is a renewable resource; it has provided respectable amounts of iron to many past societies. Still, there's no need to rely on bog iron; most of the billions of tons of metals extracted from deep within the Earth are now sitting conveniently on its surface, ready to be salvaged and put to new uses.

Every skyscraper in every city on the planet, just for starters, contains hundreds of tons of iron, steel, aluminum, and copper. In a deindustrial society, this is all raw material ready to be cut apart by salvage crews, hauled away on oxcarts, and turned into knives, hoes, plowshares, and other useful things. The same is just as true of most of the other artifacts of 20th and 21st century technology, from cars to tin cans to the rebar that runs through every concrete structure in the industrial world. As iron turns to rust, it simply changes itself from one form of resource to another — rust is iron oxide, FeO_2, a common iron ore that can be turned back into iron with nothing more demanding than charcoal and a good pair of bellows.

In this way, the material extravagance of the industrial age will provide a vital cushion of resources as we move down the curve of decline. The most important limiting factor here is the practical knowledge necessary to turn skyscrapers, cars, and the other detritus of the industrial system into useful goods for the deindustrial world. Not many people have that knowledge today. Our educational system (if America's dysfunctional schooling industry deserves that name) shed the old trade schools and their practical training programs decades ago. At a time when the creation and exchange of actual goods and services has become an economic sideline, this comes as no surprise, but it's a situation that has to change if anything is to be salvaged once the first major wave of crises hits.

The range of possibilities open to intelligent salvage can be measured through a practical example. Right now in the United States there are something like 500,000,000 (that's half a billion) alternators. For more than half a century, since they outcompeted generators in the Darwinian world of auto design, every car or truck with an internal combustion engine has had one. Right now, alternators are worth next to nothing; they're old technology, they rarely wear out or break down, and when they do, you can usually make them as good as new by replacing a diode or a few ball bearings.

Old tech or not, they're ingenious devices. You put rotary motion into the shaft, and 12 volts of electricity (six volts in some older
models) come out of the terminals. The faster the motion, the
higher the wattage, but the voltage always stays the same. In a car or
truck, the rotary motion comes from the engine, and the electricity goes to charge the battery, power the cooling fan, run the lights,
and so on; it's simply a way to take some of the energy produced by
burning petroleum and do things with it that burning petroleum,
all by itself, doesn't do well. In terms of the catabolic collapse theory, these alternators are part of the capital our civilization uses to
convert petroleum into air pollution and global warming.

Apply the strategy of salvage, though, and alternators become
something very different. They stop being part of a car and become a resource on their own. Rotary motion from any imaginable source can be applied to the shaft, and you still get 12 volts of
electricity. Since there are half a billion alternators in cars, trucks,
and junkyards all over North America, and because those cars and
trucks are going to lose their value as capital once petroleum becomes too scarce and expensive to waste on individual transport,
the cost of alternators is limited to the time and effort needed to
gather them, while their value soars.

In a salvage economy, each of those half a billion alternators is a
potential energy source. Take one, add some gears and a chain salvaged from a bicycle and some steel borrowed from an old truck,
spend a week carving and sanding a 5-foot length of spruce into a
propeller, and you've got a windmill that will trickle-charge a set of
scavenged lead-acid batteries and run a 12-volt refrigerator taken
from an old RV.[2] Take half a dozen more, add more bicycle parts,
wood of various dimensions, and a year-round stream, and you've
got a waterwheel-based micro-hydro plant that turns out 12 volts,
night and day, at pretty fair wattage.[3]

Care to try a solar heat engine? The French did it back in the
1870s.[4] Before diesel generators running on dirt-cheap petroleum
crashed the market for the technology, France's North African

colonies drew up extensive plans to use solar-powered steam engines for everything from pumping water to printing newspapers. Given sunshine, boiler parts, plenty of scrap metal, and alternators, you've got solar-generated electricity that you can maintain and replace with 1870s technology — that is, without access to pure amorphous silicon, monomolecular layers of rare earth metals, clean rooms with nanoparticle-free air, or the other exotica needed to make photovoltaic cells. None of these latter will be readily available in a deindustrializing world. On the other hand, boiler parts, scrap metal, and alternators certainly will.

It has to be said up front that none of these makeshift technologies will provide more than a minute fraction of the electricity needed to support a modern industrial society. None of them work at anything remotely like high efficiency, and it's an open question whether any of them produce as much energy in their lifespans as went into producing them in the first place. Still, in a salvage economy, none of that matters. The only relevant question is whether technologies will repay, on an individual basis, the effort of salvaging them and putting them to work. Is a week's worth of work on a windmill a good deal in exchange for a working refrigerator? In a world where food preservation will once again be a matter of life and death, it's hard to imagine that the answer could be anything but yes.

Such makeshifts look much less impressive than the grand projects for sustainability that have been proposed at intervals since the limits to growth came into sight in the 1970s, but the opportunity for those latter has long since passed us by. The strategy of salvage may not be pretty, by contrast, but it provides us with options that are still within reach. Alternators are useless as a way to keep industrial civilization afloat; that's why there's half a billion of them in good working order sitting in junkyards at this moment. The same thing is true of hundreds of other products of industrial society that can be transformed into resources for a deindustrializing world. A little practical knowledge about how to use salvaged materials, preferably backed up by experiment in advance, would be a good investment for those people who plan on riding the waves of change.

Renewable Energy

The gradual, stepwise nature of the decline ahead of us has to be understood in order to make sense of the possibilities of renewable energy. During the heady days of the 1970s, when it looked as though industrial society might actually face up to the challenge of building a sustainable future for itself, talk about renewable energy filled the pages of more than a dozen now-defunct journals and provided cocktail-party chatter for progressive circles across the industrial world. Solar energy, windpower, and conservation technology briefly counted as significant growth industries, while more exotic possibilities — geothermal, tide and wave power, oceanic thermal energy conversion, and others — attracted their share, or more, of attention and investment.[5]

All this went away with the political manipulations that crashed the price of oil in the early 1980s. The renewable energy industry wasn't the only economic sector flattened by the Reagan administration's decision to put low oil prices ahead of every other consideration: America's nuclear industry suffered an even more drastic meltdown, and the collapse in oil prices brought a decade of economic crisis to once-booming states around the Gulf of Mexico. In the long view, though, the early death of the renewable energy industry will probably prove to be the most disastrous result of the shortsighted policies of the Reagan era. In 1980, the United States still had some 25 to 30 years to get ready for the worldwide peak of oil production, and its energy demands were much smaller than today's. A controlled transition to sustainability would have been a massive challenge, but it could probably have been accomplished.

At the same time, the hard aftermath of the 1970s alternative energy boom showed all too clearly the shaky numbers behind

many overhyped renewable energy technologies. Crucially, too
many of them failed the test of net energy: that is, the usable energy they produced turned out to be little more than, and in some
cases noticeably less than, the energy needed to manufacture,
maintain, and run the technology. A case could be made that it's
the net energy provided by a society's energy resources that defines
the upper limit of its economic development. More than any other
factor, the huge net energy of fossil fuels — up to 200-to-1 for light
sweet petroleum from wells under natural pressure — made possible the industrial world and its extravagant energy-wasting lifestyles. Net energy in single digits, which is what the best renewable
energy technologies manage, simply won't produce enough spare
energy to support an industrial society.

These awkward facts show that renewables won't allow us to
continue living the lifestyles we take for granted today. The problem, of course, is that as things now stand, neither will anything
else. As oil production worldwide plateaus and falters, other fossil fuels are coming under strain, and no alternative — renewable
or otherwise — shows any sign of being able to take up the slack.
A steady decline in the overall production and availability of energy thus defines all the likely futures ahead of us. Extrapolate the
effects in economic and social terms, and we face what might as
well be called the Deindustrial Revolution, a period of wrenching
change in which the world's industrial societies give way to subsistence economies dominated by the agricultural sector and powered by sun, wind, water, and muscle.

The implied reference to the Industrial Revolution is deliberate, of course. The birth of industrial society in the late 18th and
19th centuries, and its global expansion in the 20th, catalyzed
sweeping changes in almost every dimension of human life, and
it left the certainties of previous ages in tatters. It seems likely
that the twilight of industrial society will drive equally sweeping
effects, overthrowing today's fundamental assumptions just as
thoroughly as the coming of fossil fuels overthrew those of early

modern Europe's agrarian societies. The economics of renewable energy technology, though, take on a very different and much more positive shape in the context of deindustrialization.

This suggestion cuts across much of the conventional wisdom in the peak oil community these days, but at least three factors back it. First and most obvious, of course, is the fact that even the most drastically deindustrialized society will still need energy. (Even hunter-gatherers systematically exploit energy resources, if only in the form of food and firewood.) Windmills with a net energy of 5- or 6-to-1 are hopelessly inadequate to power an industrial society, but deindustrial societies with grain to grind, water to pump, and many other uses for mechanical energy will find them just as economically viable as did the agrarian societies of the past. In the same way, the economics of passive solar heating are one thing when it's a question of whether to heat one's home with solar energy or fossil fuels, and quite another when fossil fuels are priced out of the heating market, firewood is scarce, and the choice is between solar heat and nothing at all.

Renewable energy technologies that can be built from readily available materials with hand tools are uneconomical today, because they have been priced out of the market by fossil fuels. Many of them, however, will be economically viable in a deindustrialized society. Windpower and waterpower head the list of crucial energy sources for the deindustrial age; as Lewis Mumford pointed out in his *Technics and Civilization*, the first phase of the Industrial Revolution (his "eotechnic" phase) used windmills, waterwheels, and sails as its prime movers.[6] Passive solar space heating and solar hot water heating also belong on the list, as do bicycles and other efficient ways of converting human muscle power into mechanical energy.

Many other renewable energy technologies don't make this particular cut. The poster child for the losers is the photovoltaic (PV) cell. PV cells can't be made without high-tech manufacturing facilities and energy-intensive materials, and, according to some calculations, their net energy is right around 1-to-1 — that is, it takes about as much energy to manufacture a cell as the cell produces in its relatively short working life.[7] In the aftermath of the Deindustrial Revolution, barring drastic changes in the technology, PV cells will be museum pieces or expensive novelties, if they can be made at all.

Yet a simple before-and-after analysis misses a crucial variable. The net energy of PV cells, like most other renewable energy technologies, is radically asymmetric over time. Essentially all the energy inputs go into PV cells at the beginning, when they are manufactured and installed; the energy output comes later on, and requires almost no further input. In effect, then, a PV cell can be seen as a way of storing energy; the energy put in at its manufacture, one might say, is extracted out of it, bit by bit, over its working life.

When energy availability is increasing or remains steady over time, this asymmetry is a drawback; it means that the user has to pay for all the energy produced by the PV cell up front, in the form of manufacturing costs, and only gets the energy back over time. Deindustrialization, though, stands this logic on its head. As energy resources decline in availability and rise in price, PV cells allow the user to arbitrage energy costs across time — to buy energy, in effect, when it's relatively cheap and available, and to use it when energy is relatively costly and scarce. The same is true of other renewable energy technologies; for example, a high-tech windpower generator can be built and stocked with spare parts now, when plentiful fossil fuel puts its manufacture within reach. For the next ten to twenty years, as fossil fuels deplete and the price of energy soars, that windmill can continue turning out electricity with only the most minimal further investment.

Such strategies won't provide energy for the long term, but it's crucial to remember that the long term is not the only thing that matters. To return to a metaphor used earlier, if you knew that tomorrow you would be taken up in an airplane to 10,000 feet or so and tossed out the cabin door, the long-term value of a parachute as an investment would probably not be the first thing on your mind, and the fact that the parachute would be of no further use to you once you reached the ground might not weigh heavily on your decision making process, either. These points would presumably take second place to the overriding need to get to the ground alive.

We face a similar situation today. Industrial society's vulnerability to fossil fuel depletion leaves us perched unsteadily in the cabin door with plenty of empty air below us, waiting for declining oil production to give us the shove that will send us on our way down. Renewable energy technologies, like the parachute of the metaphor, won't keep us from falling, but they can potentially slow the descent enough to make a difference. One of the lessons taught by (but rarely learned from) the wars and disasters of the 20th century is that the difference between a lot of energy and a little is less important than the difference between a little and none at all. Investing a portion of today's relatively abundant energy resources into tomorrow's energy technologies will make it a good deal easier to provide that "little" when it's most needed, as well as cushioning some of the impacts of the Deindustrial Revolution.

Climbing Down the Ladder

Yet the airplane of industrial society is very short on parachutes just now, and it's instructive to explore the reasons for that. One of the children's books I read when I was growing up used the metaphor of a ladder to represent progress; this rung is a chariot, the next a stagecoach, the one after that a locomotive, the next a car, and so on. The problem with this metaphor is that it makes it look as though the earlier rungs are still there, so if the top one starts to crack, you can step down to the next one, or to the one below that. In most fields of technological progress, that isn't even remotely true. How many people nowadays, faced with a series of complicated math problems and denied a computer, could whip out a slide rule or sit down with a table of logarithms and solve them?

These days even grade school students in math class do arithmetic on pocket calculators.

The same thing is true in nearly any other branch of technology you could name. Each new generation of technology is more complex, more resource-intensive, and more interdependent with other technologies than the one before it. As each new generation of technology is adopted, the one before it becomes "obsolete" and is scrapped — even if the older technology does the job just as well as the newer one. Twenty years later only a handful of retired engineers still remember how the old technology worked, and in many cases not even they would be able to build it again from scratch.

In effect, as we've climbed from step to step on the ladder of progress, we've kicked out each rung under us as we've moved to the next. This is fine so long as the ladder keeps on going up forever. If you reach the top of the ladder unexpectedly, though, you're likely to end up teetering on a single rung with no other means of support — and if, for one reason or another, you can't stay on that one rung, it's a long way down. That's the situation we're in right now, with the rung of high-tech, high-cost, and high-maintenance technology cracking beneath us.

In the last few years, fortunately, people have begun to replace a few of the lower rungs. Once again there are working farmers who use draft animals or their own muscles instead of tractors and who fertilize the soil with compost and manure instead of petroleum-based chemicals. Once again there are blacksmiths who make extraordinary things using only hand tools, and there are home brewers who turn out excellent beer with the ordinary kitchen gear and raw materials their great-great-great-grandparents knew well. Even the lowest rung of all, making stone tools by flint knapping, has had a modest renaissance of its own in recent years.

One of the most hopeful features of this side of our predicament is that the revitalization of old technologies can be done successfully by individuals working on their own. It's precisely those technologies that can be built, maintained, and used by individuals that formed the mainstay of the economy in the days before cheap, abundant energy made a global economy seem to make sense. These same technologies — if they're recovered while time and resources still permit — can make use of the abundant salvage of industrial civilization, help cushion the descent into the deindustrial future, and lay foundations for the sustainable cultures that will rise out of the ruins of our age.

Another practical example shows how this can work. Some time ago, after mulling over the points just mentioned, I started looking into the options for climbing down the ladder a rung or two in the field of practical mathematics. The slide rule was an obvious starting place. A few inquiries revealed that most of my older friends still had a slipstick or two gathering dust in a desk drawer, and not long afterward I found myself being handed a solid aluminum Pickett N903-ES slide rule in mint condition. The friend who gave it to me is getting on in years and has a short white beard, and though he looks more like Saint Nicholas than Alec Guinness, I instantly found myself inside one of the fantasies burned into the neurons of my entire generation:

> "This," Obi-wan Kenobi tells me, "is your father's slide rule."
> I take the gleaming object in one hand, my gaze never leaving
> his face. "Not so wasteful or energy-intensive as a calculator,"
> he says then. "An elegant instrument of a more sustainable age."
> I press my thumb against the cursor, and…

Well, no, a blazing blue-white trigonometric equation didn't come buzzing out of the business end, and of course that's half the point. The slide rule is an extraordinarily simple, low-tech device that lets you crunch numbers at what, at least in pre-computer terms, was a very respectable pace. Even by current standards it's not slow. I've only begun to learn the ways of the Force, so to speak, but I can easily multiply and divide on my Pickett as fast or faster than I can punch buttons on a calculator.

Beyond its practical uses, however, the slide rule has more than a little to teach about what sustainable technology looks like. It's quite literally pre-industrial technology — the basic principle was worked out in 1622 by Rev. William Oughtred, though it took many more years of experimentation to produce the handy ten-inch device with multiple scales that played so important a role in 19th and 20th century science and engineering. This simple device crunched most of the numbers that put human footprints on the moon. Set a slide rule side by side with an electronic calculator and certain points stand out.

First, *a slide rule is durable.* By this I don't simply mean that you have to use more force to break a slide rule than a pocket calculator, though this is generally true. More important is the fact that a pocket calculator has a limited shelf life. Over fairly modest time spans, batteries go dead, memory and processing chips break down, and plastics depolymerize into useless goo. Even the cheap plastic slide rules once mass-produced for schoolchildren will outlast most pocket calculators, and a good professional model can stay in working order for something close to geological time.

Second, *a slide rule is independent.* You don't need to rely on any other technology to make it work or to do something useful with the output. Pocket calculators depend on a certain level of battery technology to work, though admittedly this puts them toward the independent end of the spectrum. By contrast, think of the number and extent of the technological systems needed to keep a car or an Internet terminal functioning and useful.

Third, *a slide rule is replicable.* If you have one, it doesn't take advanced industrial technology to make another, or a thousand more; a competent cabinetmaker with hand tools and a good eye can produce them as needed. Making a pocket calculator, by contrast, demands a mastery of dozens of extraordinarily complex and energy-intensive technologies: clean rooms with nanoparticle-free air, solvent chemistry, and manufacture of monomolecular metallic films are but a few. Once these technologies can no longer be sustained — a dead certainty in the deindustrial age — pocket calculators become a nonrenewable resource. Slide rules remain viable as long as something like the technology of Oughtred's time remains available.

Fourth, *a slide rule is transparent.* By this I mean that it's easy to work out the principles that make it function from the device itself. This is crucial, because a transparent technology can communicate much more than its own output.

Imagine for a moment that the deindustrial age turns out much more severe than we have reason to expect, and nearly all mathematical knowledge gets lost. A thousand years from now, a surviving slide rule ends up in the hands of a scholar who has laboriously learned how to read ancient numbers and has learned all the arithmetic known in her time. A few minutes of fiddling would show her how the C and D scales can be used to multiply and divide numbers, and a few more would reveal that the A scale shows the squares of corresponding numbers on the D scale. Once she realizes that each scale shows a different mathematical operation, the device itself becomes a mathematical Rosetta stone that can teach her all about fractions, decimals, squares and square roots, cubes and cube roots, reciprocals, and logarithms, because all the mathematical relationships are right there in plain sight.

If our imaginary scholar gets an ancient pocket calculator instead, none of this happens, because the algorithms that make a calculator work are hidden away in its circuitry. Even if the thing still works, it's a black box that spits out numbers, and the relationships between the numbers would have to be worked out the hard way, by trial and error. For that matter, how would our future scholar realize that the calculator was a calculator rather than, say, a remote control or some other enigmatic ancient relic?

Science fiction writer Arthur C. Clarke unknowingly pointed out one of the potential long-term weaknesses of our present technology in his famous Third Law: "Every sufficiently advanced technology is indistinguishable from magic."[8] What makes one technology more or less advanced than another is a subtler question than it may appear at first glance, but Clarke's point remains valid: once a technology becomes complicated enough that it loses transparency, it can be very hard to recognize the technology for what it is — and very easy to turn it into a stage property for ritual use. A number of today's technologies have already become ritual props in industrial society's mostly unacknowledged ceremonial life, and that process could accelerate drastically as education levels decline and technologies become rare.

The effects of Clarke's law thus have to be dealt with if the technologies we pass on to the deindustrial future are going to be of value to anyone. For that matter, all four of the principles suggested by the humble slide rule — durability, independence, replicability, and transparency — make good criteria for any technology meant to outlast the industrial age. Too many of the technologies currently being touted as answers to peak oil fail one or more of these tests, and many fail all four. As the world begins to move beyond debating the fact of fossil fuel depletion and starts tackling the challenges of planning for a difficult future, a careful study of potential technologies in something like the terms I've outlined may be a good place to start.[9]

Scores of other technologies, skills, and traditions of high value to a low-energy future can be found with a little searching. Consider the haybox or fireless cooker, a container full of insulating material with a well in the center to hold a pot of food. Hayboxes were a standard piece of kitchen equipment in the industrial world a century ago; if your great-grandmother lived in Europe or North America she very likely had one. She brought food to a boil, popped it into the haybox, and left it there to cook by residual heat, saving most of the fuel she would have needed to cook the same dish on the stove.[10] Haybox technology could make a future of energy shortages much more livable, but only if it's brought out of museums and put back into circulation before knowledge about it is lost.

Technological Triage

As the previous section suggests, one of the main blind spots that
has to be overcome in facing the deindustrial future is the habit of
thinking of technology in the singular, as though it's all of a piece.
Like so many common mistakes, this one gets its strength from the
fact that it's not entirely mistaken. Among the dominant features
of modern industrial society, as Lewis Mumford pointed out,[11]
is the way that most technologies depend on other technologies,
forming an intricate web of interconnections.

One of the most widely cited apocalyptic writers of my teen
years, Roberto Vacca, argued in his 1973 book *The Coming Dark
Age* that this extreme interdependence would turn out to be the
Achilles' heel of industrial society. His argument was that too
much interconnection among unstable systems would lead to cascading systems failures and the collapse of industrial civilization.
Although his ideas impressed the likes of Isaac Asimov (who con-
tributed an introduction to the book), in retrospect it's clear that
Vacca was embarrassingly wrong. Like so many others at that time,
Vacca put the cart before the horse; the rising tide of interdependence and interconnection he saw moving through the industrial
world was a reaction to improvements in information processing,
not a force in its own right, and further developments along the
same lines — especially the explosive growth in computer technology — proved more than adequate to keep the process moving.

Still, Vacca was right to see the web of interconnections that
unites today's industrial technology as a critical vulnerability. It's
just that the vulnerability comes into play further along the arc of
catabolic collapse. Many of today's technologies depend so completely on the support of an intact industrial system that they cannot operate without it. Many more could operate without it, at
least in theory, but have been designed in a way that maximizes
their dependence on other technologies and will have to be reengi-
neered in a hurry as the fabric of the industrial system comes apart.
A third class of technologies are largely or wholly independent of

the system, and will likely carry on without a hitch while industrial society comes apart around them.

These three classes of technologies — the wholly dependent, the somewhat dependent, and the independent — have an uncomfortable similarity to the three categories used by battlefield medics in the process known as triage. Triage — the word comes from French and means "trying" or "testing" — is a care-rationing process used when the number of wounded overwhelms the people and resources available to treat them. Incoming wounded are sorted into three classes. The first consists of those who will die even if they get care. The second consists of those who will survive even if they receive no care. The third consists of those who will live if they get help, but will die without it. In a triage situation, all available resources go to the third category. When the need for care outruns available time and resources, this harsh but necessary logic maximizes the number of survivors.

The coming of deindustrial society will require us to approach technologies in much the same way. Technological triage requires more complex judgments than the battlefield variety, however. Not all technologies are of equal value for human survival; it won't do us any good to preserve video game technology, let's say, if by doing so we lose the ability to grow food. Some technologies necessarily depend on other technologies — firearms, for example, presuppose a certain level of metalworking ability. Finally, technological triage involves four categories, not three. There will be technologies that can't be saved no matter what we do, technologies that are certain to be saved even if we do nothing, and technologies that will be saved if we act and lost if we do not; there will also be technologies that have gone out of existence, but could be brought back and put into use if action is taken now.

Another difference, of course, is that we can begin the triage process on current and past technologies right now — and it's important that this process start soon. The more work people put into understanding the issues and sorting through potential technologies in advance, the less wasted effort and missed opportunities there are likely to be. In the case of technologies that have to be brought back from the heap of discarded tools our civilization has left behind it, starting now — when information and, in many cases, working examples of old technologies can still be located — could easily make the difference between success and failure.

The differences outlined earlier in this chapter between the slide rule and the pocket calculator offer a starting point for carrying out triage on today's technologies, but more precise issues need to be addressed as well. What sort of questions, then, need to be asked when wounded technologies start showing up at our imaginary triage station? The following list might do as a starting point for discussion.

1. *How long can it be fueled and maintained in a deindustrializing world?* The imminence of peak oil makes this point obvious, but there are twists that many people in the peak oil community may not have recognized. Declining production and rising costs of petroleum cut into the supply of lubricants, solvents, and plastics as well as fuels; and anything that needs any of these things in order to operate must either be adapted for an alternative source or land in history's junkyard. These same factors affect the whole supply chain for fuel, maintenance supplies, and spare parts, among many other things.

2. *How long can it be manufactured or replaced in a deindustrializing world?* This represents a much higher threshold than the previous question, since the capacity to manufacture complex technologies — for example, most of today's digital electronics — will likely be lost sooner than the inputs needed to keep them running. A whole class of technologies — call it "legacy tech" — falls between the two thresholds; these are machines that can be kept running for years or decades after they can no longer be made. The struggle to control various items of legacy tech may become a fruitful source of conflict as the deindustrial age proceeds down the curve of catabolic collapse.

3. *How long will it be useful in a deindustrializing world?* Many of the technologies we have today aren't useful even now — I defy anyone to give me a meaningful definition of "useful" that includes, say, dancing mechanical Santa Claus dolls — but many more have value only because they provide services to other technologies that will not be viable in an age of limits. When rising fuel costs, for example, bring down the curtain on the age of mass air travel, whole constellations of technologies currently needed to keep airlines and airports running will lose their reason for existence. Unless they have other uses, saving them would be pointless.

4. *How long will it take to become useful in a deindustrializing world?* The flip side of question 3 is that many technologies that survive today only as hobbies or museum pieces are likely to become valuable and even essential at some point along the curve of catabolic collapse. Consider the technologies needed to build, rig, and sail square-rigged wooden ships. Right now, they survive only in relic form, preserved by our society's fascination with its own past, but a century or two from now they could easily become the foundation of maritime trade networks like the ones that linked the continents in 1800. Steps taken now or in the near future to keep this "outdated" maritime technology viable on the downslope of Hubbert's peak could pay off big later on.

5. *How broad a set of human needs and other technologies can be supported by it?* Some technologies fill narrow niches, some fill broad ones. Organic agriculture can be used to produce food, herbal medicines, oil crops for fuel and lubricants, and a dizzying assortment of raw materials for craft and small-scale industry. This puts it in a different category from, say, lens grinding, which can make lenses and not much else. Both have value in their own contexts, but might reasonably be given different priorities in times of resource scarcity.

6. *How crucial a set of human needs and other technologies can be supported by it?* Some needs and technologies are more important

than others. The basic human essentials of food, drink, shelter, and safety outrank most other considerations. Technologies that provide these efficiently belong at the top of the triage list. This is another reason why organic agriculture deserves special attention in sorting out potential technologies for the deindustrial age — it can provide the raw materials for most of the core necessities. Beyond the basics, priority lists differ, as indeed they should. If it's necessary to choose one or the other, is the capacity to print books more or less important than the capacity to treat illnesses that herbs won't cure? Such questions need to be taken seriously as people begin the process of deciding what to save.

7. *What commitments follow from investing in it?* All technologies — without exception — have consequences and entail commitments. By investing in automobile technology nearly to the exclusion of all other transportation choices, for example, the United States and several of its allies committed themselves to maintaining the flow of cheap, abundant oil at all costs — a commitment that has landed them in a no-win situation in Iraq and made their national interests hostage to centuries-old religious and ethnic quarrels in a dozen different corners of the globe. Few other technologies entail commitments so disastrous, but every choice of technology closes some doors as it opens others. As we consider different models for the deindustrializing societies of the near future and the fully deindustrialized cultures further off, attention to the implied commitments of proposed technologies might keep us out of a variety of blind alleys.

All this implies, of course, that technologies exist to meet human needs, and not vice versa. The habit of mind that subordinates human values to the needs of technology is one of the strangest outgrowths of the mythic narrative of progress, and it needs to be outgrown as soon as possible. It's crucial to realize that in some cases — when a job doesn't actually need to be done, or when tech-nological means aren't the best way to do it — the best technology for the purpose is no technology at all. We'll return to this theme in the last chapter of this book.

Feeding the Deindustrial Future

One conclusion that follows from these points is that the techno-logical advances we consider most important today may not get the same rating from future generations. Ask people today what they think is the greatest scientific achievement of the 20th cen-tury and the answers will likely focus on the Apollo moon land-ings, computer technology, the discovery of the genetic code, or what have you. Past ages, though, were notoriously bad judges of the relative importance of the legacies they've left to the future, and ours will likely be no different.

In the Middle Ages, for example, scholastic theology was thought to be the crowning achievement of the human mind. On the other hand, Gothic cathedrals, the spectacular technological advances chronicled by Jean Gimpel in *The Medieval Machine*, and the English feudal laws that evolved into parliamentary gov-ernment and trial by jury were considered minor matters. Today, nobody outside the University of Chicago and a few conservative Catholic colleges pays the least attention to scholasticism, while Gothic architecture still shapes how we think of space and light; a good half of the machinery that surrounds us every day runs on principles evolved by the inventors of the clock and the windmill; and the political and legal systems of a majority of the world's na-tions come from that odd Saxon tribal custom, borrowed by Nor-man kings for their own convenience, of calling together a group of yeomen to discuss new laws or decide who committed a crime.

When it comes to the long-term value of a culture's accom-plishments, in other words, the future has the deciding vote. I don't pretend to know for certain how that vote will be cast. Still, I'm willing to risk a guess. A thousand, or two thousand, or ten thousand years from now, when people look back through the mists of time to the 20th century and talk about its achievements, the top of the list won't be moon landings, computers, or the double helix, much less the political and cultural ephemera that occupy so much attention just now. If I'm right, it will be something much humbler — and much more important.

In the first decades of the 20th century, Albert Howard, an English agronomist working in India, began experimenting with farming methods that focused on the health of the soil and its natural cycles.[12] Much of his inspiration came from traditional farming practices used in India, China, and Japan that had maintained and even improved soil fertility for centuries or millennia. Howard fused these practices with Western scientific agronomy as well as the results of his own experiments to create the first modern organic agriculture. Later researchers, notably Alan Chadwick in England and John Jeavons in America, combined Howard's discoveries with methods of intensive gardening developed in France not long before Howard began his work. Combining the result with the biodynamic system developed in the 1920s by Austrian philosopher Rudolf Steiner, Chadwick and Jeavons developed the system that is now the current state of the art in organic intensive farming.

The result of their work is potentially a revolution in humanity's relationship to the land and the biosphere as dramatic as the original agricultural revolution itself. To begin with, the new organic methods are astonishingly productive. Using them, it's possible to grow a spare but adequate vegetarian diet for one person on 1,000 square feet of soil.[13] (For those with math phobia, that's a patch of dirt 20' by 50', about the size of a small urban backyard, $\frac{1}{45}$ of a football field, or a bit less than $\frac{1}{43}$ of an acre — not much, in other words.) These yields require no fossil fuels, no chemical fertilizers or pesticides, and no soil additives other than compost made from vegetable waste and human manure. Hand tools powered by human muscle are the only technological requirements —

and yet organic methods of intensive production get yields per acre significantly higher than you can get with tractors and pesticides.

What makes organic farming even more of an achievement is that these yields are sustainable indefinitely. The core concept of organic agriculture is that healthy soil makes a healthy farm. Instead of treating soil like a sponge that needs to be filled with chemical nutrients, the organic method treats it as an ecosystem that will provide everything plants need so long as it's kept in balance. The insect pests and plant diseases that give conventional farmers so much trouble can be managed by fine-tuning the soil ecosystem, changing the timing and mix of plants, and introducing natural predators (name any organism you need to get rid of, and there's another organism that wants to eat it for you). Where conventional farming depletes the soil, requiring heavier applications of fertilizer and pesticides every season, organic methods produce improved soil, increased yields, and decreased pest problems year after year.

The third factor that makes today's organic methods revolutionary is their portability. Many traditional cultures around the world have worked out farming methods that are sustainable over the long term, but nearly all of those depend on specific environmental conditions and plant varieties. The growing methods practiced in the New Guinea highlands, for example, are brilliantly adapted to their native ecosystem and produce impressive yields, but they only work for the specific mix of food crops, weather and soil conditions, and ecological factors found where they evolved. Intensive organic farming, by contrast, was developed simultaneously in the very different ecosystems of England and northern California, and it has been put to use successfully in temperate, semiarid, and semitropical environments around the world. Like everything natural, it has its limits, but some 80% of the world's population lives in areas where it can be practiced.

Some people at the apocalyptic end of the peak oil community have argued that starvation and mass dieoff will ensue when today's petroleum-fueled agricultural system grinds to a halt and nothing takes its place. This is a good example of what I've called the "Y2K fallacy," because at least part of the solution is already in place. Rising prices of petroleum products and fertilizers, most of which are manufactured from natural gas, have already started to price chemical agriculture out of the market. At the same time, organic crops command premium prices. One unsurprising result has been the rapid spread of organic agriculture in most of the world's industrial nations. In the United States alone, more than 4 million acres were newly certified for organic production in 2005, a figure up more than 1 million acres from the year before.[14] The next round of energy crises may well see the chemical model of agriculture abandoned wholesale because organic methods can produce equal or better yields for less money — an equation even the most conservative farmer can understand.

The rise of organic agriculture suggests that in America, at least, the great agricultural challenge of the next century or so may not be producing food but rather getting it to people who need it. Very large cities may become difficult places to live in as the deindustrial age kicks into gear, precisely because there isn't enough farmland within easy transport range to feed their populations. On the other hand, most North American cities of half a million or less are close to agricultural land that could, in a pinch, be used to grow food intensively and feed the smaller population that will remain as declining public health takes its toll. What's needed is the framework of a distribution system around which this can take shape.

The good news is that this framework already exists; it's called the farmers market movement. The last three decades or so have seen farmers markets spread with remarkable speed across North America, from 340 markets nationwide in 1970 to 4,385 in 2006.[15] At these weekly markets, local farmers set up stalls and sell produce directly to local consumers, bypassing distributors and grocery chains. Like the slide rule or the haybox, it's a technology — a social technology, in this case — remembered from an earlier time, dusted off and put back to work to solve a contemporary problem. As fossil fuels become more expensive and the cost of long distance transport begins to cripple today's food distribution system, farmers markets are likely to become even more economically viable than they are today, taking over a steadily larger role in getting food from farm to table.

In many ways, the conjunction of organic agriculture and resurgent farmers markets provides a working model for a constructive approach to catabolic collapse. Systems that are economically viable as well as ecologically sustainable are the key to this approach. If people can earn a living by building the foundations for the deindustrial societies of the future, those foundations are a good deal more likely to get built.

The examples just given also show that under these conditions, the systems needed to manage the Long Descent can spring up with impressive speed. Forty years ago organic agriculture was the special interest of a small group of enthusiasts on the fringes of society, and the last of North America's farmers markets were fighting for survival against city governments that dismissed them as anachronisms. In the same way, recycling forty years ago was practiced by a tiny minority of environmentalists; today it is a way of life for most urban Americans and a growing fraction of the small town and rural population as well. Other systems needed to deal with the consequences of the deindustrial age will likely develop in the same way — if people are willing to commit the time, effort, and resources to make them happen.

How Not To Save Science

The tools and technologies discussed so far in this chapter represent one side of the heritage of our industrial and preindustrial past that would be worth saving. Another side, less tangible and thus potentially more vulnerable, comprises the knowledge gathered over the last three hundred years or so of the intellectual adventure of modern science. Now it's true that some elements of that knowledge might be better off lost — I'm not at all sure the far future really needs to know how to build nuclear warheads or synthesize nerve gas — but on the whole, the heritage of modern science forms one of the great triumphs of our civilization and deserves a shot at survival.

It's all the more impressive, in an age dominated by the myth of progress, that the challenge of preserving this heritage into the future has already been discussed in scientific circles. Most of that discussion has centered around a proposal made by ecologist James Lovelock in his 1998 essay "A Book for All Seasons."[16] Lovelock proposed that a panel of scientific experts be commissioned to write a book outlining everything modern science has learned about the universe, forming — in his words — "the scientific equivalent of the Bible." This book, he urges, ought then to be produced en masse on durable paper, so that some copies make it through the decline and fall of industrial society and reach the hands of future generations.

It's hard to think of a better proof that most scientists don't learn enough about the history of their own disciplines — or a better piece of evidence that they need to. A book of the sort Lovelock proposes would be a disaster for science. I don't simply present this claim as a matter of opinion. The experiment has been tried before, and the results were, to put it mildly, not good.

In the twilight years of Roman civilization in western Europe, as the old institutions of classical learning were giving way to the Dark Ages, Isidore of Seville (560–636) — a Christian bishop and theologian in Spain (who was recently named by the Vatican as the patron saint of the Internet) — compiled a book along the same lines as the one Lovelock envisions. Titled *Etymologiae* (*Etymologies*), it was the world's first encyclopedia, a summary of what Isidore's contemporaries defined as useful knowledge, and it was a huge success by the standards of the time.[17] The most popular general reference work in medieval libraries, it was still so widely respected when printing became available that it saw ten print editions between 1470 and 1530.

During the Dark Ages, the *Etymologiae* served a useful purpose as a compendium of general knowledge. Over the longer term, though, its effects were far less positive. Because Isidore's book quickly came to be seen as the be-all and end-all of learning, other books — many of which would have been much more useful to the renaissance of learning that spread through Europe after the turn of the millennium — were allowed to decay, or had their parchment pages recycled to produce more copies of the *Etymologiae*.

Worse, the reverence given to Isidore's work gave a great deal of momentum to the medieval belief that the best way to learn about nature was to look something up in an old book. That same reverence came to be applied to the works of Aristotle and other Greek classics after they were translated from the Arabic, beginning in the 12th century. The resulting conviction that scientific research ought to consist of quoting passages from ancient authorities succeeded in hamstringing natural science for centuries. It took the social convulsions of the 16th and 17th centuries to finally break Aristotle's iron grip on scientific thought in the Western world and make it acceptable for people to learn from nature directly.

This could all too easily happen with Lovelock's "scientific equivalent of the Bible." Like Isidore's encyclopedia, a modern compendium of scientific theories about the world would inevitably contain inaccurate information — today's scientists are no more omniscient than those of 50 years ago, when continental drift was still considered crackpot pseudoscience, or 110 years ago, when Einstein and the quantum physicists hadn't yet proved that the absolute space and uniform time of Newtonian cosmology were as imaginary as Oz. Because the compendium Lovelock imagines would be a collection of knowledge, rather than a guide to scientific practice, it would teach people that the way to learn about nature was to look facts up in a book, rather than paying attention to what was actually happening in front of their noses —

and it might well ensure that, in a time that had limited resources for the preservation of books, copies of a book of scientific doctrines could be preserved at the expense of, say, the last remaining copy of Newton's *Principia Mathematica*, Darwin's *The Origin of Species*, or some other scientific classic that would offer much more to the future.

A book of scientific doctrines of the sort Lovelock proposes could also ensure that the most important dimension of science itself would be lost. Science, it's crucial to remember, is not a set of teachings about the universe, however accurate those might be. At its core, science is a system of practical logic, a set of working rules that allow hypotheses to be tested against experience so that they can be discarded if they're false. That set of rules isn't perfect or flawless, but it's the best method for investigating nature that our species has invented so far, and it's worth far more to the future than any compendium of currently accepted scientific opinions.

In his essay, Lovelock imagines a survivor in some postcollapse society faced with a cholera epidemic, equipped with nothing but a book on aromatherapy. It's a compelling image. What, though, if the survivor has to deal with a new disease — one that hasn't yet jumped to human beings from its original animal host, let's say — or an old disease that has mutated into a new form? What if the antibiotics and treatments we use today have become useless due to the spread of antibiotic resistance in microbes? A textbook focused on existing knowledge circa 2008 might not offer much help. Nature is constantly changing. Science as a method of inquiry can keep track of those changes; science as a set of doctrines can't.

A book that might actually succeed in saving science for the future would be a very different book from the one Lovelock has envisioned. Rather than projecting the infallibility and misplaced reverence that a phrase like "the scientific equivalent of the Bible" suggests, this new book would present the scientific method as an open-ended way of questioning nature, providing enough practical tips and examples to help readers learn how to create their own experiments and ask their own questions. It would treat its readers in the present and future alike as participants in the process of science, not simply consumers of the knowledge it produces. The role of participant is not one that many scientists today are comfortable seeing conferred on laypeople, but if today's science is going to be saved for the future, getting past that discomfort is one of the first and least negotiable requirements.

Whatever its flaws, though, Lovelock's proposal has at least had the positive effect of focusing attention on one of the biggest challenges of the deindustrial age — preserving as much as possible of the cultural heritage of the last six thousand years or so. That's a tall order because nearly all of that heritage is brutally vulnerable to an age of decline. Nearly all books printed in the last century and a half are on high-acid paper, which gradually turns back to sawdust; librarians are already struggling to preserve collections of disintegrating 19th-century books. CDs and DVDs, like other electronic media, have even shorter lifespans; moreover, they won't even be playable in a low-tech future. During the most challenging parts of the transition to the deindustrial age, when people are struggling to survive on a day-by-day basis, literature, music, art, and science may not rank very high on their list of priorities anyway.

Any effort toward cultural survival, in other words, will demand ruthless sorting. Today's sprawling libraries will need careful winnowing to sort out collections small enough to be copied by hand if it comes to that. Musical forms that can be passed on as living traditions will be more likely to make it, which means folk music has a better chance than Beethoven's Ninth Symphony. A huge amount of our present cultural heritage will inevitably be lost; the job at hand is to try to make sure that the best possible selection gets through.

Those cultural, artistic, and spiritual traditions that will be sustainable and relevant in a future of modest energy supplies and limited resources belong at the top of the list of what to save. These traditions will be crucial during the crisis periods of the catabolic collapse process, when they will provide desperately needed balance to the grim realities of a disintegrating society. They will be even more crucial in the long term. Just as the creative minds of the early Middle Ages drew much of their inspiration from classical poetry and philosophy that had been preserved by Irish monks through the worst of the intervening years,[18] cultural legacies handed down over the decades and centuries to come will form crucial parts of the inheritance on which our successor societies will build.

Building Tomorrow's Societies

One core concept that has to be grasped to make use of any of the possibilities mentioned in this chapter, however, is the rule that the community, not the individual, is the basic unit of human survival. History shows that local communities can flourish while empires fall around them; the Chinese towns and villages mentioned earlier in this book have remained viable while dynasties rose and fell, and they have countless parallels around the world. Any attempt to bring today's local communities through the approaching crises, however, depends on having viable communities in the first place, and viable communities are in short supply just now.

The reason for this shortage deserves discussion. In the second half of the twentieth century, most of the industrial world abandoned modes of social organization based on local communities in favor of mass society.[19] Most of the fragmented communities that remain depend on mass society not only for economic survival but for the subtler but equally important support that comes from common goals and worldviews. Many of the social changes that have made viable communities scarce will have to be undone in a hurry, so that local society can survive and flourish as the larger systems of society disintegrate. The rebuilding of civil society in the industrial world has already begun, but it still faces many challenges. At least three factors in short supply need to be brought on line for communities to have a good chance at survival in the deindustrializing world of the near future.

1. **A community needs local organizations.**

   Our present culture here in North America has discarded most of the local organizations it once had, in favor of a mass society where individuals deal directly with huge government and corporate institutions. This has to be reversed. Some recent moves toward reinvigorating civil society have been made, and these are a step in the right direction, but much more needs to be done. One often-neglected but useful resource, mentioned earlier in this book, consists of the old fraternal orders — the Masons, the Odd Fellows, the Grange, and so on — which once included in their memberships more than 50% of adult North Americans. Many of these organizations still exist, and they're far less exclusive than people outside them tend to think. Joining such an organization, or some other local community group, and helping to revive local civil society is a crucial step that will provide your community with essential networks of cooperation and mutual aid in difficult times.

2. **A community needs a core of people who know how to do without fossil fuel inputs.**

   An astonishing number of people, especially in the educated middle class, have no practical skills whatsoever when it comes to growing and preparing food, making clothing, and providing other basic necessities. An equally astonishing number are unable to travel more than a mile or two by any means that doesn't involve burning fossil fuels — and how many people in the developed world can light a fire without matches or a lighter? Survival skills such as organic gardening, low-tech medicine, basic hand crafts, and the like need to be learned and practiced now, while there's time to do so. Similarly, those people who cut their fossil fuel consumption drastically now — for example, by getting rid of their cars and using public transit or bicycles for commuting — will be better prepared for the inevitable shortages.

3. **A community needs to be able to meet basic human requirements.**

Above all else it must be able to obtain food. The ability to feed people without wrecking the Earth will be the bottom line for human survival in the future. The revolutionary advances of modern organic farming offer one way to meet this set of needs. Other approaches such as permaculture also have a wealth of valuable methods and perspectives to offer. The more completely such methods are preserved and expanded, the better off we and our descendants will be.

The ability to meet basic human requirements also calls for the establishment of local networks of production and distribution, especially of food and other necessities. Here, farmers markets, food co-ops, and the like are of central importance. Functioning networks of exchange and food distribution will become the frameworks around which new social forms coalesce; it's a routine event in the aftermath of collapsing civilizations. Helping to support these right now, and in the years to come, will ensure that some of them make it through the crises of the next century and are in place, in some form, for successor societies.

The availability of a range of ecologically balanced, renewably powered, sustainable technologies will also be of crucial importance in establishing these local networks. Food is the foundation, but the more technically adept a community is, the more likely it is to survive and grow. We live in a society in which most people have totally neglected their own innate abilities in favor of ersatz mechanical imitations. Even our schoolchildren use pocket calculators instead of learning how to add and subtract. All this has to be reversed as soon as possible, at least by those people who hope not only to survive the approaching waves of crisis but to contribute to the great project of making a better future.

Those people who can use their own hands and minds to make tools, grow food, brew beer, treat illnesses, generate modest amounts of electricity from sun and wind, and the like, will have a major survival advantage over those who can't. Those communities that focus their efforts on helping members achieve skills like these, and pass them on to others, will become the seedbeds of the sustainable societies of the future. Whatever they preserve and develop will not need to be laboriously reinvented by their descendants.

None of these things can be left until the first wave of crises hits, though. During the last two centuries, the quickest way to prosper was to ride the wave of progress, using more energy, more resources, and more technology than your competitors. For the next two centuries, the quickest way to prosper will stand this rule on its head. Those who accept the reality of decline and get by on less energy, fewer resources, and less technology than their competitors will win out. Now, before the immense knowledge base of industrial society begins to come apart, is the best time to look for ways of living that use less of what we won't have soon.

Organic farming, again, is an excellent case in point. The extraordinarily effective methods used by today's organic farmers may turn out to be our civilization's greatest gift to the future, but only if they survive the approaching age of decline. Today they're covered in detail in dozens of readily available books. Whether that will be true in a hundred years depends, at least in part, on what we do right now. If people come to terms with the future now, and begin assembling and using skills and lifeways our deindustrial descendants can follow, the approaching age of decline can be made less traumatic than it will otherwise be.

The
Spiritual
Dimension

One of the things that gives the mythology of progress its emotional power is the circular logic at its center. From within the worldview defined by the narrative of progress, what's new is better than whatever it replaces simply because it's newer; whatever our technology happens to be good at doing is the most important thing to do, and whatever our technology does poorly, or doesn't do at all, doesn't really need to be done. Thus the much-repeated claim that our technological worldview is bound to triumph because it works better than any other approach begs the question. Modern industrial technology does certain things better than any other suite of tools we've got, to be sure, but it's by no means a given that the things it does best are the things that we most need to do as the industrial age winds down.

There's an old saying that if the only tool you have is a hammer, everything around you starts to look like a nail. This variety of mental blindness — the habit of redefining our problems to fit the solutions we happen to have on hand, rather than looking for solutions that fit the problems we're actually facing — pervades current discussions about the future of industrial society.

It's crucial to remember, too, that there's no such thing as "technology" in the singular, only technologies in the plural. The notion that technology is a single, monolithic thing is a convenient bit of mystification that is used to hide the fact that our society, like all others, picks and chooses among available technological options, implementing some and neglecting others. This fact needs hiding because most of these choices are made by influential factions of America's political class for their own private profit, very often at the expense of the rest of us. Wrapping the process in a smokescreen of impersonal inevitability is a convenient way to keep awkward questions from being raised via what remains of the democratic institutions of an earlier age.

In a broader sense, of course, technologies of some sort will be an inevitable part of whatever society comes into being out of the ruins of the industrial world. Toolmaking is as natural to human beings as singing is to finches. Every human culture across space and time has had its own technologies, each of which draws on available resources to meet culturally recognized needs in culturally desirable ways. It's habitual in our own culture to think of the particular suite of technologies we've come up with as not only better than anybody else's, but more advanced, more progressive. Think about what these two phrases imply, and you'll see how they derive from and feed into the core narrative of the myth of progress — the way of telling the story of our species that turns every other culture and every past technology into a stepping-stone on the way to us. From within this narrative, all earlier technologies are simply imperfect attempts to achieve what we've got.

Again, this is mystification, and it serves a socially necessary purpose in a culture where talking about the goals and values of specific technologies is taboo. The frequently repeated claim that "technology is value-free" is fatuous nonsense, but as long as we think about tools and techniques as a single thing called "technology," it's also plausible nonsense. In reality, of course, individual technologies embody the values and goals of their designers, and they are selected by users on the basis of the technology's relationship to values and goals. Look at the suite of technologies used by a person or a culture, and it's an easy matter to divine the values that person or that culture holds and the goals they pursue. This is unmentionable in our culture because, among other reasons, the values and goals our technologies reveal to the world are a very long distance indeed from the ones we claim to embrace.

Thus it's crucial that any meaningful discussion about the future finds its way out of debates about technology in the abstract and addresses at least two other, more specific questions:

- First, which technologies, out of the many available options, will still be useful as we wake up from the dream of perpetual progress and start down the far side of Hubbert's peak?
- Second, what are the values and goals that might usefully govern our technologies — and the rest of our society — as the deindustrial age dawns around us?

The first of these questions was central to Chapter 5 of this book; the second forms the core of the present chapter. The latter issue can't be settled, or even meaningfully discussed, without asking hard questions about some of the most basic assumptions of the modern world. It's one thing to talk about which technology to use for a given project, but it's quite another to ask whether the project itself is worth doing and, if so, whether applying some form of technology is the best way to go about it at all. Questions like these may start out in the most pragmatic terms, but they lead inescapably into the dimension of human thought that our society is least comfortable discussing: the dimension of spirituality.

After the Prosthetic Society

It's often said that generals prepare to fight the last war rather than the next one, and the same thing deserves to be said at least as much of societies in general. In every age, most people believe that the current state of affairs can be counted on to keep on going forever, and they plan for the future on the assumption that it will be just like the present, only more so. Political, economic, and cultural institutions do the same thing, and too often spiritual traditions — which have the social function of pointing out inconvenient realities — get caught up in the same way of thinking. Then the future comes along and turns out different, and everyone who thought they knew what was coming ends up sitting in the wreckage wondering what happened.

Prophecies about the future made on the basis of conventional wisdom just don't wear very well. When I was growing up in the suburban America of the 1960s, everyone knew that by 2000 we'd have manned bases on the Moon and a Hilton hotel in orbit. Back here on the ground, our homes would be run by nuclear power that would literally be too cheap to meter; you'd just pay a monthly hookup fee and use all the juice you wanted. The decaying inner cities would be replaced by huge, terraced megastructures or Paolo Soleri's gargantuan arcologies, while Sealab (does anybody remember Sealab any more?) was going to be the prototype for whole cities under the sea. It would have been quite a world, but somehow it got lost in the 1970s energy crises, and we ended up instead with SUVs, metastasizing suburban sprawl, and the short-term political gimmicks that papered over fossil fuel depletion for twenty years and lost us our best bet of getting through the next century without some form of collapse.

So it may not be out of line to suggest that many current ideas about where we're headed are as misplaced as the atomic Utopia of 1960s futurists turned out to be. One trend usually pointed out as the wave of the future seems particularly likely to end up in history's compost heap in much the same way: the replacement of human abilities with electronic and mechanical devices.

This mechanization of everyday life has become a huge trend, especially, but not only among the middle classes of the industrial world, who set fashions for the rest of the planet. Think of something that people used to do, and the salesman at your local mall can probably sell you something to do it for you. My favorite example is the breadmaking machine. A hundred years ago nearly every family baked its own bread; it's a simple, enjoyable task that can be done with Stone Age technology. Now, though, you can drop hundreds of dollars on a countertop machine with buttons and flashing lights that will do it for you.

Similarly, people used to entertain themselves by singing and playing musical instruments, but now we have CDs and iPods. They used to exercise by taking walks in the park, but now we have treadmill machines. In place of memories, we have Palm Pilots; in place of imagination, we have TVs, and so on. At the zenith of the mechanizing trend came that bizarre figure of the late 20th century, the suburban couch potato, whose sole activity outside of work hours and commuting was sitting on a couch clicking a baroque array of remote controls while delivery drivers came to the door with an endless supply of consumer products ordered, bought, and paid for online.

In effect, the 1980s and 1990s witnessed the creation of a prosthetic culture. A prosthetic is an artificial device that replaces a human function. They are, of course, valuable technologies for those who have lost the use of the function in question; if you've lost a leg via accident or illness, for example, an artificial leg that lets you walk again is a very good thing to have. Still, when a society starts convincing people to saw off their own legs so businesses can sell them artificial ones, something has gone decidedly wrong — and that's not too far from the situation we're in today.

There are at least two drastic problems with our prosthetic culture. First, the abandonment of human abilities in favor of mechanical replacements has no little impact on who we are and what we can be. As E. M. Forster pointed out in his harrowing 1909 short story "The Machine Stops," it's hard to imagine that anyone's highest potential as a human being can be achieved in a lifestyle that consists solely of sitting in a chair and pushing buttons. On the other hand, Forsteresque remote-control dystopias are about as likely now as those orbital hotels and undersea cities because the basis for the couch potato lifestyle is trickling away as I write these words.

The driving force behind the prosthetic culture of the 20th century's last decades was the final hurrah of the age of cheap oil. The manipulations that crashed the price of petroleum in the early 1980s made energy cheaper than it has ever been in human history. At several points in the 1980s and 1990s, oil dropped to $10 a barrel, its lowest price ever, once inflation is factored in. During those years, oil was the single largest component in the industrial world's energy mix, and the "gateway resource" that gave access to all other forms of energy: the machines that mine coal, drill for natural gas, build hydroelectric dams, and so on, are all powered by oil. The plunging price of oil thus pulled the bottom out from under the cost of energy as a whole, and it put the world's industrial societies into a historically unprecedented situation. For the first (and probably only) time in history, it was cheaper to build a machine to do almost everything than to have a human being do it.

In some ways, of course, this was simply the culmination of a process that got started at the beginning of the Industrial Revolution, and then went into overdrive with the birth of the petroleum economy in the years just before the First World War. Earlier efforts to replace human skills with machines had to deal with much more limited and expensive energy supplies, which forced a reliance on economies of scale; machine-made bread, for instance, had to be made in big factories (rather than home breadmaking machines) to keep costs within reach of most consumers. The pinnacle of the age of cheap oil made energy so abundant and so inexpensive, at least in the more privileged industrial countries, that it was briefly possible to ignore economies of scale and make each middle-class person the beneficiary of a microfactory designed to produce, or at least deliver, whatever goods and services were wanted.

All this, though, depended on cheap energy, and with today's plateauing of world oil production and the approach of inevitable declines in the near future, the prosthetic culture of the last few decades is headed for the recycling bin of history. The reasons for this have nothing to do with the romanticism of which people who question today's technological triumphalism are so often accused. Rather, they're a matter of cold, hard economics.

The modern faith in progress has its blind spots, and one of the most pervasive is the tendency for people to believe that the present arrangement of society is somehow inevitable and the natural result of all those centuries of progress. To this way of thinking, for example, it seems inevitable that every culture will end up relying on machines rather than people for tasks like data processing, simply because that's the way we do things. Behind the grand facade of progress, though, lies a simple economic fact: in an age of abundant fossil fuel energy, it's cheaper — a lot cheaper — to build and power a machine to do something than it is to train and employ a human being to do the same thing. As long as that equation holds, the only constraint that limits how many people get replaced by machines is the sophistication of the machines, and so the same equation drives technological advances. Because machines powered by cheap fossil fuels do things at lower costs than people do, investment in new technology tends to pay for itself. The last three centuries of the Western world's history show what happens when this process goes into high gear.

The whole process depends, though, on having a cheap, abundant source of mechanical and electrical energy. For the last three centuries, fossil fuels have provided that, but the lesson of peak oil is that this was a temporary situation, possible only because human beings found and exploited the huge but finite reserves of cheap energy in the Earth's crust. Everything based on that fact is subject to change — including the equation that makes machine labor cheaper than human labor.

In a world where fossil fuels are expensive and scarce, the equation works the other way. Modern machines require very

829473702865716094

specialized and resource-intensive inputs of energy and materials, and if those aren't available within tight specifications, the machines don't work. Human beings, by contrast, can be kept happy and productive with very simple, generally available resources — food, drink, warmth, shelter, companionship, and mental stimulation, all of which have wide tolerances and a great deal of room for substitution. In a society that has to operate within the energy budget provided by renewable resources, ordinary human needs are a good deal less challenging to provide than the pure, concentrated, and precisely controlled inputs needed by complex machines.

This disparity explains why the steam turbine, invented in ancient Greek times by Hero of Alexandria, remained a philosopher's toy, and why the brilliant mechanical inventions of medieval China never caused the sort of social and economic transformations the Industrial Revolution launched in the modern West. Machines existed, but without the energy resources to power them — more exactly, without the realization that coal, oil, and natural gas can be turned into mechanical energy if you have the right kind of machine — human labor was more economical, and so the machines languished. In the deindustrial world of the future, when human labor will again be less expensive than mechanical energy, counting on machines to maintain some semblance of today's prosthetic society may turn out to be an expensive mistake; focusing on human potential may be a better option.

All this suggests that current visions of the future, and the policies based on them, are in desperate need of a rethink. The decades to come will see many things that are now done by machines handed back over to human beings for the eminently pragmatic reason that it will again be cheaper to feed, house, clothe, and train a human being to do those things than it will be to make, fuel, and maintain a machine to do them. How many things? That depends on how much renewable energy capacity gets brought online before production rates of oil and natural gas start slipping down the steep slopes of Hubbert's peak.

In a worst-cast scenario in which nothing significant is done until major crises start to hit (and in the United States especially, we're uncomfortably close to that scenario right now), energy shortages could be severe enough that during the worst phases of crisis, essentially everything will have to be done with human labor alone. In any realistic future, however, old skills are likely to be in high demand again. Professions that involve doing useful things with one's hands, brain, and a relatively simple muscle-powered toolkit should be high on any list of hot career tracks in the 21st century.

The Butlerian Future

One of the ironies of this situation is that science fiction, the branch of modern literature most often caught up in the uncritical celebration of progress, has more than once worked through the consequences of the equation just discussed. Now it's true that science fiction has a very mixed track record for predicting the future, and quite a few of the major trends of the last half century were missed entirely by science fiction's would-be prophets. Manned landings on the moon were a staple of science fiction from Jules Verne until Apollo 11, yet nobody in the SF scene even guessed at the immense cultural impact that television coverage of that first lunar landing would turn out to have. The thought that the Apollo flights would turn out to be, not the beginning of a golden age of space exploration, but an extravagant gesture too costly to push further out into the solar system, would have been rejected out of hand in science fiction's own golden age between the two World Wars.

Still, it's when science fiction isn't actually trying to anticipate our immediate future that its predictions often prove the most prescient. Though it anticipated all too much of today's online culture, the E. M. Forster story mentioned earlier in this chapter wasn't an attempt to foresee the Internet; Forster described his imagined future as "a counter-blast to one of the early heavens of H. G. Wells,"[1] and he used it mostly to talk about the downside of his own culture's obsession with ideas as a substitute for lived experience. In the same way, a science fiction novel widely considered to be one of the greatest works in the genre — Frank Herbert's sprawling classic *Dune* — doesn't claim to talk about the near future of our own society, but several of its central themes are likely to make the transition from speculative fiction to hard reality in the decades ahead of us.

An important element of the backstory in *Dune* was the Butlerian Jihad, a massive and violent popular movement against computer technology that took place centuries before the events in Herbert's novel. "Once," one character in the book explains to another, "men turned their thinking over to machines in the hope that this would set them free. But that only permitted other men with machines to enslave them." [2] In the aftermath of the Butlerian Jihad, the human race went down a different path. As the same character comments a bit later in the same conversation: "The Great Revolt took away a crutch...It forced human minds to develop. Schools were started to train human functions."

By the time *Dune* opens, human beings fill many of the roles now entrusted to machines. Mentats, people trained in mnemonic and analytic skills who function as living computers, handle data processing; struggles between major power blocs employ assassins and highly trained special forces rather than massed military technologies; secret societies such as the Bene Gesserit sisterhood pursue disciplines of mind-body mastery that give them astonishing powers over themselves and other people as well.

Under present circumstances, mind you, a Butlerian Jihad is about as likely as a resumption of the Punic Wars. Even radical neoprimitivists who think we all ought to go back to hunting and gathering rely on websites and podcasts to get their message out. Still, Herbert may turn out to be a prophet after all; there's a real chance that we may find ourselves backing into a Butlerian future without intending anything of the kind. The same economic forces that will make human labor more viable than mechanical prosthetics will open a door through which some of the possibilities Herbert suggested might be accessible.

It's not often noticed that the sort of exotic labor performed by Herbert's characters is well within the range of human capacity. The skills of *Dune*'s Mentats, for example, have a close equivalent in the art of memory, a system of mnemonics first devised in ancient Greece and passed on via classical Roman schools of rhetoric to the Middle Ages and the Renaissance.[3] Students of the art learned to encode material to be memorized in the form of visual images and to file them in mental matrices of various kinds that allowed instant recall.

Adepts of the art accomplished feats of memorization that stagger the modern imagination. Peter of Ravenna, a renowned exponent of the art in the 14th century, and the author of one of the most widely read memory treatises of the age, was famous in his time for having the entire body of medieval canon law, word for word, at his mental fingertips.[4] Could similar mental disciplines replace at least some of the functions of today's computer technology once catabolic collapse puts modern data processing out of reach? This is likely to be a more viable option than trying to maintain our current technologies as the resources needed to build and power them slip away from beneath our feet.

In the process of creating a prosthetic society over the last three hundred years, we have vastly expanded our technological capacities at the cost of systematically neglecting the potentials within our own bodies and minds. The body-mind disciplines worked out in other cultures over the centuries, or practiced in subcultures within the industrial world itself, could become important resources for the deindustrial age. If we have the imagination to let go of the monkey trap that fastens us to a purely technological approach to life, we can see these traditions as resources rather than irrelevancies.

The ideologies of the industrial age either devalued human potential in favor of the possibilities opened up by fossil-fuel-powered

machines, or they reacted against this sort of thinking by glorify-
ing whatever human beings could do that the machines of any
given time couldn't do. The 19th century clash between industrial
triumphalism and its Romantic opposition still defines most of
the terms in which we think of machines, human beings, and their
interactions today. Herbert's imagination leapt beyond this clash
to offer a glimpse of what we might be capable of if we pursued human potential with as much enthusiasm as today's engineers push
the limits of machines. In a world where energy-intensive high
technologies may not be supportable for much longer, Herbert's
glimpse into a possible future is worth thinking about.

     Herbert's novel also places spirituality at the center of this vi-
sion of expanded human possibilities, and this is only fair. The
skilled professions that will have to be revived in the deindustrial
age treat human potential as means, but spirituality treats the fulfillment of human potential as an end in itself, the proper goal of
human life. As the prosthetic society fades into memory, ways of
life that focus our attention on goals we can reach without trash-
ing the planet are likely to prove more useful than those modern
belief systems that treat the accumulation of consumer gewgaws
as the ultimate goal of human existence. The world's spiritual traditions offer a rich selection of such lifeways, and as the deindustrial age dawns around us, they may prove to be the most relevant
force of all.

Magic and the Enlightenment

The idea that spirituality might have anything useful to impart to
the future can, of course, be counted on to offend a sizeable seg-
ment of today's population. Our culture insists that modern scientific methods of solving problems rendered all other methods
obsolete, and it upholds this claim with the same conviction that
ran through the religious dogmas of past ages. Yet this declara-
tion of faith begs questions on a far deeper level because scientific
methods are only really well suited to certain kinds of questions

relating to the ways matter and energy interact — and these questions aren't as relevant to the current predicament of industrial society as they sometimes seem.

Peak oil is a case in point. What happens to today's industrial economy when world petroleum production peaks and begins its long decline will likely have very little to do with how matter and energy interact. The forces that will take the lead in the opening phases of the deindustrial age will be political, cultural, and psychological, not scientific. About these issues the methods of the scientist and the engineer have very little useful to say, and most of what they do have to say was drowned out decades ago by the louder voices of political opportunism and middle-class privilege.

In the same way, the technical issues of the approaching deindustrial transition were either solved long ago or could have been solved readily with modest investments in research and development. What could *not* be solved by scientific methods is the problem of finding the motivating factors and the political will to get these solutions put into place. Since this latter problem could not be solved by scientific methods, in turn, it has not been solved at all. This is the downside of the superlative technological efficiency of our age: those things we can't do with our machines, or with the ways of thinking that we evolved to manage our machines, are for all practical purposes beyond our reach.

Thus, discussions about how to respond to peak oil, when these have not simply been exercises in denial or utopian fantasy, have tended to focus on finding ways to redefine the issues in technical terms so they can be dealt with by technical methods. We hear endless talk about finding new ways to fuel our cars, and very little about the tangled and dysfunctional human motives that make it seem logical to us to ghettoize our homes, worksites, and marketplaces at such distances from one another that a preposterously inefficient system of freeways, roads, and automobiles has to be used to bridge the distances among them. It's all very reminiscent of the old fable about the drunkard who dropped his keys in a dark street and went to look for them under the streetlight half a block away, since there, at least, he could see what he was doing.

There's a rich irony, in other words, in the common dismissal of the lessons of spirituality as "magical thinking," because magical thinking is exactly the form of human thought that deals with the realm of motivations, values, and goals that technical and scientific thinking handle so poorly. Americans dream of living in suburbs not because suburbs have any particular grace — most of them have all the worst features of cities and rural areas, while lacking the amenities of either — but because the modern suburban house, surrounded by its protective moat of grass, is a magical symbol brimful of potent cultural meanings. Americans drive preposterously oversized and overpowered cars, not because these are better than smaller and more sensible vehicles in any objective sense, but because they magically symbolize the freedom and power most Americans long ago surrendered to the cultural machinery of a mass society. For that matter, the hallucinated wealth that keeps our economy churning away with the mad single-mindedness of some legendary goblin consists of sheer enchantment, with even less substance behind it than the moonbeams and fairy dust of a child's wonder tale.

To speak of these issues in terms of magic is not, by the way, just a metaphor. Dion Fortune, one of the premier magical theorists of the 20th century, defined magic as the art and science of causing changes in consciousness at will.[5] It's predictable that a society fixated on seeing its own technology as the be-all and end-all of human achievement would misunderstand magic as a kind of failed physical technology, but that predictability makes modern attitudes about magic no less mistaken. This is hardly the place for a detailed discussion of magic, but for present purposes magic can be seen as the use of psychologically potent symbolism to influence consciousness and, through consciousness, the universe as we experience it. The advertising campaigns that seduce so many people into buying, say, fizzy brown sugar water, by associating it with symbols of happiness, self-esteem, or love, are good examples of magic at work — a debased magic, force-fitted into the manipulative mold of physical technology, but magic nonetheless.[6]

In recent years I've watched people in the peak oil community shake their heads in bafflement at the way that so many people seem to be sleepwalking toward the abyss, oblivious to the signs of imminent crisis all around them. Many of these reactions come from people who have no knowledge of magic and who wrinkle their noses in disgust at the mere mention of the word — yet they frequently use words like "trance" and "spell" in their discussions. The crucial insight toward which they are moving, it seems to me, is that attempts to change the course of industrial civilization without changing the narratives and symbols that guide it on its way are doomed to failure; at the same time, those narratives and symbols cannot be changed effectively with the toolkit that peak oil advocates have used up to this point. Behind this difficulty lies a much vaster predicament — the failure of the Enlightenment project of rebuilding human civilization on the foundations of reason.

The Enlightenment (for those of my readers who received an American public school education — which in matters of history, at least, amounts to no real education at all) was an 18th century movement in European thought that laid most of the intellectual foundations for the modern world. The leading lights of the movement argued that the transformations that Galileo, Newton, and their peers made in the sciences needed to be made in the realms of social, political, and economic life as well. To them, the traditional ideologies that then framed European society amounted to one vast, festering mass of medieval superstition that was centuries past its pull date. Voltaire's famous outburst against the Catholic church — *Écrasez l'infâme!* ("Chuck the wretched thing!") — gave voice to a generation's revulsion against a worldview that in their minds had become all too closely bound to bigotry and autocracy.

Mind you, there was quite a bit of truth to the charge. The upper classes of 18th century Europe had been as strongly affected

by the Scientific Revolution's disenchantment of the world as anyone else, and in their hands, traditional ways of thinking that once
wove a bond of common interest among people of different classes
turned into abstractions veiling brutal injustice. Like so many social critics, though, the thinkers of the Enlightenment combined a
clear if one-sided view of the social problems of their day with un-
workably utopian proposals for their solution. They argued that
once superstition was dethroned and public education became
universal, rational self-interest and dispassionate scientific analysis would take charge, leading society progressively toward ever
better social conditions.

If this sounds familiar, it should. The ideology of the Enlightenment swept all before it, forcing even the most diehard reac-
tionaries to phrase their dissent in terms the Enlightenment itself
defined. That same ideology remains the common currency of
social, economic, political, and religious thought in the Western
world to this day. Though the myth of progress provided it with
its most important narrative, it quickly evolved its own apocalyptic myths; some of these, like the narrative of Marxism, appealed
to those who thought that the Enlightenment was not moving fast
enough, while others, like the narrative of radical conservatism,
appealed to those who thought the Enlightenment was moving
too fast and in the wrong direction.

One of the consequences of the Enlightenment's revolution in
myth is our habit of producing rational plans for social improvement — a habit that spawned the torrent of peak oil solutions
on the market today. Since Voltaire's time, the idea that building
a better social mousetrap will cause the world to beat a path to
one's door has pervaded our civilization. The irony, of course, is
that neither in Voltaire's time nor in ours has social change actually happened that way. The triumph of the Enlightenment itself
did not happen because the social ideas circulated by its proponents were that much better than those of their rivals. It happened because the core mythic narrative of the Enlightenment,

the myth of progress, proved to be more emotionally powerful than its rivals.

The resulting mismatch between our rationalist assumptions and the myths and symbols that still shape our behavior defines a faultline running through the middle of the modern mind. On the one hand, our economists treat human beings as rational actors making choices to maximize their own economic benefit. On the other hand, the same companies that hire those economists also pay for advertising campaigns that use the raw materials of myth and magic to encourage people to act against their own best interests, whether it's a matter of buying overpriced fizzy sugar water or the much more serious matter of continuing to support the unthinking pursuit of business as usual in the teeth of approaching disaster. The language of rational self-interest and dispassionate scientific analysis itself has been incorporated into exactly the sort of mythic narrative it attempts to dismiss from serious consideration.

The crux of the problem, as I've suggested throughout this book, is that human thought is mythic by its very nature. We think with myths as inevitably as we see with eyes and eat with mouths. Thus, any attempt to bring about significant social change must start from the mythic level, with an emotionally powerful and symbolically meaningful narrative, or it will go nowhere. The founders of the Enlightenment recognized this and brought about one of the great intellectual revolutions of Western history by harnessing the power of myth in the service of their project. The very nature of their legacy, though, has made it much harder for others to recognize the role of myth in social change.

Thus it's not accidental that the great storytellers of recent history, the figures who catalyzed massive changes in the world by the creative use of myth, have mostly come from the fringes of the Western cultural mainstream. Two examples are particularly worth citing here. The first is Mohandas Gandhi, who broke the grip of the British Empire on India by retelling the myth of

European colonialism so powerfully that even the colonial powers fell under the spell of his story. He accomplished this by drawing on his own Hindu culture, as well as his Western education, to
pose a challenge to the reigning narratives of the West that Western people had no way to counter. On the other side of the scale,
but no less powerfully, Adolf Hitler came out of the crawlspaces
of Vienna's urban underclass with a corrupted version of Central
European occult traditions, and he turned them into a myth that
mesmerized an entire nation and plunged the planet into the most
catastrophic war in its history. In rational terms, the story of either man's achievements seems preposterous — another measure
of the limits of reason and its failure to plumb the depths of human motivation.

If something constructive is to be done about peak oil and the
rest of the predicament of industrial society, in other words, yet
another round of reasonable plans will not do the trick. The powers that must be harnessed are those of myth, magic, and the irra-
tional. What remains to be seen is whether these will be harnessed
by a new Gandhi…or a new Hitler.

The City of Progress

All these issues can be phrased in a more forthright way, if we start
with the admission that the present situation is ultimately a religious crisis. As the aspect of human life that links it back (in Latin,
re-ligere, the root of the word *religion*) to its roots in the realm of ultimate concern, religion undergirds and defines every other aspect
of a culture. When events bring a civilization's most basic assumptions into question, it's high time to look to the religious dimension of that civilization for the ultimate cause.

Mind you, the last few centuries of intellectual history make
statements about religion remarkably easy to misunderstand. Like
those people who use the word "superstition" only for those folk
beliefs they don't hold themselves, many people in the contemporary industrial world use the word "religion" purely for those belief

systems that they don't consider absolutely true. Equally, they insist that nothing can qualify as a religion unless it contains a set of beliefs (for example, the real existence of gods and the possibility of personal survival after physical death) that are specifically excluded from the religion most people in the industrial world follow today. This odd habit of thought has its roots in the complicated compromise between Protestant piety and nascent scientific materialism in 17th century Britain, but it remains firmly fixed in place today, and it makes clarity a real challenge in talking about the spiritual dimension of peak oil.

When I suggest that our current predicament has its roots in a religious crisis, then, I don't mean to say Christianity has much to do with the matter. In most of the Western world, Christianity in its historic forms sank to the status of a minority religion several centuries ago. The illusion that it remained a majority faith rose because a newer faith took over its outward forms, in much the same way that a hermit crab takes over the cast-off shell of a snail and pulls it along behind it through the sand. That newer faith is the religion of progress, the established church and dogmatic faith of the modern industrial world.

Cultural critic Christopher Lasch, in his scathing study *The True and Only Heaven*, anatomized the way that the faith in progress eclipsed older religious traditions in the modern Western world, but even he didn't take the argument as far as it can go. As I've suggested elsewhere in this book, to speak of progress as a religion is not to indulge in metaphor. Progress has its own creation myth, rooted in popular distortions of Darwin's theory of natural selection that twisted the messy, aimless realities of biological evolution until it fit the mythic image of a linear ascent from primeval pond scum to the American suburban middle class. It has its saints, its martyrs, and its hagiographies, ringing endless changes on the theme of the visionary genius disproving the entrenched errors of the past. It has its priests and teachers, of whom the late Carl Sagan is probably the best known. Sagan, in fact, was arguably one of the most innovative theologians of the last century, with his mythic "We are star-stuff" narrative that fused 19th century positivist philosophy with the latest theories out of astrophysics and evolutionary biology.[7]

Finally, of course, it has its own heaven, a grand vision of perpetual improvement toward a Promethean future among the stars. It's impossible to make sense of the predicament of the industrial world, it seems to me, without recognizing the sheer intellectual and emotional power of this vision. The religious revolution that made faith in progress the defining religious idiom of the modern world happened, in large part, because the progressive myth proved more emotionally appealing to more people than the narratives of Christianity it replaced. It's one thing to expect people to anchor their hopes for a better world in the unknowable territory on the far side of death and trust completely in the evidence of things not seen; it's quite another to encourage them to re-imagine the world they know in the light of technological and social changes going on right in front of them, trace the trajectory of those changes right on out to the stars, and embrace the changes themselves as vehicles of redemption and proofs of the imminence of a better world.

What the mythic power of the vision made it all but impossible to grasp, though, was that the progress of the last three hundred years, while very real, was the product of two temporary and self-limiting sets of circumstances.[8] One of these unfolded from the wars of conquest and colonization that gave European nations control of most of the planet in the 16th, 17th, and 18th centuries, enabling them to prosper mightily at the expense of the world's other peoples, just as previous empires did in their times. The second and far greater circumstance was the discovery that fossil fuels could be used in place of wind, water, and muscle to power human technologies. From the perspective of the myth of progress, these things were simply side effects of the Western world's embrace of a true doctrine of nature. The possibility that they were the causes of progress, not its effects, was unthinkable.

The weakness of the religion of progress, though, forms a precise mirror to its strengths. A religion that claims to justify itself by
works rather than faith stands or falls by its ability to make good
on its promises, and for the last few decades the promises of the
religion of progress have been wearing noticeably thin. Despite a
flurry of media ceremonies parading new technological advances
before the faithful like so many saints' relics, most people in the
industrial world have begun to notice the steady erosion in standards of living, public health, and the quality of products for sale
since the energy crises of the 1970s. Compare the lifestyle that was
possible in the United States on a single working-class income in
1970, let's say, with the lifestyle possible in the same country on a
single working-class income today, and it becomes very hard to
cling to the assurance that the future will inevitably be better than
the past.

While the religion of progress is a relatively new thing, the predicament of a faith that fails to make good on its promises is not.
One of the fundamental documents of the civilization that industrial society replaced, Augustine of Hippo's *The City of God*,
maps out that predicament with the brutal clarity only the eyes of
a triumphant doctrinal opponent can manage. A few years before
Augustine set pen to parchment, the Visigothic king Alaric tossed
the most basic assumptions of the Roman world into history's
rubbish heap when his horsemen swept across southern Europe to
the gates of Rome and sacked the city of the Caesars. The empire's
Pagan population, then still close to a majority, argued that the
gods had deserted Rome because Rome had deserted her gods.

Augustine's response launched shockwaves in the Western
zeitgeist that have not entirely faded even today. In place of the
pax deorum, the Roman Pagan concept of a pact between humanity and divinity that guaranteed the blessing of the gods on human
society, Augustine argued that it was a fatal mistake to conflate the
world of social life in historical time with the world of spiritual
truth in eternity. The hard line of division he drew between two

cities, the City of Man doomed to perish and the City of God destined to reign forever, put a full stop at the end of the long and by no means inglorious history of classical Pagan civil religion, and it defined a new religious consciousness that was able to cope, as classical Paganism could not, with the implosion of the ancient world and the coming of the Dark Ages.

Augustine's distinction is typical, in many ways, of religious consciousness in ages of decline, just as the confident belief that ultimate truths stand guarantor to current social arrangements is typical of religious consciousness in ages of progress; the *pax progressus* of the last few centuries mirrors not only the emotional tone but a surprising amount of the rhetoric of the *pax deorum* of ancient Rome. To the extent that anything like the medieval Christianity that Augustine played so large a role in founding survives in today's Christian churches, it might conceivably become a significant social as well as religious resource as industrial civilization slides down the slope into its own dark ages. Yet there are many other possibilities. History never repeats itself exactly, and, as the industrial age draws toward its end, the prospect of a revival of some traditional Western faith must be balanced against the opportunities open to faiths from other cultures as well as newly created visions of destiny.

The Next Spirituality

It may be prophetic that science fiction — that cracked but not always clouded mirror of our imagined futures — so often makes religion central to narratives about a world after industrial civilization. That fashion was set in a big way by Walter M. Miller's 1959 bestseller *A Canticle for Leibowitz*, which leapt past the then-popular genre of nuclear holocaust novels to envision a centuries-long reprise of the Dark Ages, complete with Catholic monks guarding the knowledge of the past. Miller's book covered quite a bit of philosophical and theological ground, but among its core themes was the argument that religion — specifically, of course,

Catholic Christianity — was the wellspring of humanity's better possibilities, and it would be more important than ever once progress betrayed the hopes of its votaries.

In the hothouse environment of mid-20th century science fiction, a retort from the opposition was not long in arriving. It came from Edgar Pangborn, whose award-winning 1964 novel *Davy* was in large part a counterblast aimed at Miller's vision. In Pangborn's future history, the collapse of industrial civilization was followed by the slow rise of a neomedieval society shackled to superstition and ignorance by the Holy Murcan Church. Like *A Canticle for Leibowitz*, *Davy* covered quite a bit of intellectual ground. Pangborn's invented Murcan religion was at least as much a scathing satire on the American Protestant religiosity of his own time as it was an attempt to imagine a religion of the future. Central to Pangborn's vision, though, was the argument that religion — any religion — was the zenith of human folly, an arrogant claim to privileged knowledge about the unknowable that inevitably lashed out violently against those too sane to accept its pretensions.

Of course these two arguments have been fodder for countless debates since Christianity lost its hold on the collective imagination of the Western world some centuries back. One feature of the dispute that deserves more attention than it has usually received, though, is the extent to which both sides present the choice between them as the only option there is. Such recent antireligious polemics as Richard Dawkins' *The God Delusion*, for example, found their arguments explicitly on the insistence that the kind of religion represented by conservative Christians is the only kind worth debating, just as the equal and opposite polemics from conservative Christians commonly claim that any religion different from theirs is tantamount to Dawkins' evangelical atheism. This sort of dualistic thinking comes so naturally to most people in the industrial world that those few works of science fiction that tried to suggest a third option languished in obscurity. Marvin Kaye and Parke Godwin's 1978 novel *The Masters of Solitude*, for example, a richly ambivalent tale of three-way struggle among Wiccans, Christians, and rationalists in a world two thousand years after the fall of the industrial age, received little attention, while *Davy* and *A Canticle for Leibowitz* both went through many editions.

One of the great factors fostering this sort of dualist thinking, of course, is the way it's proven to be immensely profitable for the two mutually dependent sides of a great many disputes. Behind the quadrennial antics of the interchangeable Demublican and Repocratic politicians in the United States (or their equivalents in other industrial countries) lies a canny good cop-bad cop routine in which each side shakes down an assortment of captive constituencies by bellowing as loud as possible about how terrible a victory by the other side would be. The same routine underlies the relationship between atheism and fundamentalism. Yet it's a mistake to assume that a dualism of this sort necessarily remains fixed in place forever.

The classical world provides a good example of the way such relationships can unravel. Well before the beginning of the Common Era, the religious landscape of the Greco-Roman world broke open along a line of fracture defined by the gap between an archaic polytheism rooted more in poetry than theology, and a rationalist movement among the political classes that sought individual perfection through moral philosophy. Relations between the two sides were never quite as bitter as the equivalent strains in our own culture; the decision of the Athenian court that condemned Socrates to death for introducing new gods was mirrored in Plato's insistence that poets ought to be driven out of his imaginary Republic, but at the same time many Roman intellectuals argued that the *religio Romana* was justified by its role in maintaining social order.

In classical times, the religious stalemate lasted until a third force — Christianity — entered the picture from outside. One of the foundations of Christian victory in the theology wars of the late classical world was the polemic the two older forces used against one another. Christian apologists could, and did, copy the philosophers in denouncing the gods of Olympus for their dubious morals, then turn around, borrow the rhetoric of the religious party, and assail the philosophers for their arrogance and impiety. It wasn't until the end of the third century CE that philosophers such as Iamblichus and Proclus tried to build a united opposition to Christianity, and by then it was far too late. The classical world was already sliding down the slope of its own catabolic collapse, and the future of the Mediterranean world belonged to the new religious vision exemplified by Christianity and, a little later, Islam as well.

It's very popular to see this transition as historically inevitable and to point to features in Christianity that make it "more advanced" than classical Paganism, but this simply rehashes the myth of progress in a different key. Comparative history from other societies suggests that things could just as well have turned out differently. In Nara- and Heian-period Japan, for example, a very similar divide between imported Buddhism and indigenous Shinto took a very different course. Japan found its equivalents of Iamblichus and Proclus much earlier, in the persons of Buddhist leaders such as Kobo Daishi and Dengyo Daishi who worked to establish common ground with the older faith, and the resulting accommodation proved to be so durable that a millennium and a half later, most Japanese still practice both faiths.

Despite all the arguments of historical determinists, history does seem to be contingent rather than determined — which is to say, of course, that in human affairs slight causes can have vast effects, so trying to predict the future is a risky proposition at best. This is true, above all, of religious history, where the blazing spiritual vision of a vagabond prince, a camel driver, or a tentmaker on the road to Damascus can catch fire in the imaginations of millions, sending the world careening down an unexpected path. Thus it would be a waste of time to point to one religious movement or another and proclaim it as the inevitable wave of the future. A glance at some of the possibilities might be worthwhile, but such a glance must be tempered with the recognition that history seems to take a perverse delight in embarrassing would-be prophets.

Still, for the religion of progress in any of its forms — the straightforward atheist anthropolatry of Richard Dawkins and his peers, or the quasi-theistic versions that use the forms of older faiths but redefine them in progressive terms — the coming of the deindustrial age promises a major crisis and most likely an epitaph in the bargain. As the limits to growth push industrial civilization further into its own spiral of catabolic collapse, the most fundamental assumptions of our modern faith in progress are likely to be tested severely, if not shattered. As I've suggested earlier in this book, the likely outcome is a social, psychological, and spiritual crisis of no small order. Nearly every dimension of today's industrial society relies on the religion of progress to cover it with meaning and justification in the eyes of the political classes and the general public alike, and without that clothing many of today's familiar social and economic arrangements will stand exposed to an almost indecent degree. In the resulting scramble for new garments, the likelihood is very high that our current faith in progress will be trampled underfoot.

The same fate lies in store for the secular apocalyptic faiths that have hijacked the rhetoric of the Enlightenment for their own uses. All of them, from old-fashioned Marxism to the latest neoprimitive ideologies, depend on the same assumptions as the myth of progress; they simply stand one or another of them on its head to suit the requirements of their particular challenge to the status quo. It's quite possible that one or more of them will attract a mass following as industrial civilization winds down; such things happen often in the twilight years of civilizations, not least because blaming hard times on scapegoats is so easy. Still, if such ideologies do rise to power their success itself is likely to prove their undoing. Once their vision of Utopia stops being a tool for social critique and becomes a promise on which their leaders are expected to make good, few apocalyptic faiths survive for long.

The future will also probably not be kind to the various currently popular brands of religious fundamentalism. These present themselves as alternatives to today's secular mythologies, but they have made themselves just as vulnerable to a future that shows no sign of conforming to their prophecies. A profound irony underlies the fundamentalist challenge to secular culture, for, in the process of confronting the religion of progress, the fundamentalist faiths have made their own religious traditions over in its image, seeking a fulfillment of their mythic visions as tightly focused on the world of history and political affairs as any atheist could imagine. It's not accidental that most fundamentalist movements put conservative social issues at the center of their agenda, as though crusading for the social mores of a previous decade or century is what religion ought to be about, or that most of them have reduced their teachings to a collection of sound bites and slogans for convenience in marketing.[9]

The conservative wing of contemporary Protestantism, in many ways, has gone furthest in this process, just as the liberal wing has gone furthest in surrendering its traditional religious content and replacing it with platitudes about progress. It seems likely that both are on their way out, and they may well succeed in taking Protestantism with them. Catholicism, on the other hand, is potentially a very different matter. While American Protestantism has been losing members steadily for decades, the Catholic church has been holding steady, not least because so much immigration into North America today comes from predominantly Catholic countries. Demographics have worked very much in Catholicism's favor, and they will very likely continue to do so. The great weakness of Catholicism is the immense financial burden of its current organizational superstructure, a burden that will become increasingly hard to bear as poverty spreads and Catholic laity find themselves forced to choose between supporting the hierarchy and their own economic survival. If the Catholic church can find a way to meet this challenge, perhaps by returning to its early medieval roots in a reaffirmation of the old monastic value of poverty, *A Canticle for Leibowitz* may not be as farfetched as it looks.

Buddhism, it seems to me, is also very much worth watching. While it still carries the reputation of an exotic foreign import, Buddhism has had a substantial presence in the Western world for more than a century, and of course it has successfully made the leap from culture to culture many times in the past. Buddhist monasteries can be found all over North America these days — there are three of them within a short drive of the small Oregon town where I live — and a religion that centers on the quest to find an answer to human suffering is likely to find attentive audiences over the decades and centuries to come, when the decline and fall of industrial civilization is likely to cause a great deal of unavoidable human suffering. If it can finish the process of acclimatizing itself to its new cultural settings in the West, as it did long ago during its spread across Asia, it could easily become a major factor in the North American religious scene for many centuries to come.[10]

Yet it's also worth watching the fringes, and keeping an eye out for wild cards. Christianity, after all, was a legally proscribed minority faith only a few generations before it seized control of a crumbling Roman world. In a world shaped by the contingent and the unexpected, where slight causes can drive vast effects, some religious movement barely large enough to be noticed today might turn into the dominant religion of North America a few centuries down the road. Arnold Toynbee noted in his massive *A Study of History* that the downslope of civilizations forms the great incubator of religious movements.[11] Rarely does this happen so dramatically as in times when the most basic assumptions of a civilization are visibly disproving themselves. This is such a time, in case you haven't noticed.

My own Druid faith, for all that, seems vanishingly unlikely to become anything like a major force in the religious landscape of the deindustrial future. Born in the 18th century out of a three-way pileup between mystical Anglicanism, fragmentary Celtic traditions, and the first stirrings of what we now call environmental awareness, the modern Druid movement is distinguished more by its tolerance of diversity and a wry sense of humor than by any sort of missionary fervor or mass appeal.[12] Many contemporary Druids are aware of peak oil and the other dimensions of the predicament of industrial society, and they are taking action to respond to it. Most likely, though, it would take the abject failure of any other religious tradition to respond constructively to that predicament to push Druidry out of its current place as a relatively minor player in the alternative spirituality scene and make it a significant factor in the religious history of the future.

Still, whatever religion or combination of religions rises to prominence as industrial society slides down the rough slope of the Long Descent, the religious dimension will very likely play a massive role in the way that people adapt, or fail to adapt, to the world of harsh limits and harsher choices that the missed opportunities of recent decades have made inevitable. As the aspect of human life that deals with ultimate concerns, religion harnesses the most powerful of all human motivations, and it seems to me that any serious attempt to make something positive out of the approaching mess will have to draw on religious motivations, in one way or another, if it is to have any chance of meeting the challenges of our future. Thus, those who attempt to imagine the next economy, the next society, or even the next energy system might be well advised to take at least a passing glance in the direction of the next spirituality as well.

Afterword

Our civilization, as historian John Lukacz has suggested,[1] has been haunted since its birth by an extraordinarily intense awareness of historical change. Other civilizations have been fascinated by history, of course. The medieval world that preceded modern industrial society, to name only one example, showed its passion for its own history in a wealth of local and national chronicles that scholars still study today. Still, the same monastic scribes who noted down every baronial feud and outbreak of plague in some small corner of medieval Europe saw nothing wrong in rewriting Biblical narratives and Classical history in the social terms of their own day, turning the patriarch Abraham and Alexander the Great into feudal grandees indistinguishable from the ones who galloped past their monastery gates.

When industrial civilization embraced a mythic narrative that centered on its sense of its own uniqueness, though, it set out on a course toward a radically different consciousness of history. Historians of the 18th century Enlightenment liked to contrast the reasonable consensus of their own time with the discarded beliefs of earlier ages. Their successors in the 19th century set themselves the task of chronicling those discarded beliefs and working out the ways of thinking that undergirded them. They succeeded well enough that by the middle of the 20th century, historians of ideas found themselves facing the uncomfortable realization that those discarded beliefs made just as much sense in their own time as the equally unproven assumptions of our own age make today.

That recognition offers views at least as sweeping as the one over Caernarfon I described in the opening lines of this book. From such a vantage point, as from the Welsh hill, the approaching Long Descent of industrial civilization can be seen in the light of earlier examples of decline and fall, and the arrival of the successor civilizations that will build on the ruins of today's proud towers can be sensed, if not yet seen, in the context of past equivalents. Still, the awareness of historical change has an even more precious gift to offer.

With a clear sense of the differences that separate one age and civilization from another, it's possible to compare the many ways that cultures of the past have responded to their own declines. This sort of comparison does not reflect particularly well on industrial civilization's claim to superior rationality, as many cultures of the past have done far better at managing their own declines than ours has accomplished so far. Yet the possibility of learning from the past, and using the resulting knowledge to prepare for an uncertain future, remains open — at least for the time being.

One much-repeated lesson history offers is that in the twilight years of a civilization, the shape of reality itself is open to question. The industrial world's own fundamental certainties came to birth in the bitter cultural struggles of the Renaissance, marking the twilight of a medieval civilization with its own sharply different ways of looking at the world. Behind the medieval world, in turn, lay the cultural and spiritual chaos of the last years of classical Greco-Roman civilization. Trace that civilization back to its origins, in turn, and you'll find another time of social disintegration in the terrible dark ages that followed the fall of Knossos and Mycenae in the 14th century BCE.

The choices we make in our turn, the insights we achieve, and the stories we choose to tell in the twilight of our own civilization have the potential to build foundations for the cultures of an age not yet born. At this point in the trajectory of industrial society, as our resource base falters and our political, economic, and religious leaders keep on following the path of least resistance toward a head-on collision with ecological reality, the chance to turn aside from the Long Descent lies back among the missed opportunities of past decades. Much can still be done, though, to cushion the way down, to preserve cultural and natural resources for the future, and to hand on to the builders of future societies the ideas and tools they will need to help build a more humane and sustainable world.

The hilltop view in Caernarfon, after all, held its own ambiguities. Standing in the sun and wind over the gray roofs of the town, I could see enough of the past to sense the fate waiting for the civilization that left its mark on the shores of the Menai Strait in the last few decades. What remains hidden is the shape of the civilization that will replace it, turning old structures to new uses and leaving its own unique imprint on the world. When other travelers climb up to the same hilltop a thousand years from now, what will they see below? Our own actions here and now have the power to help shape the answer.

Appendix

How Civilizations Fall:
A Theory of Catabolic Collapse

Introduction

The collapse of complex human societies, while a subject of perennial scholarly and popular fascination, remains poorly understood. Tainter (1988), surveying previous attempts to account for the demise of civilizations, noted that most proposed explanations of collapse failed to adequately describe causative mechanisms, and relied either on ad-hoc hypotheses based on details of specific cases or, by contrast, essentially mystical claims (e.g., that civilizations have lifespans like those of individual biological organisms). In another recent survey of collapses in history (Yoffee and Cowgill 1988), contributors proposed widely divergent explanatory models to account for broadly similar processes of decline and breakdown.

Tainter (1988) proposed a general theory of collapse, in which complex societies break down when increasing complexity results in negative marginal returns, so that a decrease in sociopolitical complexity yields net benefits to people in the society. This theory has much to offer students of collapse, and it models many features of the breakdown of civilizations, but it fails to account for other factors, especially the temporal dimensions of the process. Tainter

Table 1: Timescales of collapse

Civilization	Onset of collapse	Time to collapse
Minoan Crete	c. 1500 BCE	c. 300 years
Mycenean Greece	c.1200 BCE	c. 150 years
Hittite Empire	c. 1200 BCE	c. 100 years
Western Chou empire	934 BCE	163 years
Western Roman Empire	166 CE	310 years
Medieval Mesopotamia	c.650 CE	c. 550 years
Lowland Classic Maya	c.750 CE	c. 150 years

Note: all dates from Tainter 1988)

defines collapse as a process of marked sociopolitical simplification
unfolding on a timescale of "no more than a few decades" (Tainter
1988, p. 4); in this process an unsustainably high level of complexity is replaced with a lower, more sustainable level. Many of the examples he cites, however, fail to fit this description because they
occurred over centuries rather than decades (see Table 1) and involved an extended process of progressive disintegration rather
than a rapid shift from an unsustainable state to a sustainable one.

The best documented examples of collapse, such as the fall of
the western Roman empire, show a distinctive temporal pattern
even more difficult to square with Tainter's theory. Thus, during
the collapse of Roman power, each of a series of crises led to loss of
social complexity and the establishment of temporary stability at
a less complex level. Each such level then proved to be unsustainable in turn, and was followed by a further crisis and loss of complexity (Gibbon 1962; Tainter 1988; Grant 1990). In many regions,
furthermore, the sociopolitical complexity remaining after the empire's final disintegration was far below the level that had existed in
the same area prior to its inclusion in the imperial system. Britain
in the late pre-Roman Iron Age, for example, had achieved a stable and flourishing agricultural society with nascent urban centers

and international trade connections, while the same area remained depopulated, impoverished, and politically chaotic for centuries following the collapse of imperial authority (Snyder 2003).

An alternative model based on perspectives from human ecology offers a more effective way to understand the collapse process. This conceptual model, the theory of catabolic collapse, explains the breakdown of complex societies as the result of a self-reinforcing cycle of decline driven by interactions among resources, capital, production, and waste. Previous work on the human ecology of past civilizations (e.g., Hughes 1975; Sanders et al. 1979; Ponting 1992; Elvin 1993; and Webster 2002) and attempts to project the impact of ecological factors on present societies (e.g., Catton 1980; Gever et al. 1986; Meadows et al. 1992; Duncan 1993; and Heinberg 2003) have yielded data and analytical tools from which a general theory of the collapse of complex societies may be developed. This will be attempted here.

The Human Ecology of Collapse

At the highest level of abstraction, any human society includes four core elements: resources, capital, waste, and production. Resources (R) are factors naturally present in the environment that can be exploited by a particular society, using methods and technologies available to the society, but which have not yet been extracted and incorporated into the society's flows of energy and material. Resources include material resources such as iron ore not yet mined, naturally occurring soil fertility that has not yet been exhausted, human resources such as people not yet included in the workforce, and information resources such as scientific discoveries not yet made. While the resources available to any society, even the simplest, are numerous and complex, this conceptual model treats resources as a single variable. This radical oversimplification is acceptable solely because it allows certain large-scale patterns to be seen clearly, permitting one model to be applied to the widest possible range of societies.

Capital (C) consists of all factors (derived from any source) incorporated into the society's flows of energy and material that can be put to further use in other applications. Capital includes physical capital such as food, fields, tools, and buildings; human capital such as laborers and scientists; social capital such as social hierarchies and economic systems; and information capital such as technical knowledge. While a market system is a form of social capital, and currency and coinage are forms of physical capital, it should be noted that money as such is a mechanism for allocating and controlling capital rather than a form of capital in its own right. While the capital stocks of every society are diverse and complex, again, for the sake of exposition, this model treats all capital as a single variable.

Waste (W) consists of all factors incorporated into the society's flows of energy and material that are already fully exploited and have no potential for further use. Materials used or converted into pollutants, tools and laborers at the end of their useful lives, and information garbled or lost — all become waste. All waste is treated as a single variable for the purpose of this conceptual model.

Production (P) is the process by which existing capital and resources are combined to create new capital and waste. The quality and quantity of new capital created by production are functions of the resources and existing capital that go into the production process. Resources and existing capital may be substituted for one another in production, but the relation between the two is nonlinear and complete substitution is impossible. As the use of resources approaches zero, in particular, maintaining any given level of production requires exponential increases in the use of existing capital, due to the effect of decreasing marginal return (Clark and Haswell, 1996; Wilkinson 1973; Tainter 1988). For the purpose of this model, all production is treated as a single variable.

In any human society, resources and capital enter the production process; new capital and waste leave it. Capital is also subject to waste outside production — uneaten food spoils, for example, and unemployed laborers still grow old and die. Thus maintenance of a steady state requires new capital from production to equal waste from production and capital:

$$C(p) = W(p) + W(c) \longrightarrow \text{steady state (1)}$$

where $C(p)$ is new capital produced, $W(p)$ is existing capital converted to waste in the production of new capital, and $W(c)$ is existing capital converted to waste outside of production. The sum of $W(p)$ and $W(c)$ is $M(p)$, maintenance production, the level of production necessary to maintain capital stocks at existing levels. Thus, Equation 1 can be more simply put:

$$C(p) = M(p) \longrightarrow \text{steady state (2)}$$

Societies which move from a steady state into a state of expansion produce more than necessary to maintain existing capital stocks:

$$C(p) > M(p) \longrightarrow \text{expansion (3)}$$

In the absence of effective limits to growth, this expansion can become a self-reinforcing process, because additional capital can be brought into the production process, where it generates yet more new capital, which can be brought into the production process in turn. The westward expansion of the United States in the 19th century offers a well-documented example: in a resource-rich environment, increases in human capital stemming from immigration and increases in information capital that came with the development of new agricultural technologies increased production; this drove increases in physical capital derived from geographical expansion, settling of arable land, manufacturing, etc., which in turn increased production again and drove increases across the spectrum of capital (Billington 1982). This process may be called an *anabolic* cycle.

The self-reinforcing aspect of an anabolic cycle is limited by two factors that tend to limit increases in $C(p)$. First, resources may

not be sufficient to maintain indefinite expansion. (Here the use of
"resources" as a single variable must be set aside briefly.) Each resource has a replenishment rate, $r(R)$, the rate at which new stocks
of the resource become available to the society. For any given resource and society at any given time, $r(R)$ is a weighted product
of the rates of natural production, new discovery of existing deposits, and development of alternative resources capable of filling
the same role in production. Over time, since discovery and the
development of replacements are both subject to decreasing marginal returns (Clark and Haswell 1996; Wilkinson 1973; Tainter
1988), $r(R)$ approaches asymptotically the combined rate at which
the original resource and replacements are created by natural processes.

Each resource also has a rate of use by the society, $d(R)$, and the
relationship between $d(R)$ and $r(R)$ forms a core element in the
model. Resources used faster than their replenishment rate, $d(R)/r(R) > 1$, become depleted; a depleted resource must be replaced by
existing capital to maintain production, and the demand for capi-
tal increases exponentially as depletion continues. Thus, unless all
of a society's necessary resources have an unlimited replenishment
rate, $C(p)$ cannot increase indefinitely because $d(R)$ will eventually exceed $r(R)$, leading to depletion and exponential increases
in the capital required to maintain $C(p)$ at any given level. Liebig's
law of the minimum suggests that for any given society, the essential resource with the highest value for $d(R)/r(R)$ may be used as a
working value of $d(R)/r(R)$ for resources as a whole.

Resource depletion is thus one of the two factors that tends
to overcome the momentum of an anabolic cycle. The second is
inherent in the relationship between capital and waste. As capital stocks increase, $M(p)$ rises, since $W(c)$ rises proportionally
to total capital; more capital requires more maintenance and replacement. $M(p)$ also rises as $C(p)$ rises, since increased production requires increased use of capital and thus increased $W(p)$,
the conversion of capital to waste in the production process. All

other factors being equal, the effect of $W(c)$ is to make $M(p)$ rise faster than $C(p)$, since not all capital is involved in production at any given time, but all capital is constantly subject to conversion to waste. Increased $C(p)$ relative to $M(p)$ can be generated by decreasing capital stocks, thus decreasing $W(c)$; by slowing the conversion of capital to waste, thus decreasing $W(c)$ and/or $W(p)$; by increasing the fraction of capital involved in production, thus increasing $C(p)$; or by increasing the intake of resources for production, thus increasing $C(p)$. If these are not done, or prove insufficient to meet the needs of the situation, $M(p)$ will rise to equal or exceed $C(p)$ and bring the anabolic cycle to a halt.

Broadly speaking, a society facing the end of an anabolic cycle faces a choice between two strategies. One strategy is to move toward a steady state in which $C(p) = M(p)$, and $d(R) \leq r(R)$ for every economically significant resource. Barring the presence of environmental limits, this requires social controls to keep capital stocks down to a level at which maintenance costs can be met from current production, so that intake of resources can be kept at or below replenishment rates. This can require difficult collective choices, but as long as resource availability remains stable, controls on capital growth stay in place, and the society escapes major exogenous crises, this strategy can be pursued indefinitely.

The alternative strategy is to attempt to prolong the anabolic cycle through efforts to accelerate intake of resources through military conquest, new technology, or other means. Since increasing production increases $W(p)$ and increasing capital stocks lead to increased $W(c)$, however, such efforts drive further increases in $M(p)$. A society that attempts to maintain an anabolic cycle indefinitely must therefore expand its use of resources at an ever-increasing rate to keep $C(p)$ from dropping below $M(p)$. Since this exacerbates problems with depletion, as discussed above, this strategy may prove counterproductive.

If the attempt to achieve a steady state fails, or if efforts at increasing resource intake fall irrevocably behind rising $M(p)$, a society enters a state of contraction, in which production of new capital does not make up for losses due to waste:

$$n\,C(p) < M(p) \longrightarrow \text{contraction (4)}$$

The process of contraction takes one of two general forms, depending on the replenishment rate of resources used by the society. A society that uses resources *at or below* the replenishment rate $(d(R)/r(R) \leq 1)$, when production of new capital falls short of maintenance needs, enters a maintenance crisis in which capital of all kinds cannot be maintained and is converted to waste: physical capital is destroyed or spoiled, human populations decline in number, large-scale social organizations disintegrate into smaller and more economical forms, and information is lost. Because resources are not depleted, maintenance crises are generally self-limiting. As capital is lost, $M(p)$ declines steeply, while declines in $C(p)$ due to capital loss are cushioned to some extent by the steady supply of resources. This allows a return to a steady state or the start of a new anabolic cycle once the conversion of capital to waste brings $M(p)$ back below $C(p)$.

A society that uses resources *beyond* the replenishment rate $(d(R)/r(R) > 1)$, when production of new capital falls short of maintenance needs, risks a depletion crisis in which key features of a maintenance crisis are amplified by the impact of depletion on production. As $M(p)$ exceeds $C(p)$ and capital can no longer be maintained, it is converted to waste and unavailable for use. Since depletion requires progressively greater investments of capital in production, the loss of capital affects production more seriously than in an equivalent maintenance crisis. Meanwhile further production, even at a diminished rate, requires further use of depleted resources, exacerbating the impact of depletion and the need for increased capital to maintain production. With demand for capital rising as the supply of capital falls, $C(p)$ tends to decrease faster than $M(p)$ and perpetuate the crisis. The result is a catabolic cycle, a self-reinforcing process in which $C(p)$ stays below $M(p)$ while both decline. Catabolic cycles may occur in maintenance crises if the gap between $C(p)$ and $M(p)$ is large enough, but they tend to be self-limiting in such cases. In depletion crises, by contrast, catabolic cycles can proceed to catabolic collapse, in which $C(p)$ approaches zero and most of a society's capital is converted to waste.

A society in a depletion crisis does not inevitably proceed to catabolic collapse. If depletion is limited, so that decreased demand for resources as a consequence of diminished production brings $d(R)$ back below $r(R)$, the accelerated fall in $C(p)$ may not take place and the crisis may play out much like a maintenance crisis. If the gap between $C(p)$ and $M(p)$ is modest, nonproductive capital may either be diverted to production to raise $C(p)$ or preferentially converted to waste to bring down $M(p)$, forcing $C(p)$ and $M(p)$ temporarily into balance in order to buy time for a transition to a steady state. A society in which depletion is advanced and $M(p)$ rapidly increasing relative to $C(p)$, though, may not be able to escape catabolic collapse even if such steps are taken. Cultural and political factors may also make efforts to avoid catabolic collapse difficult to accomplish, or indeed to contemplate.

Testing the Model

These two forms of collapse, maintenance crisis leading to recovery, and depletion crisis leading to catabolic collapse, are to some extent ideal types, forming two ends of a complex spectrum of societal breakdown. Most historical examples of collapse fall somewhere in between the two. The limitations of the abstract and extremely simplified model on which the theory is based should also be kept firmly in mind when attempting to apply it to past or present examples. Still, a survey of historical examples shows that many of them have features which support the model proposed in this section.

Closest to the maintenance-crisis end of the spectrum are tribal societies such as the Kachin of Burma. Kachin communities cycle up and down from relatively decentralized to relatively

centralized social forms without significant losses of physical, human, or information capital. In this case, anabolic cycles lead to the
growth of organizational capital in the form of relatively centralized social forms, but the maintenance costs of this organizational
capital turn out to be unsustainable, leading to maintenance crises, loss of social capital, and the restoration of more decentralized
and thus less resource- and capital-intensive social forms (Leach
1954).

Essentially the same process on a larger and more destructive
scale characterizes the history of imperial China from the 10th
century BCE to the end of the 19th century CE. Efficient cereal agriculture and local market economies provided the foundation for a
series of anabolic cycles resulting in the establishment of centralized imperial dynastic states (Gates 1996; Di Cosmo 1999). These
anabolic cycles drove increases in population, public works such
as canals and flood control projects, and sociopolitical organization, all of which proved unsustainable over the long term. As
maintenance costs exceeded the imperial government's resources,
repeated maintenance crises led to the breakup of national unity,
invasion by neighboring peoples, loss of infrastructure, and steep
declines in population (Ho 1970; Di Cosmo 1999). Imperial
China's resource base had a relatively high replenishment rate, due
largely to the long-term sustainability of traditional Chinese agriculture and the use of human and animal muscle as the primary
energy sources, so any significant resource depletion could be reversed once population levels dropped (Elvin 1993). Though resource depletion played a limited role, the maintenance crises of
imperial China were self-limiting and resulted in contraction to
more modest levels of population and sociopolitical organization,
rather than the total collapse of the society.

The collapse of the western Roman Empire, by contrast, was
a catabolic collapse driven by a combined maintenance and resource crisis. While the ancient Mediterranean world, like imperial China, was primarily dependent on readily replenished

resources, the Empire itself was the product of an anabolic cycle fueled by easily depleted resources and driven by Roman military superiority. Beginning in the third century BCE, Roman expansion transformed the capital of other societies into resources for Rome as country after country was conquered and stripped of movable wealth. Each new conquest increased the Roman resource base and helped pay for further conquests. After the first century CE, though, further expansion failed to pay its own costs. All remaining peoples within the reach of Rome were either barbarian tribes with little wealth, such as the Germans, or rival empires capable of defending themselves, such as the Parthians (Jones 1974). Without income from new conquests, the maintenance costs of empire proved unsustainable, and a catabolic cycle followed rapidly. The first major breakdown in the imperial system came in 166 CE, and further crises followed until the Western empire ceased to exist in 476 CE (Grant 1990; Grant 1999).

The Roman collapse has an instructive feature which offers further support to the model presented above. In 297, the emperor Diocletian divided the empire into western and eastern halves. Co-ordination between them waned, and by the death of Theodosius I in 395, the two halves of the empire were effectively independent states. Since the western empire produced one-third the revenues of the eastern empire, but had more than twice as much northern frontier to defend against barbarian encroachments, this placed most of the original empire's vulnerabilities in the western half and most of its remaining resources in the eastern half. In terms of the catabolic collapse model, the eastern empire allowed massive quantities of relatively unproductive, high-maintenance capital to be converted to waste, bringing its $M(p)$ below its remaining $C(p)$ and breaking out of the catabolic cycle. The eastern empire's territory decreased further with the Muslim conquests of the seventh and eighth centuries CE; while this was involuntary, the effects were the same. Successfully shifting to a level of organization that could be supported sustainably by trade and agriculture within a more manageable territory, the eastern empire survived for nearly a millennium longer than its western twin (Bury 1923).

Near the depletion crisis end of the spectrum is the collapse of the Lowland Classic Maya in the eighth, ninth, and tenth centuries of the Common Era. The most widely accepted model of the Maya collapse depends on demographic and paleoecological evidence that Maya populations grew to a level that could not be indefinitely supported by Mayan agricultural practices on the nutrient-poor laterite soils of the Yucatan lowlands. In terms of the present model, the key resource of soil fertility was used at a rate exceeding its replenishment rate, suffering severe depletion as a result. Mayan polities also invested a large proportion of $C(p)$ in monumental building programs, which raised maintenance costs but could not be readily used for production, and they maintained these programs up to the beginning of the Terminal Classic period. The result was a "rolling collapse" over two centuries, from c. 750 CE to c. 950 CE, in which Lowland Maya populations declined precipitously and scores of urban centers were abandoned to the jungle (Willey and Shimkin 1973; Lowe 1985; Webster 2002).

The Lowland Classic Maya collapse is particularly suggestive in that it appears to have been preceded by at least two previous breakdowns. Preclassic sites such as El Mirador and Becan show many of the same artistic and cultural elements as Classic Maya urban centers, but they were abandoned in a poorly documented earlier collapse around 150 CE (Webster 2002). A second episode, the so-called Hiatus between the Early Classic and Late Classic periods (500–600 CE), saw sharp declines in monumental building and the breakdown of centralized political systems (Willey 1974). Whether these events were maintenance crises preceding the final resource crisis of the Terminal Classic, or whether some other explanation is called for, is difficult to determine from the available evidence.

Features of comparative sociology outside the realm of collapse processes also offer support to the catabolic collapse model.

One implication of the model is that societies that persist over extended periods will tend to have social mechanisms for limiting the growth of capital, thus artificially lowering $M(p)$ below $C(p)$. Such mechanisms do, in fact, exist in a wide range of societies. Among the most common are systems in which modest amounts of unproductive capital are regularly converted to waste. Examples include aspects of the potlatch economy among Native Americans of northwest North America (Kotschar 1950; Rosman and Rubel 1971; Beck 1993) and the ritual deposition of prestige metalwork in lakes and rivers by Bronze and Iron Age peoples in much of western Europe (Bradley 1990; Randsborg 1995). Such systems have been interpreted in many ways (Michaelson 1979), but in terms of the model, one of their functions is to divert some of $C(p)$ away from capital stocks requiring maintenance, thus artificially lowering $W(c)$ and making a catabolic cycle less likely.

Such practices clearly have many other meanings and functions within societies. Nor does this interpretation require any awareness within societies themselves that systems of capital destruction prevent catabolic cycles. Rather, if such systems make catabolic collapse less likely, cultures that adopt such systems for other reasons are more likely to survive over the long term and to pass on such cultural elements to neighboring or successor societies.

Conclusion: Collapse as a Succession Process

Even within the social sciences, the process by which complex societies give way to smaller and simpler ones has often been presented in language drawn from literary tragedy, as though the loss of sociocultural complexity necessarily warranted a negative value judgment. This is understandable, because the collapse of civilizations often involves catastrophic human mortality and the loss of priceless cultural treasures, but like any value judgment it can obscure important features of the matter at hand.

A less problematic approach to the phenomenon of collapse derives from the idea of succession, a basic concept in the ecology of

nonhuman organisms. Succession describes the process by which
an area not yet occupied by living things is colonized by a variety
of biotic assemblages called "seres," each replacing a prior sere and
then being replaced by another, until the process concludes with a
stable, self-perpetuating climax community (Odum 1969).

One feature of succession true of many different environments
is a difference in resource use between earlier and later seres. Species characteristic of earlier seral stages tend to maximize control
of resources and production of biomass, even at the cost of inefficiency; thus, such species tend to maximize production and distribution of offspring even when this means the great majority
of offspring fail to reach reproductive maturity. Species typical of
later seres, by contrast, tend to maximize the efficiency of their resource use, even at the cost of limits to biomass production and
the distribution of individual organisms; thus, these species tend
to maximize energy investment in individual offspring even when
this means that offspring are few and the species fails to occupy all
available niche spaces. Species of the first type, termed "R-selected"
species in the ecological literature, have specialized to flourish op-
portunistically in disturbed environments, while those of the second type, or "K-selected" species, have specialized to form stable
biotic communities that change only with shifts in the broader environment (Odum 1969).

Human societies and nonhuman species cannot be equated in
a simplistic manner, but the radical differences that exist in subsistence and production strategies among human societies allow
them to be compared to distinct biotic groups in certain contexts.
Human societies enter into common ecological relationships such
as symbiosis, commensality, parasitism, predation, and competi-
tive exclusion with other societies. Thus processes by which human societies are replaced by others may be usefully compared to
succession to see if common features emerge.

The model of catabolic collapse suggests one such common
feature. As outlined above, societies differ in their response to

changes in resource availability and maintenance costs. Some societies succeed in maintaining a steady state through timely adjustments; others experience a history of repeated maintenance crises and partial breakdowns followed by recoveries; still others undergo severe depletion crises followed by total collapse. These differences, according to the model presented here, unfold from differing relationships among resources, capital, production, and waste, especially the relationships between capital production and maintenance, $C(p)/M(p)$, and between use and replenishment rates of resources, $d(R)/r(R)$.

These variations among human societies parallel differences between R-selected and K-selected nonhuman species. A society that maximizes its production of capital, like an R-selected species, prospers in an environment with substantial uncaptured resources, but falters once these are exhausted. Its successors are likely to be societies that, like K-selected species, use key resources more sustainably at the cost of decreased production of capital. Nonhuman climax communities also typically display a higher diversity of species — but a lower population per species — than earlier seral stages, and they produce notably lower volumes of biomass than do earlier stages over equal time frames (Odum 1969).

Broadly similar changes often distinguish precollapse and postcollapse societies. Thus the collapse of the western Roman Empire, for example, could be seen as a succession process in which one seral stage, dominated by a single sociopolitical "species" that maximized capital production at the cost of inefficiency, was replaced by a more diverse community of societies, consisting of many less populous "species" better adapted to their own local conditions, and producing capital at lower but more sustainable rates. Analyses that portray this transformation as pure tragedy miss something important; the Roman collapse enabled other societies to emerge from Rome's shadow, launching major cultural initiatives such as vernacular literatures in the ancestors of today's Celtic, Germanic, and Romance languages (Wiseman 1997). As with any succession process, there were gainers as well as losers. If a lapse into fantasy may be excused, were nonhuman biota literate and interested in their past, a history of lake eutrophication written by meadow grasses would differ sharply from one written by fish.

Since humans have capacities for change that most species lack, the same human individuals can change from fish to grass, so to speak, composing an R-selected production-maximizing society at one time and its K-selected sustainability-maximizing replacement at a later time. The example of the Kachin cited above shows that this is not merely a theoretical possibility. However, as other cited examples and the general evidence of history suggest, such a change is not inevitable. Whenever a society shows signs of being unable to maintain its existing capital, a maintenance crisis may follow, and whenever capital production depends on the use of resources at rates significantly above their rate of replacement, a depletion crisis followed by catabolic collapse is a significant possibility.

Such assessments of past and present societies, in order to achieve a high degree of analytic or predictive value, require careful quantitative analysis of a sort not attempted here. Since each element in the conceptual model presented here stands for a diverse and constantly changing set of variables, such analysis offers significant challenges; in many historical examples it may be impossible to go beyond proxy measurements of uncertain value for crucial variables. However, general patterns corresponding to the catabolic collapse model may be easier to extract from incomplete data. Any society that displays broad increases in most measures of capital production coupled with signs of serious depletion of key resources is a potential candidate for catabolic collapse.

Bibliography

Abelson, Philip A., "A potential phosphate crisis," *Science* 283 (1999), p. 2015.

Agricultural Marketing Service, United States Department of Agriculture, *National Directory of Farmers Markets* (US Department of Agriculture, 2006).

Barkun, Michael, *A Culture of Conspiracy: Apocalyptic Visions in Contemporary America* (University of California Press, 2003).

Beck, M. G., *Potlatch: Native Ceremony and Myth on the Northwest Coast* (Alaska Northwest, 1993).

Becker, Charles M., and David Bloom, "The demographic crisis in the former Soviet Union," *World Development* 26:11 (1998), pp. 1913–1919.

Beyer, Paul, *When Time Shall Be No More: Prophecy Belief in Modern American Culture* (Harvard University Press, 1992).

Billington, R. A., *Westward Expansion: A History of the American Frontier* (Macmillan, 1982).

Bradley, R., *The Passage of Arms: An Archaeological Analysis of Prehistoric Hoards and Votive Deposits* (Cambridge University Press, 1990).

Braithwaite, Timothy, *Y2K Lessons Learned* (Wiley, 2000).

Brierley, Corale L., et al., *Coal: Research and Development to Support National Energies Policy* (National Academies Press, 2007).

British Museum, *Coin Hoards from Roman Britain*, 11 vols. (British Museum, 1982–).

Bury, J. B., *History of the Later Roman Empire* (Macmillan, 1923).

Butler, W. E., *Magic: Its Ritual, Power and Purpose* (Aquarian, 1975).

Butti, Ken, and John Perlin, *A Golden Thread: 2500 Years of Solar Architecture and Technology* (Cheshire Books, 1980).

Byrne, Rhonda, *The Secret* (Atria Books, 2006).

Cahill, Thomas, *How the Irish Saved Civilization* (Doubleday, 1995).

Carnes, Mark C., *Secret Ritual and Manhood in Victorian America* (Yale University Press, 1989).

Carruthers, Mary, and Jan M. Ziolkowski, eds., *The Medieval Craft of Memory* (University of Pennsylvania Press, 2002).

Catton, William R., Jr., *Overshoot: The Ecological Basis of Revolutionary Change* (University of Illinois Press, 1980).

Chawla, Mukesh, Gordon Betcherman, and Arup Banerji, *From Red to Gray* (World Bank, 2007).

Clarke, Arthur C., *Profiles of the Future*, rev. ed. (Harper and Row, 1973).

Clark, C., and M. Haswell, *The Economics of Subsistence Agriculture* (Macmillan, 1996).

Corning, P. A., *The Synergism Hypothesis* (McGraw-Hill, 1983).

Corning, P. A., "'Devolution' as an opportunity to test the 'synergism hypothesis' and a cybernetic theory of political systems," *Systems Research and Behavioral Science* 19:1 (2002), pp. 3–24.

Costanza, Richard, "Social traps and environmental policy," *Bioscience* 37(6) (1987) pp. 407–412.

Costanza, R., R. d'Arge, R. de Groot, S. Farber, M. Grasso, B. Hannon, K. Limburg, S. Naeem, R. O'Neill, J. Paruelo, R. Raskin, P. Sutton, and M. van den Belt, "The value of the world's ecosystem services and natural capital," *Nature* 387 (1997), pp. 253–260.

Couliano, Ioan, *Eros and Magic in the Renaissance* (University of Chicago Press, 1987).

Cross, J., and M. Guyer, *Social Traps* (University of Michigan Press, 1980).

Daly, Herman, *Toward a Steady State Economy* (William Freeman, 1973).

Danaher, Kevin, *Fifty Years is Enough: The Case Against the World Bank and the International Monetary Fund* (South End Press, 1994).

Darley, Julian, *High Noon for Natural Gas: The New Energy Crisis* (Chelsea Green, 2004).

Dawkins, Richard, *The God Delusion* (Bantam, 2006).

Dean, Carolyn, with Trueman Tuck, *Death by Modern Medicine* (Ash Tree, 2005).

Deffeyes, Kenneth, *Hubbert's Peak* (Princeton University Press, 2003).

deMoll, Lane, ed., *Rainbook: Resources for Appropriate Technology* (Schocken, 1977).

Diamond, Jared, *Collapse: How Societies Choose to Fail or Succeed* (Penguin, 2005).

Di Cosmo, N., "State formation and periodization in inner Asia," *International History Review* 20:2 (1999), pp. 287–309.

Drachman, A. G., *The Mechanical Technology of Greek and Roman Antiquity* (University of Wisconsin Press, 1963).

Drury, Nevill, *The New Age: The History of a Movement* (Thames & Hudson, 2004).

Duhon, David, *One Circle* (Ecology Action, 1985).

Duncan, Richard C., "The life-expectancy of industrial civilization: The decline to global equilibrium," *Population and Environment* 14:4 (1993), pp. 325–357.

Economic Research Service, United States Department of Agriculture, "Briefing room: Organic farming and marketing," ers.usda.gov/ Briefing/Organic/

Elvin, M., "Three thousand years of unsustainable growth: China's environment from archaic times to the present," *East Asian History* 6 (1993), pp. 7–46.

Epstein, Paul R., "Climate and health," *Science* 285 (1999), pp. 347–348.

Festinger, Leon, Henry W. Riecken, and Stanley Schachter, *When Prophecy Fails* (University of Minnesota Press, 1956).

Fields, Rick, *How the Swans Came to the Lake: A Narrative History of Buddhism in America* (Shambhala, 1985).

Forster, E. M., *Collected Stories* (Penguin, 1947).

Forster, E. M., "The Machine Stops," in *The Machine Stops and Other Stories* (André Deutsch, 1997).

Freeman, John, *Survival Gardening* (John's Press, 1983).

Freeth, Tony, et al., "Decoding the ancient Greek astronomical calculator known as the Antikythera mechanism," *Nature* 444 (2006), pp. 587–591.

Galbraith, John Kenneth, *The Culture of Contentment* (Houghton Mifflin, 1992).

Galbraith, John Kenneth, *The Great Crash 1929* (Houghton Mifflin, 1954).

Garrett, Laurie, *The Coming Plague* (Penguin, 1994).

Gates, H., *China's Motor: A Thousand Years of Petty Capitalism* (Cornell University Press, 1996).

Gever, John, Richard Kaufman, Dennis Skole, and Charles Vörösmarty, *Beyond Oil: The Threat to Food and Fuel in the Coming Decades* (Ballinger, 1986).

Gibbon, Edward, *The Decline and Fall of the Roman Empire* (Britannica Books, 1962).

Gimpel, Jean, *The Medieval Machine* (Holt, Rinehart and Winston, 1972).

Goldstein, Joseph, *One Dharma: The Emerging Western Buddhism* (HarperSanFrancisco, 2002).

Grant, Michael, *The Fall of the Roman Empire* (Weidenfeld and Nicolson, 1990).

Grant, Michael, *The Collapse and Recovery of the Roman Empire* (Routledge, 1999).

Greer, John Michael, *The Druidry Handbook* (Weiser, 2006).

Gross, Bernard, *Friendly Fascism* (South End Press, 1980).

Gross, William H., "Haute con job" and "Con job redux," *PIMCO Investment Commentary*, October 2004, archived at pimco.com.

Hanayama, Shinsho, *A History of Japanese Buddhism* (Bukkyo Dendo Kyokai, 1960).

Hanegraaf, Wouter J., *New Age Religion and Western Culture* (E. J. Brill, 1996).

Hanley, Susan B., "Tokugawa society: Material culture, standard of living, and life-styles," in John W. Hall, ed., *The Cambridge History of Japan* vol. 4, *Early Modern Japan* (Cambridge University Press, 1991).

Hanson, Victor David, *The Other Greeks* (Free Press, 1995).

Harrington, Alan, *The Immortalist* (Avon, 1970).

Hearne, Derrick, *The Rise of the Welsh Republic* (Y Lolfa, 1976).

Heinberg, Richard, *The Party's Over: Oil, War, and the Fate of Industrial Societies* (New Society Publishers, 2003).

Heinberg, Richard, *Powerdown: Options and Actions for a Post-Carbon World* (New Society Publishers, 2004).

Henderson, John, *The Medieval World of Isidore of Seville* (Cambridge University Press, 2007).

Herbert, Frank, *Dune* (Ace Books, 1965).

Hirsch, Robert L., Roger Bezdek, and Robert Wendling, *Peaking of World Oil Production: Impacts, Mitigation, and Risk Management* (US Department of Energy, 2005).

Ho, P.-T., "Economic and institutional factors in the decline of the Chinese empire," in C. M. Cipolla, ed., *The Economic Decline of Empires* (Methuen, 1970), pp. 264–277.

Howard, Albert, *An Agricultural Testament* (Rodale Books, 1973).

Hughes, J. Donald, *Ecology in Ancient Civilizations* (University of New Mexico Press, 1975).

Hynes, James W., and James R. Lindner, "Lessons from the draft horse industry in East Texas," *Journal of Extension* 44:2 (2006), online edition.

Icke, David, *Children of the Matrix* (Bridge of Love, 2001).

Jacobs, Jane, *Dark Age Ahead* (Random House, 2004).

Jacobs, Margaret, *The Cultural Meaning of the Scientific Revolution* (University of Pennsylvania Press, 1988).

Jeavons, John, *How To Grow More Vegetables* (Ten Speed, 1979).

Jefferies, Richard, "After London," in *After London and Amaryllis at the Fair* (J. M. Dent & Sons, 1939).

Jevons, William Stanley, *The Coal Question* (Macmillan, 1866).

Jones, A. H. M., *The Roman Economy: Studies in Ancient Economic and Administrative History* (Basil Blackwell, 1974).

Kaplan, Jeffrey, *Radical Religion in America* (Syracuse University Press, 1997).

Kaye, Marvin, and Parke Godwin, *The Masters of Solitude* (Avon, 1978).

Kennedy, Paul, *The Rise and Fall of Great Powers* (Random House, 1994).

Kindleberger, Charles Poor, *Manias, Panics and Crashes* (Basic Books, 1978).

King, F. H., *Farmers of Forty Centuries* (Rodale Press, 1973).

Kirschner, Heidi, *Fireless Cookery* (Madrona Press, 1981).

Kohn, Livia, *Monastic Life in Medieval Daoism* (University of Hawai'i Press, 2003).

Kotschar, V. F., *Fighting with Property: A Study of Kwakiutl Potlatching and Warfare, 1792–1930* (University of Washington Press, 1950).

Kunstler, James Howard, *The Geography of Nowhere* (Simon and Schuster, 1994).

Kunstler, James Howard, *The Long Emergency* (Atlantic Monthly Press, 2005).

Kyle, Richard G., *The New Age Movement in American Culture* (University Press of America, 1995).

Lamy, Philip, *Millennium Rage* (Plenum Press, 1998).

Lappé, Marc, *When Antibiotics Fail* (North Atlantic, 1986).

Lasch, Christopher, *The True and Only Heaven: Progress and Its Critics* (Norton, 1991).

Leach, E. R., *Political Systems of Highland Burma* (Beacon Press, 1954).

Leckie, Jim, Gil Masters, Harry Whitehouse, and Lily Young, *Other Homes and Garbage: Designs for Self-Sufficient Living* (Sierra Club Books, 1975).

Lefebvre, Georges, *The Coming of the French Revolution* (Random House, 1947).

Lovelock, James, "A book for all seasons," *Science* 280 (1998), pp. 832–833.

Lowe, J. W. G., *The Dynamics of Apocalypse: A Systems Simulation of the Classic Maya Collapse* (University of New Mexico Press, 1985).

Lukacz, John, *Historical Consciousness* (Harper and Row, 1968).

MacGregor, Jerry, and Kirk Charles, *Y2K Family Survival Guide* (Harvest House, 1999).

Manuel, Frank E., and Fritzie P. Manuel, *Utopian Thought in the Western World* (Harvard University Press, 1979).

Marks, Vic, ed., *Cloudburst: A Handbook of Rural Skills and Technology* (Cloudburst Press, 1973).

McBay, Aric, *Peak Oil Survival* (Lyons Press, 2006).

McMichael A. J., A. Haines, and R. Sloof, eds., *Climate Change and Human Health* (World Health Organization, 1996).

McNeill, William H., *Plagues and Peoples* (Anchor, 1998).

Meadows, Donella, David Meadows, Jorgen Randers, and William W. Behrens III, *The Limits to Growth* (Universe, 1972).

Meadows, Donella, David Meadows, and Jorgen Randers, *Beyond the*

Limits: Confronting Global Collapse, Envisioning a Sustainable Future (Chelsea Green, 1992).

Michaelson, D. R., *From ethnography to ethnology: A study of the conflict of interpretations of the southern Kwakiutl potlatch*, Ph.D. diss., New School for Social Research, 1979.

Miller, Timothy, *The 60s Communes: Hippies and Beyond* (Syracuse UP, 1999).

Miller, Walter M., *A Canticle for Leibowitz* (Bantam, 1959).

Mills, C. Wright, *The Causes of World War Three* (Simon and Schuster, 1958).

Milly, P. C. D., R. T. Wetherald, K. A. Dunne, and T. L. Delworth, "Increasing risk of great floods in a changing climate," *Nature* 415 (2002), pp. 514–517.

Monastersky, Richard, "Health in the hot zone," *Science News* 149:14 (1996), p. 218.

Montagu, M. F. Ashley, ed., *Toynbee and History: Critical Essays and Reviews* (Porter Sargent, 1956).

Mumford, Lewis, *Technics and Civilization* (Harcourt Brace and Co., 1934).

National Agricultural Statistics Service, *2002 Census of Agriculture* (US Department of Agriculture, 2003).

National Corn Growers Association, *2007 World of Corn* (National Corn Growers Association, 2007).

Neff, Thomas, "Lack of fuel may limit US nuclear power expansion," *MIT Tech Talk*, 4 April 2007, pp. 5, 7.

Odum, Elisabeth C., "The strategy of ecosystem development," *Science* 164 (1969), pp. 262–270.

Odum, Howard, *Environmental Accounting* (John Wiley and Sons, 1996).

Olkowski, Helga, Bill Olkowski, and Tom Javits, *The Integral Urban House* (Sierra Club Books, 1979).

Orlov, Dmitry, *Reinventing Collapse* (New Society Publishers, 2008).

Pangborn, Edgar, *Davy* (Ballantine, 1964).

Patz, J. A., P. R. Epstein, T. A. Burke, and J. M. Balbus, "Global climate change and emerging infectious diseases," *Journal of the American Medical Association* vol. 275 (1996), pp. 217–223.

Ponting, Clive, *A Green History of the World: The Environment and the Collapse of Great Civilizations* (St. Martin's, 1992).

Postel, Sandra, *Pillar of Sand* (W. W. Norton, 1999).

Putnam, Robert D., *Bowling Alone: The Collapse and Revival of American Community* (Simon and Schuster, 2000).

Ramage, Janet, *Energy: A Guidebook*, rev. ed. (Oxford University Press, 1997).

Randsborg, K., *Hjortspring: Warfare and Sacrifice in Early Europe* (Aarhus University Press, 1995).

Rather, L. J, *The Dream of Self-Destruction* (Louisiana State University Press, 1979).

Reed, David, *Ancient Maya Diet at Copan*, Ph.D. diss., Pennsylvania State University, University Park, PA, 1998.

Rosman, A., and P. G. Rubel, *Feasting with Mine Enemy: Rank and Exchange among Northwest Coast Societies* (Columbia University Press, 1971).

Roy, R. N., A. Finck, G. J. Blair, and H. L. S. Tandon, *Plant Nutrition for Food Security* (UN Food and Agriculture Organization, 2006).

Sagan, Carl, *Cosmos* (Random House, 1980).

Sanders, W. T., J. A. Parsons, and R. S. Santley, *The Basin of Mexico: Ecological Processes in the Evolution of a Civilization* (Academic Press, 1979).

Shapouri, Hosein, James A. Duffield, and Michael S. Grabowski, *Estimating the Net Energy Balance of Corn Ethanol* (US Department of Agriculture, 1995).

Shilts, Randy, *And The Band Played On: People, Politics, and the AIDS Epidemic* (St. Martin's Press, 1988).

Simon, Paul, *Tapped Out* (Welcome Rain, 1998).

Snyder, Christopher A., *The Britons* (Blackwell, 2003).

Spengler, Oswald, *The Decline of the West*, tr., Charles Francis Atkinson (Knopf, 1926–1929).

Stevens, Albert Clark, *The Cyclopaedia of Fraternities* (E. B. Treat & Co., 1907).

Stiglitz, Joseph, *Globalization and Its Discontents* (Penguin, 2002).

Stone, Jon R., *A Guide to the End of the World: Popular Eschatology in America* (Garland, 1993).

Swiss Re, *Global Warming: Element of Risk* (Swiss Reinsurance Company, 1994).

Swiss Re, *Opportunities and Risks of Climate Change* (Swiss Reinsurance Company, 2002.)

Szczelkun, Stefan A., *Survival Scrapbook 3: Energy* (Schocken, 1974).

Tainter, Joseph A., *The Collapse of Complex Societies* (Cambridge University Press, 1988).

de Tocqueville, Alexis, *Democracy in America*, tr., Henry Reeve (Vintage, 1899).

Toynbee, Arnold J., *A Study of History*, 10 vols. (Oxford University Press, 1934–55).

Toynbee, Arnold J., "*A Study of History*: What I Am Trying to Do," in Montagu 1956, op. cit., pp. 3–7.

United States Department of Energy, *Annual Energy Review 2006* (US Department of Energy, 2007).

Vacca, Roberto, *The Coming Dark Age*, tr., J. S. Whale (Doubleday, 1973).

Van Boven, S., and A. T. Gajilan, "Heading for the hills: Fear of the Y2K bug is pushing some to extremes," *Newsweek* 132:22 (1998), p. 56, 58.

Voegelin, Erich, *The New Science of Politics* (University of Chicago Press, 1952).

von Franz, Marie-Louise, "The Process of Individuation," in C. G. Jung, ed., *Man and his Symbols* (Doubleday, 1964).

Watkins, Kevin, ed., *United Nations Human Development Report 2005* (UN Development Programme, 2005).

Webster, David, *The Fall of the Ancient Maya* (Thames and Hudson, 2002).

Wilkinson, R. G., *Poverty and Progress: An Ecological Model of Economic Development*. (Methuen, 1973).

Willey, G. R., "The classic Maya hiatus: A 'rehearsal' for the collapse?" in N. Hammond, ed., *Mesoamerican Archeology: New Approaches* (Duckworth, 1974), pp. 417–430.

Willey, G. R., and D. B. Shimkin, "The Maya collapse: A summary view," in *The Classic Maya Collapse*, T. P. Culbert, ed., (University of New Mexico Press, 1973), pp. 457–501.

Williams, James L., and A. F. Alhajji, "The Coming Energy Crisis?" *Oil and Gas Journal* vol. 101 no. 5 (2003).

Wiseman, John, "The post-Roman world," *Archaeology* 50:6 (1997) pp. 12–17.

Yates, Frances, *The Art of Memory* (Routledge and Kegan Paul, 1966).

Yoffee, Norman., and G. Cowgill, eds., *The Collapse of Ancient States and Civilizations* (University of New Mexico Press, 1988).

Zarnecki, George, *The Monastic Achievement* (McGraw-Hill, 1972).

Notes

Chapter One: The End of the Industrial Age

1. My summary of Hubbert's work is primarily based on Deffeyes 2003, Duncan 1993, and Heinberg 2003.
2. Rather 1979 summarizes these views.
3. See the summary of oil production in Deffeyes 2003 and Williams and Alhajji 2003.
4. See, for example, the discussion in deMoll 1977.
5. For example, see the discussion in Ramage 1997, pp. 289–90.
6. Heinberg 2003, pp. 115–6.
7. For example, Heinberg 2004, pp. 62–75.
8. Hirsch et al. 2005.
9. See, for example, Neff 2007.
10. For the National Academy of Sciences study, see Brierley et al. 2007.
11. Ramage, 1997, pp. 12–13 and 68.
12. Nature's successful fusion reactor is, of course, the sun, which produces the vast majority of its heat and light by nuclear fusion.
13. Data for this calculation are from National Agricultural Statistics Service 2003, National Corn Growers Association 2007, and Shapouri et al. 1995.
14. Ramage 1997, p. 69.
15. For the optimist's case, see Heinberg 2003, pp. 142–46. For the pessimists, see Odum 1996.
16. Harrington 1970, p. 6.
17. See Webster 2002 for a good summary of the Maya collapse.
18. Data on Maya diets is from Reed 1998.
19. Hanson 1995.
20. Reed 1998.
21. See the case studies in Tainter 1988.
22. The Olduvai theory was originally published in Duncan 1993.
23. Orlov 2008 for a good description of the Soviet collapse and its aftermath.
24. According to the 2005 UN Human Development Report, for

example, rates of child mortality in the United States in that year
were on a level with those in Malaysia. See Watkins 2005.

Chapter Two: The Stories We Tell Ourselves

1. This does not necessarily mean, as some alternative theorists claim
    today, that the ancient Egyptians had some equivalent of modern
    technology; precisely no evidence supports that claim, and it's far
    more likely that the Egyptians worked out some clever way to use
    their own Bronze Age technology for the purpose. The fact remains
    that for the last three thousand years nobody has known what that
    clever way was.
2. One of these devices was recovered from the remains of an ancient
    Greek shipwreck in 1901. See Freeth et al. 2006 for a history and re-
    construction of the device.
3. See Drachmann 1963 for information on Hero's steam turbine.
4. The term "immanentizing the eschaton" comes from Voegelin 1952.
5. See, for example, Greer 2006.
6. This is discussed in Jacobs 1988.
7. Lamy 1998.
8. See Beyer 1992 and Stone 1993 for the role of apocalyptic myth in
    contemporary culture.
9. Toynbee 1956, p. 4.
10. Danaher 1994 and Stiglitz 2002 document the consistently disas-
    trous results of World Bank and IMF "structural adjustment."
11. Catton 1980, pp. 154–55.
12. Most famous for its involvement with trance channeling and its
    claim that "you create your own reality," the New Age movement is
    extremely diverse, and my comments on its history here are in some
    ways oversimplified. See Drury 2004, Hanegraaf 1996, and Kyle
    1995 for the history of the movement.
13. Festinger et al. 1956.
14. Byrne 2006.
15. Icke's many books present the same ideas in varied forms; Icke 2001
    is representative. See also Michael Barkun's discussion of Icke in
    Barkun 2003.
16. See von Franz 1964 for the concept of "projecting the shadow."
17. Lasch 1991.

Chapter Three: Briefing for the Descent

1. Spengler 1926–29 and Toynbee 1934–55 are the works in question.
2. This is discussed in Toynbee, op. cit., vol. 4 pp. 245–584.
3. Webster 2002.
4. Elvin 1993.

5. This was originally published on the Internet and is included as an appendix to this book.

6. See, for example, Abelson 1999 and Roy et al. 2006 for emerging shortages of phosphate for fertilizer; and Postel 1999, Roy et al. 2006, and Simon 1998 for the worldwide shortage of fresh water.

7. See Darley 2004 for the imminent crisis in North American natural gas supplies.

8. This is a point usefully made by social critic James Howard Kunstler in several books, particularly *The Geography of Nowhere* (1994).

9. Compare, for example, Barkun 2003 and Braithwaite 2000 with MacGregor and Charles 1999 and Van Boven and Gajilan 1998.

10. Galbraith 1954, while it focuses on a single example, remains one of the best studies of the psychology of speculative bubbles and crashes. See also Kindleberger 1978.

11. In his book *Friendly Fascism* (1980).

12. Gross 2004.

13. Garrett 1994 is one of the few books on this problem aimed at the general reader, and it provides the background to this section. See also Lappé 1986.

14. See Lappé 1986.

15. See Epstein 1999, McMichael et al. 1996, and Monastersky 1996.

16. The population of the Russian Federation, 149 million in 1990, is expected to decrease to 111 million by 2050. See Becker and Bloom 1998 and Chawla et al. 2007.

17. Toynbee, op. cit., vol. 5 pp. 35–336.

18. Hearne 1976.

Chapter Four: Facing the Deindustrial Age

1. Meadows et al. 1992.

2. Lefebvre 1947, esp. pp. 7–34.

3. Mills 1958, pp. 10–14.

4. See Costanza 1987 and Cross and Guyer 1980 for the theory of social traps.

5. Barkun 2003 and Lamy 1998 cover the history of the survivalist movement.

6. See McBay 2006 for one example of peak oil survivalism.

7. The 11 volumes of *Coin Hoards from Roman Britain*, published by the British Museum, should be required reading for anyone who thinks hoarding precious metal coinage is a useful response to social crisis. See British Museum 1982–.

8. Compare Hanayama 1960, Kohn 2003, and Zarnecki 1972.

9. See Manuel and Manuel 1979 for a history of American communal Utopias.

10. Miller 1999 presents a capable study of the commune movement of
    the 1960s.
11. In 2006, for example, US petroleum production still exceeded 5 mil-
    lion barrels of crude oil a day, plus the equivalent of nearly 4 mil-
    lion barrels a day from natural gas liquids and other unconventional
    sources. See United States Department of Energy 2007.
12. See Hynes and Lindner 2006 for the recovery of the draft horse in-
    dustry in recent years.
13. The Homestead Act, originally passed in 1862, permitted any citizen
    (or immigrant intending to become a citizen) of the United States to
    claim up to 160 acres of public land, and to receive full legal title to
    the land after residing there and cultivating the land for three years.
14. See Hanley 1991 for standards of living in Tokugawa Japan.
15. Ramage 1994, p. 11.
16. See especially Leckie et al. 1975 and Olkowski et al. 1979.
17. Coppicing is a traditional craft that produces sustainable wood har-
    vests from tree species that regrow from the stump. Intensively prac-
    ticed in Europe from Neolithic times until the beginning of the fossil
    fuel age, it can readily be done with many species found in North
    America.
18. The paradox is discussed at length in Jevons 1866, chap. 7.
19. In 2001, for example, the toll from iatrogenic (physician-caused) in-
    juries and illnesses, nosocomial (hospital- and clinic-acquired) infec-
    tions, adverse drug reactions, and other medical causes was 783,736
    deaths, compared to 699,697 deaths from heart disease and 553,251
    deaths from cancer. See Dean 2005.
20. See Putnam 2000 for the role of voluntary institutions in American
    community life.
21. See, for example, Carnes 1989.
22. de Tocqueville 1899, vol. 1, chapter 12.
23. Stevens 1907 provides a good survey of American fraternal orders at
    their peak.

Chapter Five: Tools for the Transition

1. See, for example, Godesky, Jason, "It will be impossible to rebuild
   civilization," at anthropik.com/thirty.
2. Szczelkun 1974, among many other sources from the 1970s, gives
   plans for an alternator-based windpower unit. According to Leckie
   et al. 1975, pp. 50–52, alternators are superior to most other kinds of
   generators for home windpower for a variety of technical reasons.
3. See Marks 1973 for plans for scrap-made hydropower installations.
4. Butti and Perlin 1980, pp. 60–111, covers the history of solar heat engines in detail.

5. See Leckie et al. 1975 and Olkowski et al. 1979.
6. Mumford 1934.
7. See Odum 1996.
8. Clarke's Third Law was originally published in Clarke 1973.
9. For information on slide rules and dealers that offer them, see the website of the Oughtred Society (oughtred.org), a nonprofit group of slide rule historians and collectors.
10. The history and use of the haybox is summarized in Kirschner 1981.
11. Mumford, op. cit.
12. See Howard 1973 and King 1973 for the origins of contemporary organic farming, Jeavons 1979 for what has become its standard textbook, and Duhon 1985 for documentation of the claims made in this section.
13. This is documented in Duhon 1985.
14. See Economic Research Service, n.d.
15. See Agricultural Marketing Service 2006.
16. Lovelock 1998.
17. See Henderson 2007 for the influence of Isidore's *Etymologiae*.
18. The role of Irish monasteries in the preservation of classical culture is discussed in Cahill 1995.
19. See Putnam 2000 for a discussion of this process.

Chapter Six: The Spiritual Dimension

1. From the introduction to his *Collected Stories* 1947.
2. Herbert 1965, p. 11; the following quote appears on p. 12.
3. For the art of memory, see Carruthers and Ziolkowski 2002 and Yates 1966.
4. Yates, op. cit., p. 120.
5. Butler 1975, p. 12.
6. See Couliano 1987 for a detailed development of this point.
7. See Sagan 1980 for a presentation of this myth.
8. Catton 1980 presents the classic arguments for this analysis.
9. See Beyer 1992 and Kaplan 1997 for the deeply ambivalent relationship of fundamentalism to modern secular ideologies.
10. See Fields 1985 and Goldstein 2002 for histories of the emergence of American Buddhism.
11. Toynbee 1954, vol. 7, pp. 381–524.
12. See Greer 2006 for the history and traditions of modern Druidry.

Afterword

1. Lukacz 1968.

Index

About the Author

Since coming of age in the energy crises of the 1970s, John Michael Greer has devoted three decades to studying and practicing hands-on ecology and nature-centered spirituality. His weekly blog, "The Archdruid Report," has become a respected voice in the peak oil community. Greer also serves as national presiding officer, or Grand Archdruid, of the Ancient Order of Druids in America (AODA), a Druid church of nature spirituality founded in 1912. He lives in the mountains of southern Oregon with his wife Sara.

If you have enjoyed *The Long Descent*, you might also enjoy other

BOOKS TO BUILD A NEW SOCIETY

Our books provide positive solutions for people who want to
make a difference. We specialize in:

Sustainable Living ◆ Ecological Design and Planning

Natural Building & Appropriate Technology ◆ New Forestry

Environment and Justice ◆ Conscientious Commerce

Progressive Leadership ◆ Resistance and Community ◆ Nonviolence

Educational and Parenting Resources

For a full list of NSP's titles, please call 1-800-567-6772 or check out our web site at:

www.newsociety.com

NEW SOCIETY PUBLISHERS